Designing and reporting experiments in psychology

SECOND EDITION

Designing and reporting experiments in psychology

SECOND EDITION

Peter Harris

Open University Press

Open University Press
McGraw-Hill Education
McGraw-Hill House
Shoppenhangers Road
Maidenhead
Berkshire
SL6 2QL
United Kingdom

email: enquiries@openup.co.uk
world wide web: www.openup.co.uk

and
Two Penn Plaza
New York, NY 10121-2289, USA

First published 1986. Reprinted 1988, 1989, 1991, 1992, 1993, 1994 (twice)
1996, 1997, 1999, 2000

First published in this second edition 2002

Reprinted 2004, 2005

A catalogue record for this book is available from the British Library.

ISBN 0 335 20146 6 (pb)   0 335 20147 4 (hb)

Library of Congress Cataloging-in-Publication Data
Harris, Peter (Peter R.)
   Designing and reporting experiments in psychology / Peter Harris. —
2nd ed.
      p. cm. — (Open guides to psychology)
   Rev. ed. of: Designing and reporting experiments. 1986.
   Includes bibliographical references and index.
   ISBN 0–335–20147–4 —ISBN 0–335–20146–6 (pbk.)
      1. Psychology—Experiments. 2. Psychometrics. 3. Report writing.
I. Harris, Peter (Peter R.) Designing and reporting experiments. II. Title.
III. Series.

BF200 .H37 2001
150′7′24—dc21   2001021404

Typeset by Graphicraft Limited, Hong Kong
Printed and bound in Great Britain by Biddles Ltd, King's Lynn, Norfolk

To my family and friends

Contents

Preface

To students

Writing reports of practical work is an important part of many courses in psychology, from school level to degree work. This book provides advice on how to go about writing these reports, focusing especially on the reports that you will most often be asked to write – reports of *experiments*.

It is a guide to *design* as well as to report writing. Why? Because these elements are inextricably linked. It is hard to write a good report of an experiment without understanding the whys and wherefores of its design. In order to fully understand what is required of you in the report, therefore, it helps to have an idea of the function that the report of a study serves in the scientific world. This, in turn, requires you to understand something about the nature and purpose of empirical studies – such as experiments. Moreover, many of the problems and difficulties that you may face with report writing involve questions such as how to report the features of your design, or how to report adequately the outcomes of your statistical analyses. The answers to such problems depend on knowledge both of the conventions of report writing and the logic and terminology of design. Consequently, this book attempts to provide an introduction to both aspects of your practical work.

How to use this book

My aim as author of this book has been to write something that will not only serve as an *introduction* to design and report writing, but that can also be used as a handy reference source throughout your career as a student of practical psychology. I see it being used much like a thesaurus or dictionary – something that you turn to and read as the need arises. In particular, you may find yourself having to go over some of the sections a number of times before full understanding dawns. Don't be above doing this – it's what the book is for. Moreover, although you should never let yourself be overawed by the lab report, don't underestimate the task that confronts you either. Report writing is not easy – but I hope that this book will make it easier.

It is essential that you take an active part in assimilating the text rather than being a passive receiver of information. After all, you are in an extremely good position to diagnose what you already know and what you need to learn. This book will have been a complete failure if the information remains on the page rather than ending up in your head. To help you with your learning, you will find that the chapters in Part 1 typically begin with a number of "diagnostic questions" with which you should test yourself to see whether you already have the required knowledge to tackle the chapter. If you have any difficulties answering these questions then you will be directed to another section of the book for assistance. Throughout the book you will also find **self-assessment questions** (SAQs) at various points in the text. Attempting these SAQs will give you feedback on your learning and a better general understanding, and will help you to be more of an active participant than a passive reader. The answers to these questions are given at the end of the book.

The summaries at the end of each section recapitulate the main points and so provide a useful aid to revision. The index of concepts that appears at the end of the book indicates the place in the text where each concept is introduced and defined. Entries in the index are in bold print in the text.

Part 1 is about writing reports. There are chapters for each of the principal sections of the report. Part 2 is about design. There is a progression to the chapters in Part 2. That is, each chapter in Part 2 has been written on the assumption that you are familiar with the material in the previous chapter. So, make sure that you are happy with the material in each chapter before you move on to the next one. In particular, make sure that you are familiar with the material in Chapters 9–11 before tackling the remaining chapters.

Although the book deals with a number of aspects of analysis and design, it does not deal with the computation and underlying rationale of specific statistical tests. You will need also to consult a decent textbook of statistics at various stages in the process of design, analysis and reporting. Nevertheless, I hope that this book offers you useful guidance on the issues that you will need to study in greater depth in methods and statistics and provides helpful accounts of most of the basic issues. You can find recommended reading at the rear of the book and also on the Web site (see below).

To help you to develop and extend your knowledge of report writing and design, I have included towards the back of the book a separate commentary on various issues and points in the text. There is also a Web site that accompanies this book.

The commentary is designed to extend your understanding by expanding on points and issues that I don't have space to cover in detail in the core text or by clarifying something that I've written. The presence of commentary is indicated in the core text with superscript numbers. The Web site is likewise intended to help you to develop your knowledge of how to design studies and write reports. You should find yourself looking to the Web site for material more and more as you become more experienced and need to write more sophisticated reports. You will find on the Web site fuller coverage of some of the material in this book and also coverage of issues that I have not been able to talk about in the book. For example, on the Web site there is further advice on how to use and report specific statistics and also how to write reports in which you have used lengthy questionnaires. I have indicated in the text at various points some of the issues covered on the Web site. *Do* log on and find out what is there. You can find the Web site at www.openup.co.uk/harris. Tell your fellow students about it.

I hope that you will find this book useful and that it helps you to produce good reports. However, please remember that it is designed to *supplement* adequate supervision – not to replace it. The advice in this book is based on the conventions in the *Publication Manual of the American Psychological Association*, fifth edition (American Psychological Association [APA], 2001). You will find this referred to in the text as the *APA Publication Manual* (APA, 2001). Nevertheless, it is quite possible that I will have written or recommended something with which your tutors disagree. If so, I hope that your tutors will make clear to you what they want from you instead and that they will not experience fits of apoplexy or direct at me torrents of abuse in the process. So, be alert to places where your tutors expect you to depart from my suggestions.

Please *do* give me feedback. Let me know whether you like the book or not, about the bits that you found useful and any bits that you found hard to follow. This will help me when I come to produce any further editions. It will also help me to develop the material on the Web site.

To tutors

The aims of this second edition are of course substantially those of the first. However, they have also broadened, in part from a desire to extend the usefulness of the book and in part because of the changes that have taken place since the quieter times in which I wrote the original. The book is designed both for use as an introductory text for those having to write reports and think about experiments for the first time, and also as a resource for students as they progress through the years of a degree course. As with the first edition, it focuses primarily on experiments. However, there is material to assist students with reporting other types of study, on the Web site that accompanies this book.

The academic world has changed significantly since I wrote the first edition. In the UK the number of students studying psychology has expanded enormously and the number that we admit on to degree courses is many times greater than it once was. This has inevitably changed the ways in which we teach our students. If my experience is anything to go by, students receive less experience of report writing and less feedback on their efforts than was once the case. The need for a guide such as this has therefore increased.

Changes in technology have also transformed the facilities available to students when producing their reports. The book has been updated throughout to incorporate these developments with, among other things, new material on producing word-processed reports, on using statistical software and graphing packages and on finding references using electronic resources.

Above all, there have been a number of changes in custom and practice that required changes to the recommendations in the first edition. Some of these are clear – such as the move away from describing people as subjects. Others – such as the challenge to significance testing – are, at the time of writing, less clear-cut in their implications for what we teach our students. I have tried to anticipate the way that things will develop – particularly the move in published work towards dealing with issues of power and effect size and the need, therefore, to educate and train our students in dealing with and reporting these issues.

I found that the first edition was used by more advanced students than I had expected. (I even know of postgraduates who used it to help them to prepare their theses.) Certainly it was not uncommon to find final-year students using it extensively to help them to write their projects. In the light of this I have added a commentary and other pointers to help such students move towards writing the more sophisticated reports expected of them. A key element in this is the Web site that accompanies this second edition. The Web site can be found at www.openup.co.uk/harris. I have placed there fuller coverage of various issues discussed in this book and also material relevant to more advanced students. The Web site also contains advice on how to report studies involving questionnaires and non-experimental studies.

Please note that each chapter in Part 2 has been written on the assumption that students are familiar with the material in the previous chapter. The material in Chapters 9–11 covers the core material on design and analysis contained in a "traditional" introductory course on these issues. This book can therefore be used with such courses by omitting the material in Chapters 12 and 13.

I have taken this opportunity to bring the recommendations in the book into line with those in the fifth edition of the *Publication Manual of the American Psychological Association* (APA, 2001). Although not a primer in APA style per se, the aim is to encourage students from the outset to produce reports that are consistent with the style that now predominates. Those tutors for whom this is less of a concern will, I hope, find that much of what I have to recommend here nevertheless still suits their purposes. I would appreciate feedback on what works and what I might do differently.

One minor but nevertheless problematic issue was to choose terms to replace the outmoded design terminology of between- and within-subjects independent variables. There is currently no consensus on this issue, as a quick trawl of contemporary statistics textbooks will show. I have chosen the terms *unrelated samples* (for between subjects) and *related samples* (for within subjects) as these seem to be among the commoner alternatives used currently, and have the advantage of being consistent with each other and of signalling meaningfully the distinction that they denote. However, for those who wish to use alternatives, I have highlighted this issue (Section 10.2) and described the principal alternatives. I have also tried to write in such a way that my chosen terms could be easily replaced without students losing sight of the conceptual and methodological issues involved in choosing between these types of independent variable.

At the time of writing, the debate on the future of statistical significance testing continues. I have written this book on the assumption that most of the students who use it will still be asked to test for statistical significance, albeit perhaps within a broader understanding of issues to do with estimation, power and effect size. Nevertheless, it should be possible to use this book even if you do not want your students to test for statistical significance. There is also material (Section 13.8) on alternative labels for independent and dependent variables for those uncomfortable with the assumptions underlying these terms. In the interests of clarity and simplicity, especially for introductory students, I have assumed that they will generally be testing the traditional "no effect" null hypothesis rather than "minimum-effect" ones (see, for example, Murphy & Myors, 1998).

Those who are familiar with the first edition of this book will find lots of other changes. The obvious changes are the additions of a chapter in Part 1 on producing the report and a chapter in Part 2 on effect size and power. Part 1 now also contains specific advice on how to report some of the more commonly used statistics. In Part 2 I have also expanded the coverage of designs involving two or more independent variables and introduced material on graphing interactions. Part 2 also contains additional material on controlling variables, now covers internal and external validity and has an expanded section on ethics. There is also a new appendix – Appendix 3 – which covers how to use tables of critical values of inferential statistics, given that students are now likely to be less familiar with the use of these and yet will still need to refer to them from time to time.

Material on the Web site covers statistics, from using and reporting chi-square through to multiple linear regression. This is designed to be of use both to relative beginners and more advanced students who may need to run and report statistics of effect size, multiple comparisons, tests of simple effects and so on. For each statistic there is a section on things for the student to watch out for when using it or reporting the outcome of the analysis. Although this part of the Web site is not intended to replace an adequate statistics textbook, it should provide the student with a useful additional source of material and help them to have a reasonable go at reporting the statistics that they are most likely to encounter as undergraduates.

Although I have written this book primarily for students of psychology, I should imagine that many of the rules and conventions are shared by related disciplines – such as biology – and so it may prove useful to students of these subjects too.

I hope that much that was good in the first edition of the book remains and that at least most of the changes are improvements. To be frank, I didn't get much feedback on the first edition, although as an old empiricist I take its sales figures to mean that I largely got it right. Very occasionally at a conference or other function someone came up to me and said something nice about the book but sometimes also asked me to change something next time round. Wherever I've been able to remember such advice, I've tried to incorporate it. Most gratifying of all were those times when letters arrived from students who'd found the book useful and wanted to let me know and especially those occasions when they came up to me and told me the same thing. These experiences made me feel warm and happy, but in the event contributed to how daunted I became at the prospect of revising it.

This second edition has been a long time coming. I am grateful to Justin Vaughan and his colleagues at Open University Press for their patience. I would also like to thank the reviewers of the first draft of this edition – David Clark-Carter, Hugh Coolican and Judith Greene – for the time, thought and effort that they evidently put into their detailed, helpful and constructive reviews. These unquestionably enabled me to make this book better than it would otherwise have been. In the case of Judith Greene, this was for the second time of asking – her excellent and very helpful comments on the first edition undoubtedly improved that one too.

While I'm on the subject of thanking people, this is a useful opportunity for me to update my thanks to my family and to the many friends, teachers, colleagues and students who have put up with me over the years. I am fortunate to know so many splendid people. Distinguished service awards go to my brother, David, my sons, Antony and Richard, and to Julia. Thanks for various things also to Joanna Fitzgerald, Mike Inglis, Fiona Jones, Mike Parkinson and Paul Sparks and to my colleagues and friends at the University of Sussex. I would also like to thank my new colleagues and students at the University of Sheffield who provided me with the support and time that I needed to get this finished even though I'd only just arrived.

Part 1 Writing experimental reports

1 Some preliminaries

When you first signed up for a psychology course, the chances are that you didn't really expect what was coming, particularly the emphasis on methodology and statistics. For a few of you this may have come as a pleasant surprise. For most, however, it will undoubtedly have been a shock to the system.

No doubt in other parts of your course you will examine critically academic psychology's scientific aspirations. My task in this book is to help you as best I can to face up to one of its major educational consequences. This is the prominence given in most psychology courses to practical work (especially *experimenting*) and the requirement in most instances to write up at least some of this work in the form of a highly structured and disciplined *practical report*.

All a report is (really) is the place in which you tell the story of your study; what you did, why you did it, what you found out in the process, and so on. In doing this you are more like an ancient storyteller, whose stories were structured in accordance with widely recognized and long-established conventions, than a modern novelist who is free to dictate form as well as content. Moreover, like the storytellers of old, although you will invariably be telling your story to someone who knows quite a bit about it already, you are expected to present it as if it had never been heard before. This means that you will need to spell out the details and assume little knowledge of the area on the part of your audience.

The nature of your story – the things that you have to talk about – is revealed in Figure 1.1.

Our first clue as to the nature of the conventions governing the report comes with a glance at its basic structure. The report is in *sections*, and these sections (by and large) follow an established *sequence*. What this means is that, in the telling, your story is to be cut up into chunks: different parts of the story are to appear in different

1 What you did
2 Why you did it
3 How you did it
4 What you found (including details of how you analysed the data)
5 What you think it shows

Figure 1.1.   Information to be provided in the practical report.

places in the report. The typical sequence of the sections is shown in Figure 1.2.

Most of the sections are separated from each other by putting their titles as headings in the text. The exceptions are the TITLE and INTRO-DUCTION, neither of which need headings to introduce them.

TITLE
ABSTRACT
INTRODUCTION
METHOD
RESULTS
DISCUSSION
REFERENCES
Appendices (if any)

Figure 1.2.   The sections of the practical report.

The exact relationship between the elements of your story and the sections of the report is shown in Figure 1.3.

INTRODUCTION   What you did
                Why you did it
METHOD   How you did it
RESULTS   What you found (including details of how you analysed
                the data)
DISCUSSION   What you think it shows

Figure 1.3.   Where the information in Figure 1.1 should appear in the report.

The METHOD is composed of a number of subsections (Figure 1.4). There is some disagreement over the precise order in which these subsections should appear and over which are essential and which are optional. In this guide I will use the order illustrated in Figure 1.4. You may be advised to employ a different one. This is fine: the important thing is that you report the appropriate material in the right way in these subsections.

The report, therefore, is a *formal* document composed of a series of sections in which specific information is expected to appear. We will

METHOD
  DESIGN
  PARTICIPANTS
  APPARATUS (or) MATERIALS
  PROCEDURE

Figure 1.4. Subsections of the METHOD.

discuss the precise conventions governing each section as we go along. There are, however, certain *general* rules that I can introduce you to straightaway.

The first of these concerns the person to whom you should address your report, whom I shall call your **reader**. A very common mistake, especially early on, is to assume that your reader is the person who will be marking the report. In reality, however, the marker will be assessing your report *on behalf of* someone else – an idealized, hypothetical person who is *intelligent*, but *unknowledgeable* about your study and the area of psychology in which it took place. Your marker will, therefore, be checking to see that you have written your report with this sort of reader in mind. You need to make sure, therefore, that you have:

- *introduced* the reader to the area of psychology relevant to your study;
- provided the reader with the background necessary to understand what you did and why you did it;
- spelt out and developed your arguments clearly;
- defined technical terms;
- provided precise details of the way in which you went about collecting and analysing the data that you obtained.

In short, you should write for someone who is *psychologically naive*, taking little for granted about your reader's knowledge of things psychological. So, when in doubt, *spell it out!*

If you find this difficult to do, then a useful approach is to write the report as if it will be read by someone you know who is intelligent but unknowledgeable about psychology; a friend of yours, say, or your partner. Write it as if this person were going to have to read and understand it. Indeed, it is a good idea, if you can, to get just such a person to read your report before handing it in (Section 8.6).

? SAQ 1   In which sections of the report are you expected to give an account of (a) what you found in your experiment? (b) what you think your findings have to tell us?

SAQ 2   "The people who mark your reports are professional psychologists. As they know quite a bit about the subject already, you can safely assume that they will understand what you did and why you did it without this having to be spelt out by you in the report. You should, therefore, direct your report at the expert, specialized reader." True or false?

1.1   Experienced students, inexperienced students and the report

The demands and expectations placed upon you will of course vary with your experience of report writing. Early on in your career as an author of practical reports less will be expected of you than later, especially in what are really the key sections of the report – the INTRODUCTION and DISCUSSION. At this early stage you will be expected principally to show that you understand what you did in your practical and its implications, together with evidence that you have at least a basic grasp of the demands of the report's format.

In particular, little will be expected of you here in the "why you did it" part of the INTRODUCTION (Figure 1.3). There are a number of reasons for this, but the main one is that the early studies that you do in your practical course tend not to be justifiable in the terms that we use here – that is, in *research* terms. Generally speaking, these early practicals are chosen for you; more often than not, this is for reasons other than their earth-shattering research significance. It would be rather perverse of us, therefore, to expect you to fabricate some plausible research justification for undertaking such studies.

Later on, however (as you begin to take more responsibility for the design of your study), you will be expected to pay more attention to the research significance of what you did. This _why_ part will then become more important – because, in being responsible for the choice of topic and design, you will be expected to be able to *justify* this choice. So, you must be able to tell us *why* it is that, given the options available to you, you decided to conduct your particular study. Moreover, these will need to be *research* justifications, not merely ones of expediency! You will need, therefore, to develop the habit of thinking about how the ideas that you are entertaining for your experiment or study will look in the report, paying particular attention to how they will fit into the INTRODUCTION. Specific dangers that you must watch out for here are, first, a lack of adequate material (*references*) to put in this section and, second, the undertaking of a project that lacks any research justification (because it is based on assumptions that are contradicted by existing findings in the area). Thinking clearly in advance will help you to avoid making these mistakes.

Summary of Section 1.1

1 The practical report is composed of a series of separate sections in which specific information is to be reported. Your task in the report is to tell your reader all about the study that you conducted.

2 You must write, however, for someone who knows nothing about your study or the area of psychology in which it took place.

3 This means that you should spell out the precise details of your study and provide your reader with knowledge of the background relevant to it (previous findings in the area) when writing the report.

4 The demands placed upon you with regard to this task will vary with your experience as a student of practical psychology. In particular, as you progress you will need to get into the habit of thinking about how the ideas that you are entertaining for your experiment or study will fit into the report. In particular, pay attention to how you will be able to develop and defend your arguments in the INTRODUCTION.

1.2 Writing the report

Before running your study you should really have a good idea of exactly how you are going to do it, as well as why it's worth doing, and how it relates to previous work in the area. However, you will have no real idea of what you are going to find and, therefore, no precise knowledge of the implications of your study. Thus the INTRODUCTION and METHOD could, in principle, have been written before you conducted the experiment, because these sections report material that you should have decided upon in advance. The RESULTS and DISCUSSION, however, can't be written in advance, as these depend critically upon the outcome of your study.

However, although the order in which the sections appear basically reflects this historical sequence (Figure 1.2), it is ill advised to *write* them in this order. For some of the sections – such as the INTRODUCTION and DISCUSSION – require greater thought and effort to complete adequately than others. Consequently, you would be wise to work on these sections when you are at your freshest, leaving the more straightforward ones – such as those that comprise the METHOD – to those moments in which your interest in what you are doing is at its lowest ebb. In particular, never leave the DISCUSSION until last. I have seen too many reports in which students have devoted the better part of their time to the earlier sections, and lost interest in what they were doing by the time that they reached the DISCUSSION. The consequence is a perfunctory DISCUSSION, and a poorer mark than they would have obtained had they budgeted their time more sensibly. Always bear in mind that the DISCUSSION is the key section of the report; it is there that the true value of what you have done in your study will be revealed in all its glory, when you come to assess the *implications* of your findings. How much have your findings added to the stock of knowledge that you described in the INTRODUCTION? In a very real sense, the whole experimental process – from design through to the writing of all of the other sections of the report – is intended to clear the ground for the DISCUSSION. So, write your report with this in mind. (Again, this will become more and more important as you come to play a larger role in designing your own studies.)

 Finally, the ABSTRACT is invariably best left until last, even though it is the first section to appear in the report. (Indeed, it is difficult to imagine writing an abstract of an unfinished report.)

? SAQ 3   Which sections of the report could, in principle, have been written *before* you conducted the experiment? Why?

? SAQ 4   Which is the key section of the report?

1.3   The importance of referencing in the text

Whenever you write in psychology you must *substantiate all factual assertions*. A **factual assertion** is simply anything that could prompt your reader to ask "who says?" or "what's the evidence?". A factual assertion is a claim about the psychological universe, and few such claims are undeniably, self-evidently true. For example, "people want to be happy", "memory deteriorates with age", "children grow into adults". Only the last of these statements is undeniably true, and only if we take adult to mean "grown up *physically*". Be alert to this issue: you will be making many factual assertions when you write, and most of the time these will require substantiation. You will be expected to tell the reader at least *who* presented evidence or arguments for the claim and *when*. So, if you make a firm statement about *any* aspect of the psychological universe (however trivial), you must attempt to support it.

In practice, this means that statements such as "Emotion interferes with the ability to reason logically" or "Anxiety enhances the impact of a persuasive message" are not acceptable. However, statements such as "Emotion interferes with the ability to reason logically (Dwyer, 1972)" and "Anxiety enhances the impact of a persuasive message (Dale & Stant, 1996)" *are* acceptable. The reason is that they contain what we call **references**, whereas the first two statements do not.

The use of references is the preferred method of substantiating factual assertions in psychology, for references provide direct answers to the questions *who* found, argued or claimed something and *when*. If they wished to, the reader could look up the source referenced to see if it really does say what you claim it says. So, wherever possible you should cite a reference (at least a name and date) for all *findings*, *definitions*, and *quotations* at all times, even where you have made the citation before. It must be clear to which author, and to which particular piece of their work, you are referring at *any given time*. For example:

> Legg (2000) found that emotion impaired participants' ability to reason logically. Emotion did not, however, affect the female participants any more than the male participants. Indeed, the reasoning performance of the women was superior to that of the men when the emotional arousal was positive. On the basis of these data and previous findings (Legg, 1999), he argued that "the traditional viewpoint that emotion disrupts the reasoning abilities of women, but not those of men, is untenable" (Legg, 2000, pp. 12–13).

You must be aware of the importance of referencing in this way in scientific writing. The conventions governing referencing in psychology are described in Chapter 8. You must adhere to these in your reports and indeed in everything that you write in psychology.

In most cases you will be given at least some references to read for your practical. As you become more experienced, however, more will be expected of you in terms of reading around the area and even hunting down your own references. Advice on how to locate references can be found in Section 1.5.

In psychology you should *never* find yourself having made a claim about an aspect of the psychological universe without attempting in some way to shore it up. Whatever happens, therefore, *you should attempt to substantiate your viewpoint*. This is particularly true of what you will come to know as the *experimental hypothesis*. You should always attempt to justify the experimental hypothesis (or hypotheses), especially as you become more experienced.

? SAQ 5   If you make a statement that might prompt your reader to ask "who says?", what should you do?

Summary of Sections 1.2–1.3

1 The DISCUSSION is the key section of the report. It is there that the true value of your study will be revealed, for it is there that you come to assess the implications of your findings. You should therefore budget your time when writing the report so that you devote sufficient thought and attention to this section.

2 When writing the report you will be expected to substantiate all factual assertions, preferably by using *references*.

1.4   The report as a research instrument

So far, therefore, you have been introduced to the basic requirements of the report and been given some idea of how to go about writing it. Yet *why* does the report take this form: why is it in sections? Why do these sections come in a particular order? Why are there restrictions over what material is to be mentioned, where it is to come, and how it is to be expressed? These are good questions. The answers to them require you to understand something about the function of the report in its **research context**.

Those of you who have already written reports may well have found yourselves confused and frustrated at some stage or other by rules of format and principles of construction that strike you as being rigid, restrictive, inhibiting, and more or less arbitrary. One of the main reasons for this is that you meet the report in a strange environment. For the report is primarily a *research* instrument. Its natural habitat is the academic *journal*. The rules and conventions that govern its construction have evolved for the purpose that it serves there. In its educational setting, therefore (where you meet it), these conventions are often difficult to understand, because you have inherited the report divorced – at least at first – from its principal function.

What is a journal? When, as a naive undergraduate, I first encountered this term and was packed off to the library to start work on my first practical report I didn't know what people were talking about. Bewildered, I wandered around the library trying to work out in what ways a journal might look different on a shelf from a book. To me a journal was a dusty old, handwritten thing kept by some intrepid Victorian travelling through the Congo or awaiting the relief of Mafeking. Quite what psychology had to do with such things was beyond me. Now, of course, I know better. Academic journals are the main way in which researchers inform each other about their work and, therefore, the places in which much of a discipline's knowledge and understanding can be found. They are collections of what are thought to be the best papers submitted to a journal's editors and are published at regular periods (and are thus sometimes also referred to as *periodicals*, especially in libraries). Most of the studies that you will cite in a report will be published in journals. (These published reports are usually called *papers*, just to add to the confusion.)

In its research context, a journal article serves to inform those who may be interested in a researcher's work of its *nature*, *purpose* and *implications*, in as *clear*, *thorough* and *concise* a way as possible (note the conflicting demands). To this end, the idea of a general format, with clearly labelled sections in which clearly defined pieces of information are to be provided, has developed (Figure 1.5). In theory, using this format, it should be possible for readers to establish quickly and with the minimum of effort whether the reported work is of interest and to locate any particular piece of information they want. Ideally, readers should be able to rerun your study (to conduct what we call a "replication") based solely on the description in your report. This is the level of description that you should aim for, within the constraints imposed by the word limit for your report.

The conventions that govern the construction of the report, therefore, have been developed for the purpose of conveying information *clearly*, *precisely*, *quickly* and *concisely* to those who are interested. To a large extent, these are the conventions that you must obey in

INTRODUCTION	1	Summarize state of area prior to study. (Why you did it)
	2	Sketch study in broad outline. (What you did)
	3	State the *experimental hypothesis* (or hypotheses) and associated predictions (Section 9.1.4)
METHOD	4	Outline precise details of study. (How you did it)
RESULTS	5	Present relevant data, together with outcomes of appropriate inferential statistical analyses. (What you found)
DISCUSSION	6	Summarize and interpret findings.
	7	Assess implications for area (i.e., return to 1). (What you think it shows)

Figure 1.5.   The requirements of the research report.

report writing, even though very few of you are ever likely to have your work read by fellow researchers. In essence, these conventions have been *transplanted* from the research world into the educational one.

 SAQ 6   What principal purposes are served by the conventions of the *research* report?

As you progress, you will be expected more and more to emulate the research process – to design your studies with their research implications in mind and to write your reports with greater emphasis on the implications of what you have done for existing findings and ideas. As a result, more will be expected of you in the report, particularly in the INTRODUCTION and DISCUSSION. So, those of you who will be expected to progress in this way must watch out for this transition. (In the UK this will probably occur for most of you during the second year of an undergraduate course.)

As this is critical to the way in which you should write your report (and as it will obviously affect the way that your report is marked), if you have any doubts about which group you fall into, then ask your tutor. Indeed, this is a general rule for anything in this book: when in doubt, ask your tutor.

Summary of Section 1.4

1 The practical report is related to the research article. The conventions that govern the construction of the research article have been developed for the purposes of conveying information clearly, precisely, quickly and concisely to those who may be interested in a researcher's work.

2 To a large extent, these are the conventions that you must obey when writing your practical reports, particularly as you become more experienced.

1.5   Finding things to write about: how to get more references

When you start off as a student, references are generally no problem. Your tutor gives them to you, you read them and write a potted account of what they say. Indeed, in your early reports there may not be much space for anything expansive. As time goes by, however, expectations change. You will be expected to know more, write about more, and to find out more yourself. At this stage you need useful, informative and *up-to-date* things to read to help you to design studies that ask interesting questions based on an *informed* understanding of what has already been found and to help you to structure your introduction. These days anyone with access to a college or university library and a bit of time can come up with a reasonable set of references to collect and read.

 When doing your reading, you need to take it in stages. You need to discriminate *primary* from *secondary* sources (see below). You also need to differentiate material that is readily available to you – in the library or electronically – from that only available by ordering it from elsewhere, which will cause delays.

1.5.1 Where to start

Start by reading something general if you can. A decent, up-to-date textbook chapter will give you an overview of the themes and issues in the area and a sense of what are the key studies. Wander around the shelves of the library looking for something suitable if no such source is on your reading list. More advanced students should search for an up-to-date review in a journal. A recent article in a decent journal will contain some sort of review of the area. If you need further references, try to get hold of any promising-looking articles contained in the references sections of these articles. There are also journals and other sources dedicated to reviews: if in doubt, ask your tutor where you might look and what might be suitable for your level of study. Ask also what journals s/he considers to be the best in the field.

In some cases there will be an obvious starting study or studies on which your experiment is based. If so, start there.

Make sure that you differentiate primary from secondary sources. A **primary source** is the original piece of work: the paper in which the authors argued something or first published their findings. Anything in which people give a second hand account of another piece of work is a **secondary source**. Textbooks are secondary sources. In these the author provides potted accounts of people's work. Such secondary sources are useful starting points, but much of the detail is lost and sometimes mistakes and misinterpretations creep in. As you progress as a student, you should expect more and more of your reading to be of primary sources and your use of secondary sources to be limited to the first phase of your reading in the area.

1.5.2 Ways of adding to your references

Many of you, most of the time, do not read enough. However, some of you read too much. Reading just the right amount to give you an informed understanding of the area, but leaving you still able to see the wood for the trees, is an important skill. So rule one, for most of you, is: *read enough*! Rule two, for some of you, is: *know when to stop*!

If you need to add to the list given to you by your tutor, here are three useful ways of doing so. Use any or all of them.

1 Extremely useful resources are available electronically. Abstracting services, such as the *Social Science Citation Index* and *Psychological Abstracts*, contain up-to-date catalogues of titles, abstracts and reference lists of thousands of articles in psychology journals and other disciplines. You can search these electronically by keyword to find some useful articles for your report. Depending on your request, the computer will search for the keyword in the title, abstract, author names, and references section of the articles on the database and provide you with a list of the ones that it has found. Many journals themselves are also available electronically, and these usually have search facilities built in to enable you to search for articles on the topic of interest. Your library will have lists of what electronic resources are available to you (e.g., Web of Science, PsycINFO) and instructions and tips on how best to use them.

2 If your library takes journals, find out where the very latest editions are displayed and look through the ones likely to have articles relevant to the topic. (If in doubt, ask your tutor which these are.) You can also use the references sections of any articles that you find to discover the full references for other articles they cite that look like they might also be useful.

3 The World Wide Web (WWW) contains an enormous range of resources. Access the home page of your college or university to see what relevant sites it provides ready access to. Even better, see whether your department maintains a Web site and what links it gives to resources and other Web sites. The home pages of the professional associations, such as the British Psychological Society and the American Psychological Association, also contain links to other Web sites.[1] If none of this works, use a search engine to obtain lists of Web sites using relevant key words.

Finally, do not underestimate the importance of reading up-to-date material. One of the first things that I do when I look at a project or practical report, *especially from the more advanced students*, is to scan the references section to see what proportion of references are from the last two or three years. I want to see a good mix of references to classic sources but also evidence that the student has read recent, up-to-date material published in decent journals.[2]

Summary of Section 1.5

1 As you progress as a student of psychology you will be expected to find relevant things to read yourself and to read more primary sources.

2 You can use searches of electronic databases and hand searches of books and journals to help you to get additional references to read. The WWW also contains potentially useful information.

 3 More advanced students should attempt to read a good mix of references to classic articles and up-to-date ones from decent journals.

1.6   Experimental ethics

Before you even begin to think about designing and running your own experiments, let alone writing them up, you need to learn how to treat your participants ethically. Any investigation involving humans or animals is governed by a set of ethical principles, and you are required to act in accordance with these. It can be very easy when designing your experiments to get caught up in the details and the science and to lose sight of the potential for insult, upset or distress in your procedures. When you first start out your tutor will play the major part in keeping an eye on this aspect of your work. Nevertheless, you too have a responsibility to make sure that your experiments and other studies are run ethically. Make sure, therefore, that you obtain, read and understand the principles adhered to in your department. At some stage you may undertake project work for which you need prior ethical approval. Make sure that you know how to obtain approval under these circumstances, and don't start without it! You will find more on ethical issues in Section 10.10.

2 The INTRODUCTION section

 Diagnostic questions on design for Chapter 2

1 What is a *variable*?

2 What is the name of the variable that we *manipulate* in an experiment?

3 What is the name of the variable that we *measure* in an experiment to assess the effects of our manipulation?

4 From which hypothesis can we predict that there will be *no difference* between the conditions in an experiment? Is it (a) the experimental hypothesis or (b) the null hypothesis?

5 What is a *nondirectional* prediction?

If you have difficulties answering any of these questions, turn to Chapter 9.

The first major section of the report, then, is the INTRODUCTION. As its name implies, the purpose of this section is to *introduce* something. Which raises two questions, both of which you should be able to answer on the basis of your reading of Chapter 1.

 SAQ 7   So, in the INTRODUCTION, you introduce *what* to *whom*?

Essentially, in the INTRODUCTION to your report you should fulfil the following requirements, *in the following order:*

1 Review the background material (existing findings and theoretical ideas) relevant to your study.

2 Outline the precise problem that you chose to investigate and describe the way that you went about investigating it.

3 Outline the predictions derived from the experimental hypothesis (Section 9.1.4).

This means that your INTRODUCTION is effectively in *two* parts: a part in which you deal with work that pre-dated your study (which will generally be the work of *other* people), and a part in which you finally introduce and discuss your *own* study, albeit briefly. You must move, therefore, from the *general* to the *specific*. That is, you do not start with a description of your study – you build up to it. Why you do it this way should become clearer as we go along.

As the INTRODUCTION is logically in two parts, I shall deal with them separately here. So, let's now turn to the first part of your INTRODUCTION, the part in which you review the background material relevant to the study that you conducted.

2.1 The first part of the INTRODUCTION: reviewing the background to your study

First, let me issue a word of caution. If you have read around your subject, there is a great temptation, whatever your level as a student, to let your marker know this by hook or by crook. Most frequently this is achieved by weaving every little morsel into the INTRODUCTION, regardless of how contrived this becomes. *Resist this temptation*, for it is counter-productive. The material that you mention should be *directly* relevant to the problem under investigation. Moreover, you should avoid the more trivial details of the studies that you report, emphasizing instead their major findings and conclusions. For your task in this part of the report is primarily to put your study into its research context, by showing its relationship to previous work in the area. Consequently, material should be mentioned *only* if it is relevant. So, if you end up having read something that turns out to be tangential, drop it from the report, however much heartbreak this causes you. Learning to write concisely and yet clearly is one of the key skills that you are trying to develop.

At the same time, however, bear in mind that you are under no obligation to treat published work as "gospel". From the outset, you are as entitled to disagree with the viewpoints of others as they are with you. It is the *manner* in which you do this that is important.

Don't be afraid to disagree with what someone has argued if you believe that you have reasonable grounds for doing so. However, make sure that you can provide plausible support for your viewpoint. That is, *you must seek to substantiate your point of view* by showing how the evidence supports it.

2.2   Inexperienced students, experienced students and the INTRODUCTION

If you are studying to go to university, taking your first course in psychology, or are in the first year of a degree course, you will probably be considered to be a novice. At this stage in your career as a psychologist you are basically learning your trade. Consequently, your marker will generally be looking to see whether you've understood the study that you conducted and whether you have a grasp of at least the basic demands of the practical report format. So, he or she will assess such things as whether you've put the right material in the right sections, referenced, quoted and defined properly, and obeyed the other main aspects of the conventions.

For you, then, the more important part of your INTRODUCTION will actually be the second part – where you talk about your study. The first part of your INTRODUCTION needs only to provide a general orientation that gives your reader some idea of the area in which your practical took place. In order to do this, you will generally need to include accounts of one or two of those studies most directly relevant to the one that you conducted. However, you probably won't be expected at this stage to spend much time attempting to *derive* your study from the work that went before it.

It is difficult to give general advice here because studies vary so much, as do markers' expectations. However, if you're completely bewildered, one general strategy that you might employ runs as follows:

1 Open with a statement about the general area or phenomenon under investigation (e.g., memory, attention, attitudes, rumour).
2 Then talk about the particular aspect of this topic that your study specifically addressed (e.g., the impact of mnemonics, the "cocktail party" phenomenon, attitude change, how rumours are spread).
3 Then, with the problem nicely set up, you are ready to introduce your own study to your reader.

This has been done in outline in the following example:

Memory has been defined as "the retention and use of prior learning" (Glassman, 1995, p. 411). One aspect of human memory that is of both theoretical and practical interest is how to go about improving it (Wagner, 1994). Over the years people have developed a number of techniques for improving memory (Toshack, 1965; Warboys, 1970). Collectively, these techniques are called *mnemonics*, from the Greek for "memory" (Glassman, 1995).

The *method of loci* is an example of a mnemonic. This method involves mentally placing the material that has to be remembered at various locations on a well-known route or in a familiar building. A mental "walk" around that location subsequently enables the material that is stored there to be retrieved. The method of loci is thus particularly suitable for recalling material in sequence.

Investigations of the method of loci were among the earliest experiments in psychology (e.g., Keenor, 1911; Wilson, 1899). For instance, Ferguson (1927) reported significant improvements in participants' ability to recall a list of everyday objects when using this mnemonic. In 1971, Clark found that the technique also enhanced recall of words. Moreover, participants in Clark (1971) recalled significantly more words high in imageability (i.e., words that readily suggested visual images) than words low in imageability.

Recently, however, Nugent, Ford, & Young (2000) failed in their attempt to replicate the findings of Clark (1971). In their study, Nugent et al. . . . . [Continue by telling your reader succinctly the key points of Nugent et al.'s study and findings.]

Notice that what you are doing here is *homing in* on your study. Rather than dropping readers in cold by starting with your study, you are taking it step by step and easing them in gently. Now, it may not be possible to do it quite so neatly each time, but you should always *try* to lead up to your study. This is a good rule: do not *start* with the details of your study; build up to them.

 SAQ 8   Why is it a good idea to build up to the details of your study, rather than starting the INTRODUCTION with a description of what you did?

Starting with such an approach from the outset will result in you developing good habits for later when – at least for those of you who must progress – more will be expected from you in the first section of the report. For, as you become more experienced, this first part of your INTRODUCTION will become longer. It will also take on some of the functions that the INTRODUCTION has in a research paper. By this stage you should be beginning to undertake studies that have at least some limited research justifications. Or at least you must write them *as if* they had research justifications.

In the INTRODUCTION to a research paper the author will summarize the state of the area *prior* to the study that s/he conducted. Subsequently, s/he will readdress this material in the light of the study's findings, to see whether the position has changed at all (i.e., whether the study itself has allowed us to make much progress). S/he does this in the DISCUSSION. Essentially, therefore, the report spans two separate time periods – the time immediately *before* the study was undertaken (reported in the INTRODUCTION), and the time immediately *after* the study had been completed and the data analysed (dealt with in the DISCUSSION). The report therefore embodies progress because we essentially revisit the area, looking at the problems and issues addressed in the INTRODUCTION with the benefit of the new knowledge gleaned from the study's findings. It's a bit like one of those "before and after" adverts in which the advertiser is at pains to illustrate the contrast between circumstances prior to and after the use of the product. The INTRODUCTION is the equivalent of a *before* picture. The DISCUSSION is the equivalent of an *after* picture. You can see this process built into the sections of the research report summarized in Figure 1.5.

It is now time for the INTRODUCTIONS that you write to ape this function. Thus, at this stage in your career, you should be attempting in the first part of your INTRODUCTION to show how the omissions in previous work – such as flaws in the studies conducted, or simply questions and issues that have yet to be addressed – form the basis of the study that you undertook. For it is your task to expose here the advance that you propose to make – the gap in our knowledge that your study is designed to plug. At this stage, therefore, not only should you be starting to give a rather more detailed account of the previous work of relevance to your study, but you should also be looking to *derive* your study from this work. That is, you should aim to show how your study builds on the previous research.

? SAQ 9   How does the research report, in principle, "embody progress"?

This requirement has obvious implications for how you should conduct yourself at the *design* stage. Essentially, it will be ill advised to dream up and run your studies without first doing the background reading and thinking about how you will go about *justifying* your study in the INTRODUCTION. Remember that studies evolve from the time at which you start thinking about interesting research questions, to the time at which the first participant takes part in your experiment. Thinking about how your study fits into the existing literature is a critical part of this process. In particular, you should never find yourself having undertaken a study that flies in the face of existing findings without having sound arguments for doing so. For you will, of course, need to be able to make these arguments in your INTRODUCTION.

What this means in practice is that you must *do your preparatory reading* and design your study *in the light of what you find there!* Do not jump straight into your study, or you will run the risk of conducting something for which there is no theoretical justification and which, therefore, is going to be exceedingly difficult, if not impossible, to write up. Always bear in mind that your practical work does not begin and end with the study itself – it ends with the completion of the report of that study. You will, therefore, have to be able to give an account of what you did that shows this to have been justified.

You should attempt to be both clear and concise when writing this part of the INTRODUCTION. Keep to the point. Discuss the most relevant previous work only. Do not attempt to write an exhaustive review of everything that has been done on the topic. Stick to the key features of the studies that you *do* cite – the most relevant findings and conclusions, and any methodological issues that you think are relevant.

Summary of Sections 2.1–2.2

1 The purpose of the INTRODUCTION is to put your study into its research context, by providing your reader with an introduction to the background material (existing findings and theoretical ideas) relevant to it.

2 This material is presented in the first part of the INTRODUCTION. The second part of the INTRODUCTION presents the reader with a brief introduction to your study.

3 Increasing emphasis is placed on the first part as you become more experienced and the reports that you write begin to emulate research papers.

2.3   Your own study

In the second part of the INTRODUCTION you turn – *for the first time* – to your own study. Here at last you are free to move away from talking about other people's work and are able to introduce your own. However, note that the emphasis is firmly on *introducing* your study. You will not be expected at this stage to give a detailed account of what you did; there will be room enough elsewhere in the report for that. Here all that is required is a paragraph or two succinctly outlining the following features of your study:

1 Briefly state the problem that you chose to investigate. This should, of course, be clear from what you have written in the INTRODUC-TION so far. Nevertheless, it is good policy to confirm the problem. Then neither you, nor your reader, should be confused over the issue that you tackled.

2 Give your reader a *general* idea of how you went about tackling it. There are always different ways to test the same issue. Here you need to describe in general terms the way that you actually chose to do it.

3 State clearly and accurately the predictions that you derive from the experimental hypothesis (or hypotheses) and clarify how your experiment tests these.

Please note that this is directed at all of you. Although I made exceptions in the first part of the INTRODUCTION for "inexperienced" students, *all* of you – regardless of level – should include the above material in the final part of your INTRODUCTION.

Don't be put off by this – it all sounds much more complicated than it really is. You can, in fact, generally achieve it in one or two short paragraphs. Below is an illustration of the sort of approach that you can adopt. This is an extract from the introduction that we began earlier. To recap, the experiment examines whether varying how easy it is to construct mental images from words affects the usefulness of a mnemonic (an aid to memory). The three features described above are all in this example. The first paragraph brings the discussion leading up to it to the point and summarizes the issue in question (requirement 1). The opening sentences of the final paragraph give the reader the general idea of how the problem will be tackled (requirement 2). The final sentences spell out the predictions and their rationale (requirement 3).

... However, as pointed out earlier, Nugent et al. (2000) found no evidence that the nature of the material affected their participants' ability to memorize lists of words using the method of loci. Yet, Nugent et al. did not allow their participants much time to become accustomed to using the mnemonic. It may be that their findings simply illustrate the need for practice before significant improvements in memory performance are revealed.

Consequently, Nugent et al.'s (2000) study was replicated. This time, however, those in the mnemonic condition were allowed to practice using the method of loci prior to the start of the experiment. If the method depends for its success upon the imageability of the material, then those using the mnemonic should recall more of the easily imaged words than do those not using the mnemonic. Those using the mnemonic should not, however, recall more of the hard-to-image words than do those not using the mnemonic.

Note that although the INTRODUCTION is in two parts, this is *not* indicated in the format of the section itself. That is, you *do not* separate the part in which you introduce your own study from the earlier part of the INTRODUCTION by things such as a separate title or by missing a line. Simply start a new paragraph.

No doubt some of you are still rather confused by all this. If so, don't worry – remember that good report writing is a skill. Consequently, it takes time to develop. You should not be surprised, therefore, if at times you find yourself uncertain and confused about what is required of you. Just do your best to develop this skill by practising it – by writing reports and getting feedback on your efforts from your tutor. If you're really stuck, look for examples of how other people have solved the problems that confront you. So, if you have access to a university or college library, look up some journal articles and see how their introductions have been ended.

At the beginning of this section I stated that the most important thing was for you to make a clear and accurate statement of the findings predicted from the experimental hypothesis. Here's how you go about this:

1 State the predictions clearly; mention in this statement both the independent and the dependent variables. For example: "those who eat the standard quantity of cheese 3 hours before going to bed will report more nightmares than those who do not consume cheese during this period", rather than "eating cheese will affect nightmares". Note, however, that you do not need to refer to these explicitly here as the independent and dependent variables. You do that in the DESIGN subsection of the METHOD.

2 State whether the prediction is nondirectional or directional (Section 9.1.4).

3 There is no need to mention here the predictions under the null hypothesis. You can take it for granted that your readers will assume that you are testing the null hypothesis that leads to the prediction that there will be no reliable differences between the

conditions in your experiment (which is what most of you, most of the time, will be doing). You can therefore omit the predictions under this null hypothesis. At this stage of the report you need only mention what your predictions are under the theories discussed in your INTRODUCTION.

For example:

> The experimental hypothesis leads to the directional prediction that those who eat the standard quantity of cheese 3 hours before going to bed will report more nightmares than those who do not eat cheese during this period.

However, your experimental hypotheses must relate clearly to the issues that you addressed in the first part of your INTRODUCTION. That is, they should be linked to what has gone before. So don't, for example, suddenly spring upon your reader a set of experimental hypotheses that *contradict* the ideas that have been addressed in the first part of your INTRODUCTION. If you wish to disagree with existing arguments or findings in the literature then include also arguments (ideally substantiated by *references*) in the first part of your INTRODUCTION outlining and *justifying* your own viewpoint. Similarly, don't set up hypotheses that bear no relation to what has gone before – remember that the INTRODUCTION is designed to set the scene for your experiment, and therefore principally functions to show how you arrived at your predictions. Similarly, never confuse predictions derived from the experimental hypothesis with those derived from the null hypothesis (see Appendix 2). Finally, you must not mention the *results* of the experiment in this section.

? SAQ 10   Why not?

? SAQ 11   What purpose does the INTRODUCTION serve?

Summary of Section 2.3

1 The second part of the INTRODUCTION should outline the purpose of your own experiment.

2 After confirming the specific problem that you investigated, you need to clarify the way in which your experiment tackles this problem.

3 Finally, you should describe clearly the predictions that you derive from your experimental hypothesis or hypotheses.

3 The METHOD section

 Diagnostic questions on design for Chapter 3

1 What is a *related* samples independent variable?

2 What is an *unrelated* samples independent variable?

3 What is a *mixed* design?

4 What is *random assignment* to conditions?

5 What is a *confounding* variable?

If you have difficulties answering any of these questions, turn to Chapters 9 and 10.

The next section in your report is the METHOD. This section is composed of a number of subsections. In these you talk about various aspects of the study that you conducted. For experimental studies the subsections are:

- DESIGN: here you talk about the formal design features of the experiment that you ran, using the appropriate terminology (things like the independent variable and dependent variable).
- PARTICIPANTS: here you describe the relevant features of the participants (those from whom you obtained scores on your dependent variables).
- APPARATUS, or MATERIALS, or APPARATUS AND MATERIALS: here you describe the equipment or materials that you used (or both).
- PROCEDURE: here you give a blow-by-blow account of precisely what you said and did to your participants in the experiment.

The METHOD, in the form of its various subsections, is designed to give the reader a coherent, clear and precise account of what you did in your experiment. In this part of the report, therefore, you describe who your participants were, what you told them about the experiment, how you presented your materials to them, the sequence in which you did things, and so on. In fact, this section is rather like a recipe in a recipe book: the first three sections (DESIGN, PARTICIPANTS, and APPARATUS or MATERIALS) correspond to the *ingredients* part; the final section (PROCEDURE), to the part in which you are told what to do with them.

The watchword of this particular section is *thoroughness*. Your aim should be to provide all the information necessary (and in the right sections) for your reader to be able to repeat *precisely* what you did – to undertake what we call an exact or direct **replication** of your study.

Why? Well, other researchers might not only disagree with the inferences that you draw from your experiment – the conclusions that you reach – but also dispute the actual *findings* that you obtained. They could argue that the findings on which you based your conclusions were anomalous and that if the experiment were run again (i.e., were replicated) they would obtain different results. For this reason you have to present the details of your experiment in such a way that anybody who thought this – anyone who doubted the **reliability** of your findings – could test this possibility for themselves by replicating your study.

This is an important argument. Findings that are not *reliable* – that are markedly different each time we conduct the same experiment – have no place in a science. The whole logic of experimental design – of manipulating one variable and looking for the effects of this on another (in order to determine cause–effect relationships) – relies on these relationships remaining constant. It is no good if the causal variables appear to change – that on Monday anxiety damages the body's immune system, but by Thursday it doesn't. To construct an adequate science of psychology, we have to be able to build on our findings. We must be able to take certain findings as read (as "facts") after experimental evidence has accumulated and use these as *assumptions* in the subsequent research and theorizing that we do.

In other parts of your course you will find debates about whether this is actually achievable in psychology. However, that is beyond the scope of this book. Here I am only concerned to give you the skills necessary to see for yourself whether experiments work. Moreover, there are those who argue that more straight replicating work should be undertaken in psychology in order to discover how reliable our findings are. This is another good reason why you *must* be clear and thorough in the various subsections that make up the METHOD.

? SAQ 12   What is an exact replication of a study?

Summary

1 The METHOD is composed of a set of subsections: DESIGN, PARTICIP-ANTS, APPARATUS or MATERIALS, and PROCEDURE.

2 It is designed to give a clear and accurate statement of what you did in your experiment, so that other people can *replicate* it if they so desire.

3.1   The DESIGN subsection

There are a variety of ways of going about experimenting in psychology – ways of ordering conditions, using participants, controlling for potentially confounding variables – and your experiment will involve you in having to choose one particular way of putting your ideas into practice. The method that you choose is known as the *design* of your experiment. The process by which you come to choose it is called *designing* experiments.

The DESIGN itself is generally one of the briefer subsections of the report. All you need to give here is a brief but formal statement of the principal features of the design that you employed. In describing the design you must use the terminology that has been developed over the years to enable us to talk accurately about features of experiments. In particular, you will need to state:

1 What type of design you used (i.e., whether you used an unrelated samples, related samples or mixed design).
2 What your independent variable (IV) was, including details of the conditions that you selected to represent different levels of the IV.
3 What your dependent variable (DV) was, including details of the units in which participants' scores were measured. You should do this for all of the DVs in your experiment.[1]

While we're on this topic, *please* make sure that you spell the terms correctly! I am constantly surprised by the number of reports that refer to "dependant" and "independant" variables. Misspelling them in this way is unlikely to impress your marker and may even cost you a mark or two. So, remember it is depend*ent* and independ*ent*. Watch out for this – "dependant" is one of those misspellings that will not be picked up by a computer's spell checker (see Section 8.7).

However, although students generally get the format of this section right, they sometimes get confused over things like what their IV or DV was, or whether they used *unrelated* or *related* samples. So make sure that you understand these concepts, for you will be expected to write a proper DESIGN regardless of whether or not you played a part in designing the experiment yourself. (This applies to the remainder of the METHOD as well – to the PARTICIPANTS, APPARATUS or MATERIALS, and PROCEDURE.)

Again, as with the description of your study at the end of the INTRODUCTION, this can be done comparatively simply. Indeed, the DESIGN really amplifies and clarifies this earlier statement of the purpose of the experiment.

Below is an example of how this can be done:

Design

The experiment had a two-way, mixed design. The related measures independent variable was the imageability of the words for recall, with two levels (easily imaged or hard to image). The unrelated measures independent variable was instruction in the use of the method of loci mnemonic: the experimental group received instruction and training in the use of the mnemonic, whereas the control group did not. This independent variable thus also had two levels (mnemonic or no mnemonic). The primary dependent variable was the number of words of each type correctly recalled by the participant after 10 minutes' delay. Misspellings counted as errors. Other dependent variables were the number of words correctly recalled during the pretest and, as a manipulation check, the ratings of the imageability of the words used (7-point scale).[2]

Note that it must be clear which IVs used related samples, which used unrelated samples, and the number of levels on each IV. You can find more on how to label experimental designs in Chapter 13.

Keep the DESIGN relatively brief. It should rarely need to be much longer than the above example. If it is longer than this then check that you are not including material that should appear elsewhere in the METHOD section. (This will usually be material that should be included under MATERIALS or PROCEDURE.)[3]

? SAQ 13   What purpose does the DESIGN serve?

Summary of Section 3.1

1 The DESIGN is a brief section in which you make a clear and accurate statement of the principal features of your design.

2 It is a *formal* statement and consists of a precise description of the design that you employed, and what your IV and DVs were.

3.2	**The PARTICIPANTS subsection**

The second part of your METHOD is the PARTICIPANTS. Here you are expected to give a brief description of the critical features of the *sample* in your study. These are the people from whom you obtained your data. The term *participants* is potentially misleading, so be clear about what is required. Concern yourself *exclusively* here with those people who were recruited to your study to be exposed to the different levels of the IV and to provide you with scores on the DV. Do *not* mention here any other people who played a role in the study or the analysis of the data – the experimenter, people who helped you by coding questionnaires or videotapes, or **confederates** (those who took part in the experiment as actors).

There are two aspects of your sample that are of interest to us: in general terms, who they were, and how they were distributed across the conditions.

Who your participants were is of importance because this contributes to the *generalizability* of your findings – the extent to which we can extrapolate your findings to other groups of human beings. This issue concerns the *external* validity of your findings (Section 10.8).

The other issue – how your participants were distributed among your experimental groups – concerns the *internal* validity of your study (Section 10.9). We would want there to be no systematic differences between the participants in your groups, other than those introduced by your manipulation of the IV. For example, we don't want disproportionately more of those who were better at the experimental task to appear in one or other of the conditions.

? SAQ 14   Why not?

For this reason, therefore, it is a good idea to present a breakdown of your participants by condition. For then your readers can satisfy themselves that this was the case.

As a general rule, therefore, you should describe your participants in terms of those variables that are likely to have an influence on the

DV. In practice, however, most of you, most of the time, will need only to describe your participants in terms of the characteristics generally reported in this section: sex, age and occupation (or courses of study if students). You may also be required to give the racial/ethnic breakdown of your sample. If you do, you should avoid describing the participants in ways that they would find negative.

Do not include *procedural* details here (see Section 3.4).

Typically, then, your PARTICIPANTS subsection should include the following:

1 Describe the number of participants per condition, including a breakdown of the sexes. However, please avoid here the "mixed-sex" joke. That is, saying that the participants were of "mixed sex". It'll only prompt your tutor to make some kind of idiotic remark in a strenuous effort to be funny.

2 Mention the age *range*, together with *mean* or *mode*, of the overall sample (break down by condition if there's a lot of variation between the groups).

3 Give some idea of the overall range of occupations or, if using students, courses of study.

4 State the means of selection (randomly, in response to a questionnaire, etc.). Don't lie about this!

5 Mention any inducements used to encourage participation. If the participants were paid, say how much.

6 Describe in principle how the participants were assigned to conditions (i.e., randomly or non-randomly). Describe the precise way in which this was done either here or in the PROCEDURE. Don't lie about this either!

This can in fact be done quite simply:

Participants
   Overall, there were 40 participants, 20 in each of the mnemonic and no-mnemonic conditions. There were 25 women, 13 in the mnemonic condition. The participants ranged in age from 18 to 28, with a mean age of 19.8 years (*SD* = 3.2). All participants were undergraduates at the University of Sheffield. The majority, 30, were reading for science degrees. However, none were students of psychology. Participants were a convenience sample recruited personally by the experimenters from University House, the Students' Union and the Octagon Centre. None of them were acquaintances of the experimenters. Participants were allocated to conditions randomly.

? SAQ 15   What information do readers require about the participants in your study? Why?

If you do a class experiment in which you split up into groups and take it in turns to be experimenter and participant, beware here. In all probability your experiment will be based on the whole class – in which case you should treat the *class* as a whole as your participants, rather than reporting the bit of the experiment that you carried out yourself. If in doubt, check this with your tutor.

Finally, when you run your experiment, make sure that you remember to ask your participants for the information that you need to describe them adequately in this section. It is surprisingly easy to forget this when you're so focused on your manipulation of the IV and on collecting the DVs.

Summary of Section 3.2

1 In the PARTICIPANTS section you provide a brief description of the critical features of the sample that generated your data.

2 The purpose of this account is to tell your reader *who* your participants were and *how* they were distributed across your experimental conditions, so that s/he can assess both the *generalizability* of your findings and whether there were any *confounding variables* arising from the composition of the experimental groups.

3.3   ## The APPARATUS or MATERIALS subsection

Studies in psychology vary a great deal in the amount of equipment used. At one extreme we might simply use a pen and paper. At the other, we might find ourselves using expensive equipment to monitor participants' performances in specially equipped rooms with online control of stimulus presentation and data collection. Be it hi-tech or ever so humble, the place to describe the equipment used in your study is here.

The first thing to decide is whether you used materials *or* apparatus – for this will dictate the title that you give to this section. Unfortunately, the difference between them is pretty vague: essentially, things like pencils and paper, playing cards, and so on, come under the rubric of **materials**; whereas bulkier items, such as computers, cameras and audio equipment, would be called **apparatus**. However, you must decide which of these types of equipment you employed in your study, and label this section accordingly. You should only label the section "Apparatus and Materials" if you are sure that you used *both* types of equipment.

One problem that you may face here is what to do about a questionnaire or scale that you employed in your study. Advice on what to do under these circumstances can be found on the Web site that accompanies this book.

If you only used materials, then this section will probably be little more than a description of the items that you used. Make sure, however, that you write this in coherent sentences. It must not just be a *list* of the items. Write as below:

Apparatus and Materials

A PC (Sinclair C5 Megazap PXII) was used to present the words on a monitor mounted immediately in front of the participant. There were 50 words used in the main experiment. Half of these words came from Clark's (1971) list of easily imaged words (e.g., garage, desk); the remaining 25 words came from Clark's list of hard-to-image words (e.g., conscience, love). There were 20 practice words. Of these practice words, 10 came from Clark's (1971) easily imaged list and 10 from Clark's hard-to-image list. These practice words also comprised the words used in the pretest. The experimental words were matched across conditions for length and frequency using Alston and Evans's (1975) norms. (See Appendix 1 for a full list of the words used.) Participants recorded their responses on a piece of paper.

The manipulation check comprised a list of all 50 words from the main experiment, randomly ordered, on a single sheet of paper. The instructions requested the participants to rate each item for "how easy it is to form a mental image of each of the words". Participants used a 7-point scale to make their ratings, anchored at 0 (*impossible to image*) and 6 (*extremely easy to image*).

Note that this section has been labelled "Apparatus and Materials" because the PC and monitor qualify as *apparatus*, whereas response sheets, pens, and so on, are *materials*.

If you have used visual stimuli in your experiment, provide here an illustration of each type of stimulus. Where you use apparatus, there is a little more scope for expansion in this section, especially if the layout of the equipment is either complex or theoretically important. Under these circumstances, don't hesitate to include a good, clear diagram of the layout (call this a figure; see Section 8.4). Describe the apparatus *precisely*. You would need, for instance, to mention not only that a PC or CD player was used, but also to state precisely what *make* and *model* of PC and CD player they were (as in the fictitious PC above).

? SAQ 16   What is wrong with the following subsection?

> *Apparatus*
> PC
> Audio recorder and microphone
> Playing cards
> Response buttons
> Video camera
> Pens and paper

Perhaps the commonest mistake made in this easiest of sections is to describe the *function* of the equipment – the *use* to which it was put. Strictly speaking, such detail is *procedural*, and therefore belongs in the PROCEDURE. So, do not describe *how* the equipment (material or apparatus) was used here. Simply outline *what* was used and, if relevant, how it was linked together. That is, the section should really only describe the basic *nature* and *layout* of the equipment used.

Summary of Section 3.3

1 In the APPARATUS or MATERIALS subsection you describe the equipment used in your experiment.

2 You should describe this thoroughly, accurately and clearly, using diagrams (call them figures) where these might clarify the picture.

3.4   The PROCEDURE subsection

The final part of your METHOD is the PROCEDURE. In many respects, this is one of the most difficult subsections of the report, because it requires the learning of a rather subtle distinction between procedure and other aspects of methodology. Perhaps the commonest mistake made here is to include material that should have appeared at the end of the INTRODUCTION. For in the PROCEDURE we do not concern ourselves with the broad strategy of the experiment. We are simply interested in a narrow aspect of the campaign – what *precisely* happened to participants from the moment they arrived to the moment they left. This section should provide a blow-by-blow account of what you said and did to a typical participant, in the order in which you did it.

Imagine that instead of being asked to give an account of an experiment, you are in fact writing about an episode of a soap opera that you produced. In order to produce this episode, you have to operate at a number of levels. The episode has to fit into the storyline that has been developed before. You should have established this in the INTRODUCTION, which is effectively a brief synopsis of the story so far (the existing research) for those who've missed previous episodes (the psychologically naive reader). You need equipment to record the episode and props, scenery and locations to provide the background to the action, or even to play a role in the events that take place. This you've described in the APPARATUS or MATERIALS subsection. Similarly, you need a list of the key characters who participated in the episode – those not involved on the experimenter's side of the fence have been described in the PARTICIPANTS subsection. So far, therefore, so good. All of this material provides the necessary *background* to your own episode. However, you have yet to talk in anything other than the barest detail about the actual *events* that took place: the key interactions between the characters, the critical props, and the crucial pieces of dialogue. That is, you have yet to give the reader any idea of how, in practice, you realized the action first mentioned in the latter part of the INTRODUCTION and summarized in the DESIGN. It is the equivalent of this sort of material – the key points of the script – that should appear in the PROCEDURE.

In principle, you should be aiming to tell your readers everything that they need to know in order to *replicate* your study exactly. So, *precision* and *thoroughness* are the watchwords here. Everything of relevance in your procedure should be mentioned in this subsection, therefore – it can be pedantic to the point of being tortuous. However, there are techniques that enable you to lessen the burden on your reader. For instance, you usually need only to describe the procedure in detail for one of your participants. With this done, you can generally outline where the procedure in the other conditions varied in fundamental respects from the one outlined. (There should be enough commonality between the procedures in your different conditions to enable you to do this – see below). This, of course, is where the analogy with an episode of a soap opera breaks down. If anything, in an experiment you have a number of distinctive versions of the script to report – versions that are identical in all respects other than those involving your manipulation of the IV.

? **SAQ 17**   Why should these different versions of the script be identical in all respects other than those involving your manipulation of the IV?

Where you have lengthy instructions, you can usually record the gist of them in this subsection and refer to an appendix in which the full text of the instructions is given. However, you should always report any *critical* features of your instructions (e.g., where the instructions manipulated the IV) **verbatim** here; that is, where this happens you should report *exactly* what you said, together with what you said differently to different participants.

Errors that frequently occur in this subsection are failing to state clearly whether people took part in the experiment individually or in groups, and describing how the data were scored and rendered for analysis. The PROCEDURE should end with the completion of the participant's input to the study (including follow-ups, where these have been employed), not with an account of what you as experimenter did with the scores that you'd obtained. (If you need to report this anywhere, do so at the start of the RESULTS.)

Finally, given the importance of randomization to *true* experiments (Section 13.8), describe clearly in this subsection *how* any randomization was done. It is not enough to say, for example, that you "randomly allocated participants to conditions". You must provide enough information to persuade your reader to accept that the process was indeed *truly* random (Appendix 2).

Procedure

Participants carried out the experiment individually. From the outset they sat in a soundproofed experimental cubicle, facing the monitor on which the words were to appear. Throughout, a closed-circuit video link was used to monitor the procedure and observe the participants. All written instructions appeared on the monitor. Participants read the instructions in their own time, using the mouse to move between screens of instructions. The opening instructions described the experiment as an examination of "our ability to recall lists of items." They described the equipment and its function and outlined the experimental procedure. Once participants had finished reading the opening instructions, the key points of the procedure were reiterated, and any remaining questions they had were answered. (See Appendix 2 for full instructions.)

The experimental session began once it was clear that the participant understood what s/he had to do and had no further questions. The pretest words were presented on the PC in a random sequence. The words appeared singly, on the monitor, centre-screen, with a 5-second interval between each word. Participants recalled immediately after the presentation of the final word. Following the recall period (2 minutes) participants were finally assigned to condition by the experimenter who discretely opened a sealed envelope drawn from a box in an adjacent cubicle. (The box contained envelopes placed in a sequence determined in advance by a colleague using random number tables.)

Those in the mnemonic condition read instructions on how to use the method of loci. These participants practised imagining a familiar room and placing in various parts of this room mental images of the words presented to them. The practice words appeared in a random sequence, presented in the same manner as in the pre test. There were two sets of 10 practice items, with no item appearing more than once. Participants recalled immediately after the presentation of the final word in both lists.

At this stage, those in the no-mnemonic condition simply practised recalling these items. These were the same items, presented in the same manner as above. In all other respects the groups received identical instructions.

At the end of the recall period, participants used the mouse to bring up the next set of instructions. These told them that the experimental session proper was about to commence. Subsequently, the 50 experimental items appeared in a random order, displayed as in the pretest.

After displaying the final word for 5 seconds, the PC presented a series of simple addition and subtraction calculations. This continued for 3 minutes, after which a fresh screen of instructions asked participants to recall as many of the experimental words as they could, using the pen and paper provided. Participants continued until they felt unable to recall any more words, whereupon they undertook the manipulation check. After this, the experiment ended. A brief post-experimental interview was used to explore whether those in the no-mnemonic condition had employed mnemonics on their own initiative (particularly ones that used mental imagery) and whether those in the mnemonic condition had actually used the recommended technique during the experimental session. When participants had no further questions, they were debriefed orally and also given a sheet describing the study's aims. Those wishing to receive details of the eventual findings were sent them on completion of the analyses.

3.5   Interacting with and instructing participants

As you can see, one of the most critical features of your experiment is the instructions that you give to participants – what you tell them about your study, how you tell them what to do, and so on. Consequently, an account of your instructions is a central feature of the PROCEDURE.

In the first place your instructions should be the *only* verbal communication that takes place between you and the participant during the experimental session. Second, in some studies you may actually find yourself manipulating the IV via the instructions that you give to participants in the different conditions. Even where you are not using the instructions to manipulate the IV, you may still often need to give slightly different instructions to those in the different conditions. At all times, however, it is important that you make your instructions as *similar* as you can between conditions, and *identical* within conditions.

? SAQ 18   Why?

For reasons such as these, therefore, you should always use **standardized instructions**. That is, you should make the instructions as consistent as you can *between* conditions in *style*, *content* and *delivery*, and there should be *no* variation in these elements in the same condition. Thus, if you choose to give the instructions orally, you must make sure that you do so in the same manner, and with the same inflections, to all participants – you must, in effect, become an actor delivering his or her lines. If you doubt your ability to do this, then it may be a good idea to record the instructions and to play this recording to your participants instead. Equally, you might print them out and give them to your participants to read themselves. If you are using a computer as part of the experiment, then you could display them on the screen (allowing enough time for your participant to read them, of course). I find it is generally useful to use written instructions if I can, but *always* to go over the gist of what is required of the participant once they have finished reading. (Often they take in less information when reading than they realize.[4])

Writing good instructions is, in fact, a highly developed skill. It is one that you will acquire as you go along. The instructions should be friendly and couched in language that your participants will understand. They should contain enough material for your participants to be able to perform the task that you give them adequately, but often without at this stage giving too much away. For this reason it is important to give participants an opportunity to ask questions *before* the start of the experiment. Restrict yourself, however, to answering questions about the task that confronts them, rather than addressing the wider aims of the experiment – there should be time set aside to discuss those at the end. Make sure that you do all this *before* you start the experiment in earnest. Satisfy yourself that participants understand what is expected of them before you commence – you don't want interruptions, as this will destroy the control that you have built so carefully into the design of your experiment.

Once the experiment has started, you should attempt to keep uncontrolled contact to a minimum. Thus you should avoid unscripted vocal contact, as well as any form of non-verbal contact such as head nodding or shaking, that might influence the participant's performance. At this stage you should be *friendly*, but *uninformative*. Of course this will make for a rather bizarre and artificial encounter – but that's the name of this particular game. Moreover, it may not be easy. Not surprisingly, participants may well attempt to subvert the order that you have imposed by making remarks about their performance that invite your comment. You must resist this and remain non-committal if you wish to remain loyal to your experiment. However, it is worth thinking about the extent to which this feature of experimenting in psychology influences the data that we obtain. It is another aspect of experimental psychology that has come under criticism.

As well as instructions and demeanour, you should be prepared for your participants in other respects too. Once they are with you, you should be able to devote the greater part of your attention to *dealing* with them. Participants are valuable! So, you should prepare everything that you can *in advance* – response sheets, random sequences of orders, and so on – so that you are free to attend to your participants. Also, as I said before, don't forget to acquire the information that you will need to compile your PARTICIPANTS section (gender, age, occupation, and any other information that may be relevant to your particular study, such as right- or left-handedness, quality of eyesight, ability to read English, and so on).

Summary of Sections 3.4–3.5

1 In the PROCEDURE you give a blow-by-blow account of everything that you said and did to a typical participant in your experiment, so that those who wish to are able to replicate it *exactly*.

2 Make sure that you *standardize* the instructions, so that they are identical within a condition and as similar as possible in style, content and delivery *between* the different conditions in your experiment.

3.6   Optional additional subsections of the METHOD

Under some circumstances, you may need to add one or more subsections to your METHOD describing some additional features of your study.

3.6.1   Pilot test

If you have run a pilot test (Section 13.9.3), then you should report the details of it in the METHOD. In most cases this can be done simply by inserting a subsection after the DESIGN, called "Pilot test". Describe in this subsection the participants and any changes that you made to the study in the light of the pilot test. Sometimes, especially with questionnaire-based studies, the pilot is more extensive and involves development of measures for the eventual study. Advice on how to report under these circumstances is on the Web site that accompanies this book.

3.6.2   Ethical issues

When we submit our research for publication we are usually obliged to declare to the editor of the journal that the research has received ethical clearance and has been conducted in accordance with relevant ethical principles. Hence it is rare to see a subsection covering ethical issues in published articles. In reports of your practical work, however, it may be useful to include a subsection outlining any ethical issues that your experiment raised and describing how you dealt with these. Ask your tutor for advice on whether you need such a subsection and what to put in it.

3.6.3 Statistical power

If you have never heard of this concept, ignore this subsection for now. If you have heard of statistical power, you may know that it is possible to calculate in advance how many participants you need to run to achieve a given level of power. If you did not do any such calculations before running your experiment, ignore this subsection for now.

So, congratulations, you did some power calculations before running your experiment! That is *excellent* design work. It is important to let your reader know that your chosen sample size was based on such calculations and what assumptions you made in your calculations. So, provide here the details of the key assumptions that you made in your calculations or when using power tables or a power-calculating Web site. Make it clear whether your effect size estimates were guesses or based on previous research or theory. If you did the calculations yourself put the calculations in a clearly labelled appendix.

Summary of Section 3.6

Where relevant you may need to add the following to your METHOD:

1 A subsection describing your pilot test.
2 An explanation of how you dealt with any ethical problems that you faced in your study.
3 An explanation of how you calculated power to determine your sample size before running the experiment.

4 The RESULTS section

 Diagnostic questions on statistics for Chapter 4

1 What are *descriptive* statistics?

2 What are *inferential* statistics?

3 What is a *statistically significant* difference?

4 What does it mean to say that the *5 percent significance level* was used in an analysis?

5 What is a *type I* error?

If you have difficulties answering any of these questions, turn to Chapter 11.

Of all of the sections of the report, the RESULTS is probably the one that is most frequently mishandled by students. Yet it really is one of the most straightforward sections. All that you need to do in this section is to report the **findings** of the study in the most appropriate manner, resisting in the process any temptation to *interpret* them as you go along. That is, a bit like a journalist of the old school, you must distinguish rigidly between "fact" and "comment". In this section you must not go beyond stating what you *found* ("fact") to discussing what these findings appear to you to *mean* ("comment"). That debate takes place in the DISCUSSION.

What constitutes the findings of your study depends on the nature of the study. In experiments you generate numerical or **quantitative** data (data in the form of numbers) in order to test hypotheses. This means that there are *two* aspects to your findings, *both* of which you should report here. First, you must provide a description of the key features of the *data* that you obtained, in the form of relevant *descriptive* statistics. Second, you must give an account of the type and outcomes of the *inferential* statistical analyses that you performed on these data.

Summary

1 The principal goal in the RESULTS is to report the findings of your study clearly and accurately.

2 Separate fact from comment. In the RESULTS restrict yourself to stating what you found. Consideration of how best to interpret these findings comes in the DISCUSSION.

3 Report both the descriptive statistics and the type and outcomes of the inferential statistics that you used.

4.1   Describing the data

If you reported *all* the data from your experiment – all the numbers that you gathered – it would be quite difficult for your reader to interpret what the scores of your participants had to say. For very few people are capable of grasping the essential message of a set of data from looking at the raw scores (the actual numbers obtained from the participants themselves). We therefore need a way of conveniently and simply summarizing the main features of a set of data. **Descriptive statistics** provide a way of doing this. These are statistics that *summarize* the key features of a set of data. They enable us to assess, almost at a glance, things like whether the scores of our participants tend to be similar to each or whether they vary quite a bit (measures of **variation**, such as the standard deviation or range). Likewise, we can see what score best typifies the data as a whole, or the performance of participants in each condition (measures of **central tendency**, such as the mean or mode). Answers to questions like this help us to make sense of our data and of the outcomes of our inferential statistical analyses.

For instance, imagine that we ran an experiment and obtained the numbers in Table 4.1. In this form it is difficult to make much sense of the data. It is not easy to tell much about the comparative performance of the participants in the two groups. The scores appear to vary quite a bit from individual to individual, but is the *overall* performance of the participants in the two groups all that different? This is, of course, the question that we wish to answer.

Table 4.1   Scores from an Experiment with One Control and One Experimental Condition

Control	Experimental
17.3	6.8
39.2	14.1
20.7	61.2
79.3	61.7
81.5	14.0
24.7	75.9
55.0	32.3
73.6	22.0
33.0	53.1
5.4	83.2
18.6	7.8
42.7	94.8
56.5	49.7
24.9	37.2
57.9	23.9

In Table 4.2 the same data are expressed in terms of two *descriptive* statistics. There is a measure of *central tendency* (in this case the **mean**, which tells us the average performance in each group) and a measure of *dispersion* (in this case the **standard deviation**, which tells us about the extent to which the scores within each group vary). Now our task is much easier. From Table 4.2 we can see, perhaps to our surprise, that the typical performance in the two groups is not all that much different. In addition, the scores of the participants within the two conditions vary quite a bit (the standard deviations in the two groups are high given the mean scores). Looking at this table, it would be surprising indeed if we were to find a statistically significant difference between our two groups. (If we did, we would probably want to check the analysis.)

The numbers in Table 4.1 are what we call in the trade *raw* scores. As the name implies, **raw scores** are the unprocessed scores that you

Table 4.2   The Same Data as in Table 4.1, Expressed in Terms of Two Descriptive Statistics

	Control	Experimental
M	42.0	42.5
SD	24.2	28.5

Note: *M* = mean; *SD* = standard deviation; $n = 15$ in each condition.

obtain from the participants in each condition of your experiment. Because of the difficulties inherent in grasping the essential features of raw data, we tend *not* to put such data in the RESULTS. Instead, we present an account of the principal features of the data in the form of descriptive statistics. Such material we usually display in a suitably formatted, appropriately labelled, and informatively titled *table* – like those used in the example RESULTS in this chapter.

Typically, such **tables** should contain an appropriate measure of central tendency, a measure of dispersion, an indication of the numbers of participants per condition and, once you are familiar with them, relevant confidence intervals. (You will find these measures discussed in any textbook of statistics.) Occasionally you may need more than this, but generally you will not. So, just because your statistical software package pumps out every descriptive statistic under the sun, don't dump it all into the RESULTS. Also, when reporting your descriptive statistics in tables or text, *use two decimal places* at most. Psychological measures are imprecise and do not need the false precision of lots of decimal places, whatever gets splurged out by your statistical package. Where your data are in the form of frequencies and there is only one observation per participant (as, for example, when you have used chi-square to analyse your data) then your table will consist of the counts in each category (as in Table 1 in Section 4.3).

Generally speaking, therefore, there will usually be at least *one* table in your RESULTS. You can find more on how to lay out your tables in Section 8.4. However, sometimes it is still not possible to grasp fully the main features of a set of data from even its descriptive statistics. If you wish to enhance your reader's comprehension of the data, therefore, you might go one step further and present a *graph* of it – especially as many of those who go blank at the sight of numbers have little problem in grasping the message of a well-designed graph. Be warned, however; there are some pitfalls. Advice on the use of graphs can be found in Section 8.5.

Don't be afraid, therefore, to deploy the techniques at your disposal to aid your reader's (not to mention your own) understanding of the basic features of your data. However, don't go overboard here. In an experiment, at least, this aspect of your findings is less interesting than the outcomes of your *inferential* statistical analyses. Think of the descriptive statistics as preparing the ground for the reporting of the inferential analyses.

Summary of Section 4.1

1 In the opening paragraph of the RESULTS, reiterate briefly what data were gathered from your participants (e.g., response time, number

of items recalled, number of people reporting nightmares). That is, remind the reader what the DV was. This both sets the scene and ensures that the reader does not have to hunt through the METHOD to understand your results.

2 In general, you should not include the raw data in this section. Instead, provide a potted account of your data in the form of descriptive statistics. These should generally be presented in tables.

3 However, the use of tables *alone* is not sufficient; you must include explanatory text describing what data appear in the table. (See Section 8.4 for advice about the balance between tables and text.)

4 Report descriptive statistics to no more than two decimal places.

5 Feel free to graph the data as well if you feel that this will help the reader to understand the findings better. However, read Section 8.5 first.

4.2   Analysing the data

After drawing attention to the descriptive statistics, tell your reader about the analyses that you ran on these data and the results of these analyses. These analyses involve the *inferential* statistics, such as *chi-square*, *t tests*, and *analysis of variance* (ANOVA), that you have grown to know and love. This part of the RESULTS can give you sleepless nights. Yet it is nowhere near as daunting as it might at first appear. The key point is to tell your reader *clearly* and *accurately* (a) how you analysed the data, (b) what the outcome of the analysis was, and (c) what this result tells us. There are clear rules to guide you in this. These are:

1 State precisely *in what way* the data were analysed – i.e., which inferential statistical test you used. Describe this test precisely. Do not, for example, say that a "*t* test" was used. Instead, state which *type* of *t* test – for example, a "related *t* test". If you are using ANOVA, make sure that you are precise in your description of the type that you employed (see Section 4.6.10).

2 State the significance level that you used and (where appropriate) whether your test was one- or two-tailed.[1]

3 State the precise value that you *obtained* for the statistic (i.e., the value printed in your output or that you calculated by hand). For example, the value of F or of t. Do this to no more than two decimal places. (Do not slavishly copy out all of the digits to the

right of the decimal point on your statistical output, as this looks *very* amateurish.)

4 Provide the additional information that your reader requires to look up the relevant *critical* value of your statistic should s/he want. These are usually the degrees of freedom or the numbers of participants or observations. Note that you still need to provide this information, even though most of the time a statistical software package will have calculated for you an exact probability associated with your obtained statistic. (For more on critical values, see Appendix 3.)

5 Wherever you can, report the *exact* probability associated with your obtained statistic regardless of whether the outcome is statistically significant or not. Do this to no more than three decimal places (e.g., $p = .002$). Where your output prints $p = .000$ or it is not possible to report the exact probability for other reasons, see Appendix 3 for what to do.[2]

6 State whether the obtained value was statistically significant or not.

7 State explicitly what this result tells us about the data. That is, relate the outcome of your inferential statistic back to the relevant descriptive statistics.

8 Make sure, however, that you distinguish between what you have found and what you believe it means (your inferences and conclusions about your findings). In the RESULTS restrict yourself to describing the findings. Save discussion of how best to interpret these findings until the DISCUSSION.

This sounds like a lot, but in fact the necessary information can be conveyed surprisingly succinctly. For example: "Participants using the semantically related items were significantly quicker to reach the criterion than those using the semantically unrelated items, $t(42) = 2.32$, $p = .025$ (two-tailed test)" or "The effect of reinforced practice upon the time taken to reach criterion was not significant, $t(40) = 1.30$, $p = .20$ (two-tailed test)". How to do this for some of the statistics that you are likely to use when you first start writing reports can be found in Section 4.6. Information on some of the tests not covered there can be found on the Web site that accompanies this book.

4.3   An example RESULTS section

Here is an example of how a basic RESULTS section governed by these conventions might look. In this case the data are frequencies and there is only one observation per participant, so the table of data contains counts, rather than measures of central tendency and dispersion.

Results

The number of participants reporting nightmares in each condition of the experiment is shown in Table 1. The data were analysed using chi-square and an alpha level of .05.

Table 1

The Numbers Reporting Nightmares and Numbers not Reporting Nightmares in the Cheese and No Cheese Conditions

	Nightmare	
Condition	Yes	No
Cheese	33	17
No cheese	22	28

There was a statistically significant association between the consumption of cheese and the incidence of nightmares, $\chi^2(1, N = 100) = 4.89$, $p = .027$. Participants who ate cheese 3 hours before going to bed reported a higher proportion of nightmares than did those who did not eat cheese in that period.

In the post-experimental interviews, after prompting, eight participants were able to describe the experimental hypothesis in full or in part. Five of these participants were in the cheese condition (of whom one reported a nightmare). Of the three in the no cheese condition, one reported a nightmare.

On the design front, note the use here of post-experimental interviews (Section 13.9.4) to investigate the extent to which participants reported awareness of the experimental hypotheses. These are useful things to include, as you will see when we come to the DISCUSSION of this experiment.

If you have more than one set of data and attendant analyses to report, it may be necessary to include separate tables for the different data. If so, consider the data *and* their attendant analyses as two sides of the same coin. So report them as a unit, by describing the data first and then detailing the outcomes of the analyses *before* moving on to the next data/analysis set. However, you should step through these in order of merit, starting with the data and analyses that are central to testing the main predictions of the experiment and working through to the material that is illuminating but essentially ancillary.

This, then, is the basic material that you should present in the

RESULTS. You should remember at all times that the principal aims are *clarity* and *accuracy* – you must give the reader a clear idea of the type of data that you gathered, what its main features are, and the nature and outcomes of your inferential analyses. Moreover, it should be clear at any given point *which* data you are talking about and *which* inferential analysis belongs to that set of data, especially if you have used more than one DV or wish to test more than one set of predictions. You should also make sure that you provide enough information in this section (e.g., in labelling the conditions) for the reader to be able to make sense of your data *without* having to turn to other parts of the report for clarification.

? SAQ 19   Why should you provide readers with such a clear idea of the type of data you gathered, its main features and the nature and outcomes of the inferential statistics that you employed?

? SAQ 20   If you were to come across the following in the RESULTS section of a research report, what criticisms would you have?

The data were analysed using analysis of variance. The results were statistically significant.

4.4   Mistakes to avoid in the RESULTS section

Here are some general tips to help you to avoid some of the commoner mistakes made in this section.

1 The RESULTS should never be just a collection of tables, statistics and figures. This section must *always* have useful and informative text. If you are unsure about how to strike the balance between tables and text, see Section 8.4.
2 Include enough information in this section for the reader to be able to make sense of the results without having to look elsewhere in the report. For example, take care to label conditions or groups meaningfully in tables, figures and text. Avoid using **ambiguous terms** such as "C1" or "Group A". You should not use meaningless or difficult-to-decipher abbreviations *anywhere* in the report (Section 8.2).
3 It is important to look at your data and the descriptive statistics before you analyse the data inferentially (Section 13.9.5). However,

do not **eyeball** the data by writing that there are "differences" between conditions, or that some means are "higher" or "smaller" than are others, *before* you have reported the outcome of the relevant inferential analysis. This is because these numerical differences may not turn out to be statistically significant and the convention in psychology is to talk about differences between conditions *only* if these have been shown to be statistically significant. For example, it is possible to describe the mean score for the experimental condition in Table 4.2 as higher than that for the control condition. However, this difference is extremely unlikely to be statistically significant. It would be misleading to talk about the data in this way and it is *unnecessary* to do so. Talk about differences only *after* you have reported the inferential analysis.

4 Once you *have* reported the outcome of your inferential statistic, you *are* free to comment on the presence or absence of differences among your conditions. This is no longer *eyeballing* the data, as now you know whether the sample differences are statistically significant or not. If you only have two conditions you can go even further and describe which condition was higher, better, faster (or whatever the DV measured) than the other. However, be careful here. One of the commonest and most damaging failings is to talk about differences between conditions even though these have failed to achieve statistical significance. The purpose of testing for statistical significance is to help us to decide whether to treat the means in different conditions as equivalent or as different. If your analyses tell you that you should not reject the null hypothesis, then act on that basis and assume that there are no reliable differences between the relevant conditions. If you write about differences when the analysis has not been statistically significant you are simply ignoring the analysis! Your marker is likely to assume that this is because you do not understand what the analysis means.[3]

5 You do not need to give the underlying details of the inferential statistical procedure (e.g., the rationale and workings of the *t* test) or reasoning (e.g., the principles of statistical significance testing) in this section. (Unless your tutor tells you explicitly to include such material.) One of the apparent paradoxes of the practical report is that whilst you must assume that your reader lacks knowledge of the topic that you are investigating, you *may* assume that s/he has a basic grasp of statistics and of the principles of significance testing.[4]

6 Include sufficient information in this section to enable your reader to reach his or her own conclusions about the implications of your data. Your reader should be able to disagree with your interpretation of the data purely on the basis of the information that you provide here.

7 Do not *duplicate* analyses. For example, do not report *both* a parametric test *and* its nonparametric equivalent (Section 11.4). Decide which is more appropriate for your data and report the outcomes of the one that you choose.

8 Include *all* of the data in this section that you wish to comment upon in the DISCUSSION, however impressionistic, **qualitative** (i.e., not involving numbers) and unamenable to statistical analysis. The inclusion of qualitative data, such as a selection of comments from your participants, can be very useful. However, in *experiments* such data should always be used as a *supplement* to the quantitative, numerical data.

9 Do not necessarily restrict yourself to reporting the obvious analyses – do not be afraid to squeeze all the relevant information from your data that you wish. Bear in mind, however, that your aim is to *communicate* your findings. So avoid overloading this section with irrelevant and unnecessary analyses. Nevertheless, there may be some way in which additional analyses of your data can help you to clarify or choose between alternative explanations or to resolve other issues of interpretation. So, think about ways in which further analyses might be useful.[5]

4.5   Rejecting or not rejecting the null hypothesis

Rejecting the null hypothesis entails that you accept the alternative hypothesis that there is a genuine (statistically reliable) difference between the conditions. This does not mean, however, that you can conclude that the *psychological* hypothesis underlying the experiment has been supported. After rejecting the null hypothesis you have, in fact, to *search* for the most reasonable explanation of your findings. This may well turn out to be the arguments that you addressed in the INTRODUCTION (those that led to the prediction of a difference between these conditions in the first place) – but they needn't be. You can only decide this after a suitable discussion in which you consider and examine closely *all* the plausible explanations of your findings. High on the list of issues to examine will be whether you exercised sufficient *control* in the experiment to enable you to make unequivocal inferences. This is why we require the next section – the DISCUSSION.

Of course, discussion is also needed for experiments in which you have *failed* to reject the null hypothesis. Under these circumstances you also have to work out what this means *psychologically*, as opposed to statistically. As well as examining the adequacy of the control that you exercised in the experiment, another thing to consider when you have *failed* to reject the null hypothesis is whether you had enough data (see Chapter 12).

Summary of Section 4.5

1 Once you have determined whether you have to reject or not reject the null hypothesis, you begin the search for the most reasonable explanation of the findings.

2 This process takes place in the DISCUSSION.

4.6 Reporting specific statistics

Knowing what to report can be bewildering. Even when you've chosen the correct analysis and run it properly, it can be hard to detect the bits that you need to extract from the output to report in the RESULTS. This is especially so when you are a novice, but it can be bewildering even when you are more experienced. So, do not feel alone with this problem. Do *not* under any circumstances, however, cope with it simply by copying over the output from the package, perhaps annotating it by hand, and leaving it at that. I am amazed how often I get grubby bits of second-rate printout stapled into the report, sometimes with no supportive text, often with bits of scribble by way of annotation of the output, and am supposed to be prepared to treat that as if it were RESULTS! In such circumstances I simply assume that the author is unable to detect the bits of the output s/he needs, cannot be bothered to do the hard work of locating the correct material and laying it out properly and neatly, and assumes that I'm too stupid to realize this. As you can imagine, this does not go down well and the mark is not impressive.

The main thing, especially early on in your career, is to demonstrate to your marker that you realize what needs to be reported. The basic rule when reporting inferential statistics is that you need to provide the information that will enable someone else to check whether the outcome of a test is or is not statistically significant (see Section 4.2 and Appendix 3).

The remainder of this chapter provides you with examples of how to report those specific statistics that you are most likely to use in the first year or so of report writing.[6] More information about each of these statistics, together with some of the issues to watch out for when using them, can be found on the Web site that accompanies this book. The Web site also provides examples of how to report other statistics that you may meet later on in your career as a student of psychology. Before using this section or the Web site, you should also be familiar with the issues involved in choosing tests (e.g., Section 11.4). Please note that, with the exception of the example RESULTS for the mnemonic experiment, the tables and figures referred to in these examples are hypothetical and do not appear here.

When reporting, punctuation and use of italic is important, so pay attention to this when preparing your text. In some cases the sequencing is important, as are such seemingly trivial details as whether there is a space between p and $=$ and even whether you put $p = .025$ or $p = 0.025$. This section is a veritable treasure for the anal amongst us. For the rest it can be a trial.

4.6.1 Chi-square, χ^2

The information that you need to provide to enable someone to check the significance of your obtained value of χ^2 is the degrees of freedom. The total number of observations should also be reported. This example has 1 degree of freedom and is based on 100 observations.

> An alpha level of .05 was used. Analysis of the data in Table 1 using chi-square revealed that breaking the speed limit was significantly associated with sex, $\chi^2(1, N = 100) = 10.83, p = .001$. The males tended to break the speed limit, whereas the females tended not to break the speed limit.

4.6.2 Spearman rank correlation coefficient (rho), r_s

The information that you need to provide to enable someone to check r_s is the number of participants. This example has 40 participants.

> An alpha level of .05 was used. Analysis of the data displayed in the scatter plot in Figure 1 using Spearman's rho (corrected for ties) indicated that ratings of mood were significantly positively correlated with the mean ratings of the attractiveness of the photographs, $r_s(40) = .48, p = .002$ (two-tailed test). The ratings were thus moderately correlated, with more positive mood tending to be associated with higher ratings of attractiveness.

4.6.3 Pearson's product moment correlation coefficient, r

The information that you need to provide to enable someone to check r is usually the degrees of freedom, given by the N of observations minus 2. In this example there are 40 participants, so there are 38 degrees of freedom.

> An alpha level of .05 was used. Analysis of the data displayed in the scatter plot in Figure 1 using Pearson's r indicated that age was significantly negatively correlated with the mean ratings of the attractiveness of the photographs, $r(38) = -.37$, $p = .02$ (two-tailed test). The variables were thus moderately correlated, with increases in age tending to be associated with decreases in the ratings of attractiveness.

4.6.4   Mann–Whitney U test, *U*

The information that you need to provide to enable someone to check *U* is the number of participants in group 1 and the number of participants in group 2. This example has 14 and 16 respectively in these groups.

> An alpha level of .05 was used. Analysis of the data in Table 1 using the Mann-Whitney U test indicated that ratings of overall satisfaction with the tutor's teaching were significantly lower among those receiving the positive comment than among those not receiving this comment, $U(14, 16) = 56$, $p = .02$ (two-tailed test).

4.6.5   Wilcoxon's Matched-Pairs Signed-Ranks Test, *T*

The information that you need to provide to enable someone to check *T* is the number of participants overall, not counting those with tied ranks (i.e., not counting those with the same scores in each condition). This example has 18 participants without such tied ranks.

> An alpha level of .05 was used. Analysis of the data in Table 1 using the Wilcoxon test indicated that participants rated their own chances of experiencing the diseases overall as significantly lower than they did the chances of the average student, $T(18) = 27$, $p = .01$ (two-tailed test). (Six participants had tied ranks.)

4.6.6   Kruskal–Wallis one-way analysis of variance, *H*

The information that you generally need to provide to enable someone to check *H* is the degrees of freedom, given by the *N* of groups minus 1. In this example there are 3 groups and therefore 2 degrees of freedom.

An alpha level of .05 was used. Analysis of the data in Table 1 using the Kruskal-Wallis one-way analysis of variance indicated that the ratings of overall satisfaction with the tutor's teaching were significantly different among the three groups, $H(2) = 7.38$, $p = .025$.

4.6.7 Friedman's ANOVA, χ_r^2

The information that you generally need to provide to enable someone to check χ_r^2 is the degrees of freedom, given by the N of groups minus 1. In this example there are 3 groups and therefore 2 degrees of freedom.

An alpha level of .05 was used. Analysis of the data in Table 1 using Friedman's ANOVA indicated that ratings of the chances of experiencing the diseases were significantly different for the three targets (self, best friend and average student), $\chi_r^2(2) = 9.21$, $p = .01$.

4.6.8 The *t* test (independent and related), *t*

The information that you need to provide to enable someone to check *t* is the degrees of freedom. For the independent *t* test the degrees of freedom are given by the N of observations minus 2. The first example below has 15 participants in each condition and therefore there are 28 degrees of freedom. For the related *t* test the degrees of freedom are given by the N of observations minus 1. The second example below, involving the related *t* test, has 15 participants and therefore 14 degrees of freedom.

An alpha level of .05 was used. Analysis of the data in Table 1 using the independent *t* test for equal variances indicated that performance in the end-of-course examination was significantly higher among those receiving the positive comment than among those not receiving this comment, $t(28) = 2.70$, $p = .01$ (two-tailed test).

An alpha level of .05 was used. Analysis of the data in Table 1 using the related *t* test indicated that performance in the end of course examination was significantly higher for the course in which participants received the positive comment than for the course in which they did not receive this comment, $t(14) = 2.49$, $p = .03$ (two-tailed test).

4.6.9   **Analysis of variance (ANOVA), *F***

The information that you need to provide to enable someone to check
F is *two* (NB *two*) sets of degrees of freedom: the degrees of freedom
for the numerator of the *F* ratio *and* the degrees of freedom for the
denominator of the *F* ratio. The numerator is the source under test,
such as the main effect of an IV or the interaction between two or
more IVs. (See Chapter 13 and your textbook of statistics if you are
not familiar with main effects or interactions.) The denominator (the
bit that divides into the numerator) is called the error term.

To illustrate how to go about reporting ANOVAs, here is an
example RESULTS for the mnemonic experiment. This is a more
advanced RESULTS than the earlier example. It is the kind of RESULTS
that you will be expected to write as you become more experienced
(for example, in the second year of a degree course). If you have
difficulty understanding any of the terminology in this, then don't
hesitate to turn to Chapter 13 and your textbook of statistics for
clarification.[7]

Results

An alpha level of .05 was used for all statistical tests. The
pretest data were analysed using one-way analysis of variance
(ANOVA) for unrelated samples, with condition (mnemonic or
no mnemonic) as the independent variable. This analysis was
not statistically significant, $F(1, 38) = 0.33$, $p = 0.57$, indicating
that performance was equivalent in the two conditions
(mnemonic group, $M = 10.95$ words recalled, $SD = 1.05$;
no-mnemonic group, $M = 11.15$ words recalled, $SD = 1.14$).
The groups thus appear to have had equivalent recall abilities
for lists of words before the experimental group were taught
how to use the mnemonic.

The manipulation check on the imageability of the words
used in the experiment was also satisfactory. Analysis of
participants' ratings of the imageability of these words used
one-way ANOVA for related samples with imageability (easily
imaged or hard to image) as the independent variable. This
revealed significantly higher ratings for the easily imaged
words ($M = 5.21$, $SD = .77$) than for the hard-to-image words
($M = 3.39$, $SD = .95$), $F(1, 38) = 151.72$, $p < .001$.

The mean numbers of words of each type correctly recalled
by those in the two conditions (excluding misspellings) are
given in Table 1.

Table 1

The Mean Number of Words from the Easily Imaged and
The Hard-to-Image Lists Correctly Recalled in Each Condition

		Imageability	
Instruction	n	Easily imaged	Hard to image
Mnemonic	20		
M		18.15	13.15
SD		3.79	4.17
95% confidence interval		16.38 - 19.92	11.20 - 15.10
No mnemonic	20		
M		13.80	11.00
SD		3.25	4.62
95% confidence interval		12.28 - 15.32	8.84 - 13.16

The data in Table 1 were analysed using 2 × 2 ANOVA for mixed designs, with imageability (easily imaged or hard to image) as the related samples variable and instruction (mnemonic or no mnemonic) as the unrelated samples variable. There was a statistically significant main effect of instruction, $F(1, 38) = 7.20$, $p = .01$, with those in the mnemonic group recalling more items overall than did those in the no mnemonic group ($M = 15.65$, $SD = 3.97$; $M = 12.40$, $SD = 3.74$, respectively). There was also a statistically significant main effect of imageability, $F(1, 38) = 145.22$, $p < .001$, with more items from the easily imaged list being recalled than from the hard-to-image list ($M = 15.98$, $SD = 4.12$; $M = 12.08$, $SD = 4.48$, respectively). However, these main effects were qualified by the significant Instruction × Imageability interaction, $F(1, 38) = 11.55$, $p = .002$. Figure 1 displays this interaction.

Inspection of Figure 1 suggests that the significant interaction results from the greater number of easily imaged items recalled by the mnemonic group than by the no mnemonic group (difference = 4.35) relative to the much smaller difference between the conditions in recall of the hard-to-image items (difference = 2.15). This is consistent with the experimental hypothesis. However, further analysis is required to confirm this statistically.[8]

The majority of participants (18) in the no mnemonic condition claimed to have attempted to remember the items by rote repetition, with the remainder employing simple attempts at

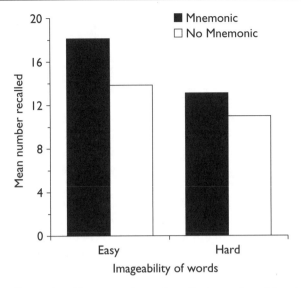

Figure 1. Mean number of easily imaged and hard-to-image words correctly recalled in each condition.

organizing the material into semantically related clusters. All those in the mnemonic condition reported using the method of loci, and most of these expressed their surprise at the impact that this appeared to have had on their capacity to recall.

Note the use in this example of the abbreviation *M* to stand for *mean* and *SD* for *standard deviation* when reporting these descriptive statistics in text rather than in tables. On the design front, note the use of a pretest to check that the groups were equivalent before being exposed to the IV and of a manipulation check to confirm that the easily imaged and hard-to-image words did differ in reported imageability. You will see the advantage of these features when we come to the DISCUSSION of this experiment.

4.6.10 Do's and don'ts when reporting ANOVA

As you are likely to use ANOVA quite frequently as a student, here are some useful do's and don'ts for reporting.

- *Make sure that you indicate precisely which type of ANOVA you used.* You will need to use different variants of ANOVA for different designs. For this reason it is important to specify *which* particular version of ANOVA you used. This is not hard: you can simply use the labelling convention that you employed in the DESIGN. For example, you can say that you analysed the data "using ANOVA for a two-way, mixed design". Alternatively, you could say that you analysed the data "using ANOVA for a 2×2 mixed design". (See Section 13.3.)

- *Make sure that you indicate the number of levels on each IV.* In either case, make sure that you specify which IVs had which number of levels and what these levels were. With mixed designs, don't forget to specify which of the IVs used related samples and which used unrelated samples.

- *Make sure that you report both sets of degrees of freedom for each F ratio.* This is an extremely common mistake and one that is both very damaging and yet easy to avoid. Remember that *every* value of *F* that you report has to have *two* sets of degrees of freedom. One set of degrees of freedom belongs to the *numerator* of the *F* ratio, the other set belongs to the *denominator* of the *F* ratio. Learn to identify each from your output and make sure that you include both.

- *Do not copy over the entire ANOVA summary table and hope for the best!* This is no solution. You have to identify in text the various sources that you are testing with your ANOVA and the precise value of *F* and associated degrees of freedom in each case. In fact researchers tend not to put ANOVA summary tables in RESULTS sections unless there are a lot of effects to report. When they do include ANOVA summary tables, they report only certain parts of the output. (You can find more about this on the Web site that accompanies this book.)

4.6.11 Statistics of effect size

Once you know how to calculate and interpret any effect size statistics, you should add these to your RESULTS. You can find out more about this in Section 12.3.

5 The DISCUSSION section

 Diagnostic questions on design for Chapter 5

1 What is *internal* validity?

2 What is *external* validity?

3 What is a *confounding* variable?

4 What is a *type II* error?

If you have difficulties answering any of these questions, turn to Chapters 10 and 11.

Researchers design experiments to test hypotheses to develop theories or to help solve practical problems. However, in psychology at least, the outcomes of experiments are *not* self-evident. That is, they require *interpretation*. It may not be apparent when you first start practical work, but we need to "discover" what we've found out. For instance, in our cheese and nightmare experiment we may have been compelled by our data to *reject* the null hypothesis that there is no reliable difference between the experimental and control conditions. Now, however, the real work begins. For we need to find out what *caused* the difference that we've found. Was it the independent variable (eating cheese)? Or are there *confounding* variables that could equally well account for this difference? The answers to such questions we can only arrive at by looking carefully at our experimental design and assessing the quality of the *control* that we employed. Only once we've done this can we decide (for it *is* a decision) which of the various options is the *likeliest* explanation for our findings. Only once we've done this will we be able to explore the *implications* of our findings for the area under consideration.

Moreover, this remains true of situations in which the data compel us *not* to reject the null hypothesis. Does this mean that the IV is *not* the causal variable after all? Or was there some aspect of the design that made it hard to detect the effect of the IV on the DV? Again, we can only decide this after a close examination of the experiment. Again, we need to sort this out before we can even begin to assess the implications of the findings for the area discussed in the INTRODUCTION.

The point is that our findings are subject to *uncertainty*. We need to interpret our results. This process is undertaken in the DISCUSSION.

There are three definable stages to the process of discussing the findings. These three stages, in sequence, provide the structure of your DISCUSSION. First, you need to say what needs to be explained. So the first task in the DISCUSSION is to state what the results of the experiment are by providing a précis (in words) of the RESULTS and describing how well they fit the original predictions. Once you have done this, you need to try to *explain* these findings. Is the IV responsible for statistically significant differences? If not, what is? Does the lack of statistical significance mean that the IV does not cause changes in the DV? The second task in the DISCUSSION, therefore, is to explore these issues, arriving if you can at a set of reasonable conclusions. Finally, you need to explore the theoretical implications of the findings, together with any practical ones that they may have. For instance, if you've concluded that the IV was indeed responsible for the changes detected in the DV, what implications does this have for the material – especially the arguments and theories – that you outlined in the INTRODUCTION? This, of course, is the key issue – the reason why we design and run experiments in the first place.

We can crystallize these three phases of the DISCUSSION around three questions:

1 How well do the findings fit the predictions?
2 What do the findings mean? (What, if anything, can you conclude about the relationship between the IV(s) and DV(s)?)
3 What are their implications (especially with regard to the issues that you outlined in your INTRODUCTION)?

Of course the balance between these three phases, and the depth to which you will be expected to follow some of the issues raised by your findings, will depend on your experience as a student of practical psychology. As a novice considerably less will be expected of you here. Your main task will be to state your findings, outline and *assess* the more plausible explanations and, in the light of this, arrive at reasonable conclusions. If you have something sensible to say about how the experiment might have been improved, then consider also including this. In particular, remember that you should be aiming to display clarity of thought and presentation when discussing the outcomes of your experiment. Demonstrate that you understand what you have done and found.

Before we go through the phases themselves, two additional points need to be made. First, if the findings of experiments are subject to uncertainty, you can imagine that findings from studies that are not experimental are even more problematic, as these methods provide us with even less control. Second, science proceeds by argument about evidence. It is important to remember that other people may disagree with your interpretation of your findings. Your task in this section, therefore, is to argue the best case that you can, given your data, and without going beyond the data.

Summary

1 The outcomes of psychology experiments are subject to uncertainty. They require interpretation in order to find out what they have to tell us about whether or not there is a causal relationship between the IV and the DV.

2 The process of assessment and interpretation takes place in three phases in the DISCUSSION. These phases revolve around three questions: (a) What are the findings of this study? (b) What do they mean? (c) What are their implications?

5.1 How well do the findings fit the predictions?

Open the DISCUSSION by describing what you have found and how well the data fit the predictions. Doing this enables you to be clear from the outset about what it is that has to be explained in the DISCUSSION. All of you, therefore, regardless of your level of experience, will need to do this adequately.

5.2 What do the findings mean?

Once you've decided what you have found, you can set about the *process* of drawing conclusions from the experiment. If you have *rejected* the null hypothesis, then you need to assess whether this was indeed due to the manipulation of the IV or whether something else is responsible. If you have *failed* to reject the null hypothesis, then how confidently can you conclude that this indicates the absence of a causal relationship between the IV and DV?

In order to answer these questions as well as you can, you need to sit down and re-examine the experiment. Have you become aware of a confounding variable that you failed to spot before running the experiment? How likely is this variable to account for the findings? In retrospect, was the design likely to have been able to allow you to reject the null hypothesis in the first place? It is only when you have satisfied yourself that there are no confounding variables (Section 9.1.3) or that your design had sufficient power (see below) that you can draw reasonable and firm conclusions.

So, how long this next bit is and how firm are your conclusions will depend on how well designed and executed the experiment was. Before starting on the DISCUSSION, therefore, take a long, hard look at your experiment, identifying its weaknesses but also recognizing its strengths. Once you have listed (to yourself) any weaknesses, then *assess* each of these. Is it a feature that undermines your capacity to attribute changes in the DV to the manipulation of the IV (*internal validity*) or does it instead compromise the extent to which you can generalize the findings (*external* validity)? Do not confuse these (see Sections 10.8 and 10.9); at this stage of the DISCUSSION we are concerned with things that affect *internal* validity. Remember that a *confounding* variable isn't any old variable that you failed to control by holding constant, but one that *systematically* co-varies with the levels of the IV. So, is the variable that you're concerned about *really* a confounding variable? If not, it relates to external rather than internal validity.

Once you have done this, decide which (if any) of these features are sufficiently important to require raising and discussing explicitly in this phase of the DISCUSSION. (Your ability to judge this *as well* as your ability to spot important design problems is being assessed here.) Be honest, but also be sensible – novices especially. Obviously, it is important not to blind yourself to flaws and weaknesses in the design that undermine the conclusions that you can draw. You will not gain marks for pretending that all is well when it is not. However, the solution is not to assume automatically that there are problems and merely catalogue every problem that you can dream up, regardless of importance. It is incredibly tedious to read a mindless list of flaws and problems, doubly so when the experiment is in fact pretty sound and could sustain reasonable conclusions.

With findings that are not statistically significant, are there features of the experiment that undermine your capacity to detect the influence of the IV on the DV? Failing to attain statistical significance may tell you more about the *power* of your experiment than about the existence or otherwise of an effect of the IV on the DV. If you are a novice, or otherwise not yet technically able to discuss power, you should at least consider whether you had enough participants – especially on unrelated samples IVs. Please note, however, that this is definitely *not* a licence to mindlessly trot out the tired old cliché that "we would have obtained significant results if we'd had more participants". This is inevitably true – any effect, however trivial, will become statistically significant if you have enough participants. The question to address is whether you might reasonably have expected to obtain statistical significance given the numbers that took part in your experiment. You can find advice on this issue in Section 12.3 and also in Section 13.1.1.

If you understand about power, then use any relevant confidence intervals that you have reported in the RESULTS to reflect on the likely power of designs that have failed to reject the null hypothesis. Comment also on any relevant statistics of effect size that you have reported there. (Remember, it is possible to estimate effect size whether or not the results are statistically significant.) You can find advice on this in Section 12.3.1.

If your findings are unexpected, especially if they contradict established findings or ideas in the area, be careful. Under these circumstances, many of you lapse into what I call the "chemistry experiment" mentality. That is, when the results don't come out as predicted, you assume that the experiment hasn't "worked" and search for where you went "wrong" – just like we used to when our test-tubes of noxious substances failed to behave as anticipated in chemistry classes (which, as I recall, was most of the time). This is *not* the way to proceed. It may well be that a flaw in your experimental design has produced "anomalous" results. However, you should not automatically assume that this is the case. As a general rule, *believe* your findings until you discover a feature of your design or procedure that casts doubt upon their validity.

On the other hand, the fact that your findings fit your hypotheses should not blind you to features that are problematic. Confounding variables can be lurking anywhere. Check your design for alternative explanations for your findings, even when the explanation that you favour seems so obvious to you as to be undeniably true. (Such as when your findings fit your predictions.)

So, it is a question of balance. Do not jump to conclusions, but do not dwell on every flaw.

If your experiment has been reasonably well designed, at the end of this process you should be in a position to say how likely it is that any difference between your conditions was caused by your manipulation of the IV, or that the absence of such a difference suggests that there is no causal relationship between the IV and DV. This is, of course, what the whole enterprise is about. This is why you spend so much time in the design phase working on such things as your controls for confounding variables. So, if at the end of this phase of your DISCUSSION you are unable to decide about the impact of your IV on your DV with *reasonable* confidence there are obviously design lessons to be learnt. So learn them! (If at this stage your findings remain equivocal, one question that you might address is whether you adequately pilot tested your experiment; see Section 13.9.3.)

5.3   What are the implications of these findings?

The first two phases of the DISCUSSION really are preliminaries for what is to follow. Having decided what it is that you have to explain, and having drawn sensible and balanced conclusions about how best to explain it, you can now get to the nitty-gritty – assessing the implications of the experiment for the work outlined in the INTRODUCTION. What, if anything, have we learned about the IV from the experiment? Does this advance our ideas in any way, or at least qualify them? To what extent can the findings be reconciled with the theoretical ideas discussed in the INTRODUCTION? Indeed, do they enable you to decide between any competing theories?

A good DISCUSSION, therefore, depends upon an adequate INTRODUCTION. Essentially, your task now is to return to the material that you addressed in your INTRODUCTION with the benefit of the findings of your study. So, what you are able to say at this crucial stage of your report depends critically on how well you prepared the ground. Indeed, unless something particularly unforeseeable has occurred, you should find yourself addressing the same themes here as in your INTRODUCTION, albeit with additional knowledge. In general, there should be no need to introduce new evidence from the psychological literature to this section.

Once you have done this you should think about the direction that future work might take. This is particularly important when your study has failed to resolve some outstanding problems and issues. At this stage you might suggest problems that need now to be addressed and, if possible, ways in which this might be done. However, be sensible about this. Think about further work that you might reasonably do yourself if you had the time – sensible next steps in the process of exploring the causal relationships that you've been investigating. Make positive and constructive suggestions. Never write "there is a need for further research" without indicating something about what form this further research should take.

This is all very well, of course, if your findings are relatively unambiguous. However, what if it has not been possible to say much at all about the relationship between the IV and DV? If this has occurred because of design flaws, then you should go some way towards improving your reputation as a designer of experiments here by indicating ways in which future experiments on the same topic might overcome the difficulties that you encountered.

5.4 What to do when you've been unable to analyse your data properly

Sometimes, however, these problems will have arisen because you experienced considerable difficulties with your study, difficulties (such as very few participants) that render your data effectively unanalysable. This, of course, will make writing the DISCUSSION that much harder. Whenever possible, avoid such circumstances *before* running the study. However, such things can occasionally happen even when the study has been well thought out in advance. In such instances, when it comes to writing the report, the important thing is to *be seen to have made an effort*.

Do not, therefore, jump at the opportunity (as you see it) of only having to write a brief and dismissive DISCUSSION, but write as thoughtfully as you would have done in the presence of suitably analysed data. Indeed, one of the most effective ways around this problem is not only to examine *carefully* the reasons for the inadequacies in the data (together with the ways in which such occurrences might be avoided in future work), but also to explore actively the sorts of implications that your data would have held had the results turned out (a) as predicted and (b) contrary to prediction. At least in doing this you will be able to demonstrate your reasoning skills to your marker – as well as being able to practise them.

You should regard this, however, as a last, somewhat desperate, exercise in damage limitation. It is not an alternative to spending time designing sensible experiments and doing adequate pilot work. The best way of dealing with this problem is by making sure that it does not arise in the first place.

Finally, one of the aspects of the implications of your findings that you should bear in mind concerns their external validity or generalizability.

5.5 External validity: the generalizability of findings

All studies have limits on their **generalizability** – that is, on the extent to which we can extrapolate the findings to situations other than those directly assessed in the study itself (Section 10.8). In some cases these limitations are severe. In others, they are not. Yet these limitations are often among the first things to be forgotten when studies are discussed in general terms.

Many factors can affect the generalizability of a study's findings: the equipment and participants that you employed, the procedure that you used, the wording of the instructions, and so on. One particularly potent source of such limitations can come from the level at which *controlled* values were held constant. For example, if you undertake an experiment in which you control for sex by using only women, then perhaps the data are applicable only to women. Or, if you run an experiment in which you test the effects of alcohol on driving performance using participants who are only occasional drinkers, then perhaps the findings will not apply to those who drink alcohol more often.

The generalizability of findings is one of the more neglected issues in experimental psychology. It seems likely that the findings of many studies have been *over*generalized. As students, this is one issue that it will be important to think about in *all* aspects of your course, not just in your practical work. Nevertheless, in your practical work consider this issue when evaluating the studies that you include in your INTRODUCTION and, of course, bear it in mind when assessing your own findings in the DISCUSSION. However, again be sensible and balanced when raising this issue. It is easy to drone on about the failure to employ a random sample of the general population. Yet this is typically to miss the point. Examine whether there are likely to be any important limitations on the generalizability of your findings and whether any simple and reasonable steps could have been taken to improve the situation. Don't waffle on in a tone of self-righteous indignation about the failure to sample adequately every sentient human being within a million-mile radius of the experimental setting.

? SAQ 21   What is the purpose of the DISCUSSION?

Summary of Sections 5.1–5.5

1 You should open the DISCUSSION by summarizing the main features of the RESULTS, so that it is clear both to you and to the reader what you have to explain in the DISCUSSION. Relate your findings to the predictions.

2 Once you've done this, search for the best available explanation of the results, examining and assessing the likely candidates in order to arrive at an overall assessment of what your findings have to say about the existence or otherwise of a causal relationship between the IV(s) and the DV(s).

3 These two stages are the necessary preliminaries for the final phase of the DISCUSSION, in which you assess the implications of your findings for the area as outlined in the INTRODUCTION. At the same time, you should think about the direction and form that future work might take.

4 Where your findings have been too ambiguous to do this, then you should examine both why this has been the case and ways in which the problems that you encountered might be avoided in future work.

 5 End with a paragraph summarizing your main conclusions.

5.6 Some tips to help you to avoid some common failings in the DISCUSSION

1 Do not repeat material that you have covered – or *should* have covered – in the INTRODUCTION. In this section you can assume that your readers have a knowledge of the relevant literature – after all, it was you who gave it to them. Where there are gaps in their knowledge that make it difficult to conduct your argument, and where these are the result of unforeseen rather than unforeseeable factors influencing your findings, then the gaps are of your own making and reflect omissions from your INTRODUCTION.

2 Include a final paragraph summarizing your main conclusions. Be careful, however, to distinguish between conclusions and mere restatements of findings.

3 Remember: do not confuse *statistical significance* (see Section 11.2) with *meaningfulness*. We can draw useful conclusions from data that are not statistically significant. On the other hand, statistically significant effects can be psychologically trivial. Neither confuse statistical significance with *proof*: statistically significant results do not *prove* that the theoretical underpinnings of your study are sound, nor do findings that are not statistically significant necessarily *disprove* your arguments. Life would be much simpler if they did, but unfortunately this isn't the case; in either instance you will still have to justify your point of view in the DISCUSSION.

4 Do not simply reformulate and repeat points that you have already

made. This is **waffle**. Markers are not *that* stupid. We know when you're waffling, so don't waste your time. Each statement should add something to the picture.

5 Do not see the DISCUSSION as an opportunity to indulge in fanciful speculation. Make conjectures with caution and keep it brief.

6 Once you know how, consider the likely effect sizes of the IVs on the DVs when discussing the implications of your findings. Remember that highly statistically significant findings do not necessarily indicate large effect sizes (see Chapter 12).

5.7   Two example DISCUSSION sections

Below are two sample DISCUSSIONS, one for the cheese and nightmare experiment, and one for the mnemonic experiment. These are only suggestions as to how you might go about writing discussions for these sections, and in some respects they provide only outlines of what might be argued. (For those unfamiliar with the term, **demand characteristics** are features of an experimental setting that provide the participant with cues about the experimental hypothesis – such as asking people to eat cheese before going to bed and then questioning them about whether or not they experienced nightmares.)

5.7.1   The cheese and nightmare experiment

Discussion

The results are consistent with the experimental hypothesis: those who ate cheese 3 hours before going to bed reported a significantly greater tendency to experience nightmares than did those who did not eat cheese at this time. Participants were randomly allocated to conditions, thus lessening the likelihood of there being differences between the groups in tendency to experience nightmares to begin with.[1]

Perhaps the most obvious explanation for this finding is that eating cheese before going to bed leads to the experience of nightmares. It may be that one or more of the ingredients in cheese affects the human nervous system and induces nightmares. However, an alternative explanation is that participant awareness of the aims of the experiment influenced the findings. Although the instructions concealed the precise purpose of the experiment from participants, those in the cheese condition ate a measured quantity of cheese at a specified time and (among other things) subsequently recorded the number of nightmares that they experienced. This may have led them by suggestion either to *experience* an increase in the number of nightmares or to *report* such an increase.

It is hard to control for this possibility. However, the questionnaire completed each morning comprised three pages of questions, many of which were "filler" items designed to draw attention away from the questions on nightmares. Careful post-experimental interviewing by an investigator blind to condition revealed few participants able to state the hypothesis of the experiment, even when strongly encouraged to do so. This suggests that the participants had little or no awareness of the experimental hypothesis.

On balance, given this apparent inability of participants to state the hypothesis, it seems reasonable to proceed on the assumption that there may be something to the common-sense idea of a link between cheese and nightmares. Further work should attempt to replicate the current findings, controlling as much as possible for demand characteristics. These studies should move away from a complete reliance on self-reports; researchers should also take less subjective measures, such as measures of rapid eye movement (REM) sleep. Although it is not possible to obtain objective measures of dream content, measures might reveal differences in the amount of REM sleep in the two conditions. In all experiments, investigators should make every attempt to mask their hypotheses.

Once further research has established that there is a link between cheese and nightmares, work can begin to determine which of the ingredients of cheese causes the problem. Isolating such an ingredient might help to reduce such unpleasant experiences (particularly if the ingredient is common to a number of foodstuffs) and may also provide useful insights into the brain's chemistry.

Thus the data from this experiment raise the possibility of a link between eating cheese and experiencing nightmares. However, it is not possible to rule out an explanation of the findings in terms of demand characteristics. The next step is to replicate this study controlling as much as possible for demand characteristics.

5.7.2 The mnemonic experiment

Discussion

Participants using the mnemonic recalled significantly more of the easily imaged words than did those not using the mnemonic. However, the groups recalled similar numbers of the hard-to-image words. Thus, as predicted, the mnemonic specifically enhanced recall of the more easily imaged words.

The pretest data suggest that, overall, the two groups had similar ability to recall lists of words prior to the experimental group being taught how to use the mnemonic. It thus seems reasonable to conclude that the randomization to conditions was successful and that it is unlikely that the findings arose from individual differences between the groups in their abilities to recall lists of words.

The manipulation check confirmed that the participants rated the words classified as easily imaged as being easier to image than those classified as hard to image. This corroborates the classification of Clark (1971) and the manipulation of word type imageability used in the current experiment.

The findings of this study are thus consistent with those of Clark (1971). The data suggest that the method of loci does make a difference to recall and does so by enhancing the recall of easily imaged words. Nugent et al.'s (2000) failure to find an improvement in recall among those using the mnemonic appears to have resulted from not allowing the participants enough time to practise using the mnemonic.

The current findings have limited theoretical implications. There is some suggestion in the data that the participants recalled easily imaged words more readily than they did hard-to-image ones. (The 95% confidence intervals for the means for the easily imaged and hard-to-image words for the no-mnemonic group overlap but only by a small amount.) Of course, despite being matched for length and frequency, there may have been other ways in which the lists differed over and above their imageability that could account for any differences in recall. However, the data in both Clark (1971, Table 2) and Nugent et al. (2000, Table 1) show differences in the same direction and of similar size. Nugent et al. used different words. In combination, these data raise the possibility that easily imaged words may be intrinsically easier to recall even without the use of a mnemonic (perhaps because they typically denote more familiar, concrete objects). Given that this difference would be theoretically interesting, future research might test whether people recall easily imaged words more easily and investigate reasons for the difference if it is shown to exist.

The practical implications of the current findings are clear. Researchers must ensure that their participants have had sufficient practice in the use of the mnemonic before the start of any experiment in this area.

In conclusion, the findings suggest that the method of loci does make a difference to recall and does so by enhancing the recall of easily imaged words. Nugent et al.'s (2000) failure to find an improvement in recall among those using the mnemonic appears to have resulted from not giving the participants enough time to practise.

6 The TITLE and ABSTRACT

Although the TITLE and ABSTRACT are the first items to appear in the report (Figure 1.1), I have left coverage of them until the end. This is partly because you need to understand something of the report's structure and purpose before you can begin to appreciate the nature and function of these sections. It is also because they are invariably better left until later in the writing sequence.

In order to understand the reasons for the form that the TITLE and ABSTRACT take, we need to remind ourselves of the function that they serve in a *research* article (Section 1.4). They are in fact vital to its research function, for they alert potential readers to the existence of an article of interest to them. These days most of us search for articles of interest among electronic databases of titles and abstracts, such as the *Social Science Citation Index* and *Psychological Abstracts* (Section 1.5). Thus it is often on the basis of the title and abstract alone that most readers will decide whether to read a paper or simply to ignore it. The TITLE and ABSTRACT, therefore, need to summarize the study clearly, concisely and (if possible!) engagingly. They should also be *self-contained*, being fully comprehensible without reference to any other part of the paper. These are your goals too, when writing these parts of your report.

6.1 The TITLE

The title should be as informative as you can make it within the constraints imposed by its length (no longer than one sentence, although you may include colons or semi-colons). It forms, in fact, the first step in the process of searching the literature. It is to a title that would-be readers turn initially in order to discover whether the paper might be of interest. You should, therefore, provide sufficient information at this stage to enable readers to make this initial decision. So, never be vague in the title. Do not title your report "Memory", for example, or "The Effect of Recall Aids" but something like "The Effect of Word Imageability on Recall Using the Method of Loci Mnemonic". If it accurately describes the findings, you can even consider a directional account of them in your title (i.e., one that specifies which direction the differences went in). For example, "The Method of Loci Enhances Recall of High-Imageability Words When Participants Have Enough Practice".

In experimental studies, if possible, you should mention the IV(s) and the DV in the title. Note also that you should begin the first word of the title, together with all subsequent key words, with a capital letter.

Avoid abbreviations and redundancy – phrases like "A Study of" or "An Experimental Investigation of" should not appear. Aim for about 10–12 words. (The directional version of the title above is therefore a bit too long.)

6.2   The ABSTRACT

The ABSTRACT constitutes the next stage in the process of searching the literature. Having gathered from the title that an article may be of interest, would-be readers will generally turn next to the ABSTRACT in order to decide whether to invest time and energy in reading the full paper. So in this section you should provide enough information to enable them to reach this decision. As well as this, however, you should attempt to be as brief as possible. The whole section, then, involves a compromise between these two aims. An abstract should rarely exceed an average paragraph in length, approximately 100–120 words.

Indeed, together with the DISCUSSION, the ABSTRACT is one of the most difficult of the sections to write; even quite experienced students (not to mention the odd member of staff, myself included) continue to encounter difficulties with this section. So don't be too dismayed if your initial attempts meet with failure. Where you experience difficulty with this section, thumb through journal articles to see how the abstracts have been written there. There really is a "feel" to a good abstract that is perhaps best absorbed in this way.

What material should the abstract contain? The *APA Publication Manual* (APA, 2001) states that the abstract of an empirical study should describe in 100–120 words the material in the left-hand column of Table 6.1. Address each of these features of your experiment in the above sequence. In doing so:

Table 6.1   What Should be Where in the ABSTRACT

What to describe	Advice
1 The problem under investigation	In one sentence, if possible. Do not repeat the title.
2 The participants	Specify pertinent characteristics, such as number, type, age, sex and method of selection.
3 The empirical method	In this case, the experiment. You should mention also any specific apparatus, key features of the data gathering procedures, and the complete name of any published scales or testing procedures used on participants.
4 The findings	Mention the statistical significance level used (if any).
5 The conclusions	Plus implications or applications.

1 Include the bare essentials. Remember that your task is to provide the minimum amount of information necessary for someone to be able to grasp fully what you did. In general, there is no need to include those procedural details that might be expected to form part of any well-designed experiment, although *unusual* procedural details, or those relevant to the conclusions, should be mentioned briefly.

2 Always look for ways of condensing this section, while retaining intelligibility and informativeness. Once you have the first draft, go back through it, eliminating extraneous details, redundancies and phrases that contain no real information (e.g., "The implications of the findings are discussed", "It is concluded that").

3 Make sure that the ABSTRACT is self-contained. Define any abbreviations and acronyms. Paraphrase rather than quote. The reader should not have to look elsewhere in the report to make sense of the ABSTRACT.

4 Make sure that the conclusions that you mention are the main ones and are those that you actually arrived at in your DISCUSSION – not ones unrelated to these or "afterthoughts".

5 Make sure that the ABSTRACT is accurate and non-evaluative. Do *not* include information that does not appear in the body of the report. Do *not* add to or comment on what is in the body of the report.

6 Despite all of this, try to make it coherent and readable! Aim for an ABSTRACT that is readable, well organized, brief, and self-contained.

As you can imagine, this is a challenging task. However, given its role, the ABSTRACT is perhaps the most important paragraph in the report, so it is worth working on. Novices should concentrate at first on the basics – providing the required information (Table 6.1, column 1) succinctly.

? SAQ 22   What functions do the TITLE and ABSTRACT serve in a research paper?

Here is an example ABSTRACT for the mnemonic study. (See if you can find ways of improving it.)

Abstract

This experiment tests whether recent research failed to show an effect of word imageability on recall using the method of loci because the researchers gave participants insufficient time to practise. A convenience sample of 40 undergraduates (both sexes) either received instruction in the mnemonic or did not. Experimental participants practised using the mnemonic. A computer presented participants with words that varied in imageability. Participants using the mnemonic recalled significantly more easily imaged words than did those not using the mnemonic, but similar numbers of hard-to-image words. (Overall alpha level was .05.) Thus the method of loci enhanced recall of easily imaged words. Researchers must ensure that participants have sufficient practice in using the mnemonic.

You might find that you are required to write a **structured abstract**. In this case the structure that is implicit in an ABSTRACT like the one above is made explicit by using headings – for example, Background, Aims, Methods, Results, Conclusions. Even if the ABSTRACT is not explicitly structured in this way, it is a good idea to write your drafts as if it were.

Summary of Sections 6.1–6.2

1 In a research report the TITLE and ABSTRACT serve to alert potential readers to an article that might be of interest.

2 They should, therefore, summarize the study clearly, concisely and attractively.

3 The TITLE should be at most a sentence in length, the ABSTRACT no longer than an average paragraph.

7 References and appendices

7.1 The REFERENCES section

This is one of the most neglected sections of the report. Do *not* neglect this section, as it helps to round off the report in style. When I mark essays and reports this is in fact the first section that I look at. It tells me a lot about the student's attitude to their work, their attention to detail and their knowledge of the discipline's writing conventions.

You will be required to write one of two types of REFERENCES. One type consists solely of a list of the sources that you used in writing the report. In such a REFERENCES section a book (e.g., your course textbook) or an article may appear *even though* you have not cited it in the text. Likewise, many citations may occur in the text but not in the REFERENCES.

The other sort of REFERENCES is the one that you see in journal articles and books. This is a complete and accurate list of *all* the citations that have been made in the text, and those alone. In the UK, final-year projects are expected to have an exhaustive REFERENCES of this sort.

Which you should use is highly contentious. Different tutors have different expectations and some can hold forth on this issue with vehemence. The safest bet, therefore, is to find out which your tutor expects and to provide it. Failing that, I advise you to opt for the exhaustive version and, if you get it wrong, to blame me. *In either case*, the citations in the REFERENCES should appear in the sequence and with the format described here.

7.2 General rules for the REFERENCES section

1 Your references should be in alphabetical order, commencing with the first author's surname and taking each letter in turn.

2 An author's one-author publications (those in which s/he is the sole author) should be placed *before* his or her *joint* publications. For example, Clinton, W. J., will come before Clinton, W. J., & Lewinsky, M. S. However, Clinton, W. J., & Lewinsky, M. S., will come after Clinton, W. J., & Clinton, H. R.

3 With *multiple* publications by the same author(s) place them in *chronological* order. For example, Blair, A. C. L., & Livingstone, K. (2002) must appear before Blair, A. C. L., & Livingstone, K. (2003).

7.3 Citing specific types of reference

There is a standard format for referencing different types of publication. Here is an example REFERENCES section. It includes illustrative examples for most of the journal articles, books and other publications that you are likely to need to reference as a student. It shows you how to reference edited books, books that have more than one volume or edition, annual publications and articles in press.

Note that, as has been the case in all the example sections in this book, the precise layout is important. This is a splendidly anal section. To look professional, the punctuation, case, order of initials, spaces and use of italic should all be as per the example.

References

Dull, V., & Boring, T. D. S. (2002). The effects of locus of control on attributions for performance outcomes among junior high school pupils. *The Journal of Tedious Research, 52,* 317–324.

Duller, M. (2001a). The effect of strip lighting on workers' attitudes towards their managers. *Journal of Incremental Studies in Occupational Psychology, 85,* 219–225.

Duller, M. (2001b). Strip lighting and managers' attitudes towards their workers. *The Work Psychologist, 1,* 3–15.

Fab, I. M., Smart, R. V., & Clever, B. (Eds.). (2003). *Mood, cognition and action* (Vol. 1). New York: University of New York Press.

Genius, T. (2003). Why we do what we do: Absolutely everything explained. In I. M. Fab, R. V. Smart, & B. Clever (Eds.), *Mood, cognition and action* (Vol. 2, pp. 1–110). New York: University of New York Press.

Genius, T., & Zealot, U. C. (2002). *Absolutely everything explained simply.* Cardiff, UK: The Patronizer's Press.

Gorbachev, M., & Reagan, R. (1986). Staring you in the face. In I. T. Botham & M. Argyle (Eds.), *If it had teeth: Fifteen years of*

  research into non-verbal communication (pp. 17–32). Moscow:
  Glasnost & Perestroika Press.

Heavy, B. C., Weather, A., & Grind, T. D. (2001). Fifteen years
  on and still staring you in the face. *Annual Review of
  Qualitative and Quantitative Psychology, 45*, 210–275.

Nasty, B., Evil, B., Demon, C. U., & Warped, T. C. (2003).
  Practical psychology for dictators (24th ed.). Hades, TX:
  Pandemonium Press.

Running from home. (1995). Brighton & Hove, UK: British
  Exercise Society.

Tired, A., & Worne, D. A., Jr. (in press). *The psychology of ageing.*
  London: Old, Young & Son.

Twit, A. I., & Daft, H. K. J. (2002). Holiday preference theory:
  A meta-analysis [Electronic version]. *Psychological Reviews, 12*,
  171–173.

7.4 Citing electronic and online sources

These days, more and more of the material that you might want to
cite in your report is available to you electronically. Some of this
material will also have been published in print form; some of it will
not. In either case, the procedure is to indicate in the references section that the material was accessed electronically.

If you have accessed a published journal article from an online
version of the journal, then add to the reference the statement [Elec-
tronic version], as in the Twit and Daft (2002) reference in Section
7.3. For anything else that you access electronically, add a *retrieval
statement*.

A **retrieval statement** gives the date on which you retrieved the
document and the source. Examples of sources are an electronic database that you used to obtain an article or abstract (such as PsycINFO)
or the URL (uniform resource locator) that leads to the material on a
Web site. For example:

Bush, G. W., Jr., & Gore, A. A., Jr. (2000). Patterns of voting
behavior by US state and region. *Machine Voting Quarterly, 25*,
536–537. Retrieved December 13, 2000, from PsycINFO
database.

Blair, E. A. (2002). *The personality profiles of winners of Big Brother.*
Retrieved June 3, 2002, from University of Newport, Psychology
Department Web site: http://www.unewp.ac.uk/research/
papers/bigbro.html

It is important to give the date of retrieval as the Internet is volatile – documents change, move or disappear from it altogether.

If you have retrieved and read only an abstract, rather than the full article, start the retrieval statement with the phrase "Abstract retrieved".

The rule is to be as precise as you can when you reference material on the Internet. So, provide a URL that directs the reader as closely as possible to the material that you have cited in your report – preferably the specific document rather than the home page or a menu page. It is also important that the address works! So, check that it does in the day or so before handing in your report and update the address if necessary.

For material from Internet sources, in text cite the names of the author(s) of the document and the year in which it had last been updated at the time of retrieval, just as with any print document. To cite specific parts of the document in text provide the usual details – chapter, figure, or table numbers and pages or paragraph numbers for quotes (where these are available).

7.5 Appendices

Some students' reports seem to have had almost as much effort expended on the **appendices** as on the rest of the report. This is invariably a waste of effort as appendices are rarely examined in any detail by your tutors – and when they are this is usually because you have included in this section something that should have appeared in the body of the report. The purpose of appendices is essentially to enable you to expand on information that you have been able to include only in abbreviated form in the body of the report itself. *However, all vital information should appear in the report, not here!* So, include in appendices things like the verbatim instructions (when these are too long to include the full text in the PROCEDURE), a copy of the questionnaire that you used in your study, examples of the stimuli or lists of words that you used, and so on. However, make sure that no vital information is mentioned here for the first time!

If you have a punitive word limit, then obviously more material than is usually the case has to appear in the appendices. However, think carefully and constructively about this. Don't put more material than is strictly necessary in the INTRODUCTION or write a self-indulgent DISCUSSION. Leave yourself room to put the key material in the METHOD and RESULTS. Strike a balance.

8 Producing the final version of the report

The material that I have presented you with so far in Part 1 of this book should go a long way towards helping you to produce good reports of your practical work in psychology. In this final chapter of Part 1, I want to talk about some general aspects of report writing that you will also need to be familiar with in order to produce the final version. I also want to give you some pointers to help you to produce reports that not only read well but also *look* as if they have been produced by someone who understands what is required of them.

8.1 Writing style

There's no doubt about it: psychology has more than its fair share of bad writing. The scientific aspirations of the discipline have led some authors, desperate to give their writing an objective, impersonal, and transhistorical flavour, to produce some quite astonishingly tortured and turgid prose. I own up to having done my bit: there are articles of mine out there written in determinedly dull, coma-inducing prose. I have also read more than my fair share, often from students trying to find the style. It is important to recognize that scientific writing has features that set it apart from creative writing. It does not follow from this, however, that the result should be jargon-laden, stuffy or pretentious.

There are numerous guides available to you on writing clearly for psychology. One I particularly recommend is Sternberg's *The Psychologist's Companion* (1988). The *APA Publication Manual* (APA, 2001) also has a good chapter on principles to follow when expressing your ideas in writing. Use the most up-to-date versions of these guides.

The objective when writing is simple: to communicate clearly. The rules are pretty straightforward: present ideas in an orderly manner, express yourself smoothly, precisely and economically, avoiding jargon, wordiness and redundancy. Despite this, it can be enormously tempting to ramble about, waffle on and obfuscate (by using words like "obfuscate"), especially when you're not quite sure what you're talking about. Resist this temptation. Above all else, learn to develop your arguments logically and to articulate them clearly. Write them down simply and clearly. Develop good habits from the outset!

In terms of writing style, there are a few rules and many guidelines. One absolute rule is that you must not use racist or sexist language. For example, only use "he" or "she" when you are actually referring to a male or female. Otherwise use alternatives (there are plenty of examples of how to do this in this book, some clumsy, some less so).

One important guideline is to use references to the **first person** (*I*, *my*) sparingly and *only* when it is necessary for you to do so. Use the plural (*we*, *our*) only when referring to yourself and the co-designers of your experiment. Another important guideline is to try to use the **active** voice rather than the **passive** voice as much as possible. A sentence in the active voice has the word order subject–verb–object. For example: "Harris wrote this book." Sentences in the passive voice tend to be longer and duller to read. For example: "This book was written by Harris." Avoid passive phrases. So, write that someone did, found, argued, claimed, used something, rather than that something was done, argued, found, claimed, used by someone.

8.2 Definitions and abbreviations

Always define the critical terms that you use in your report. If you cannot decide whether or not to provide a definition, provide one – at least then you can guarantee that people know for sure how you intend to use the term. *Never* make the definition up yourself. Search for a *professional* definition rather than one from an ordinary dictionary. This is because we generally use terms in psychology (e.g., attitudes, perception, emotion) in ways that are different from those in which lay people use them. You can obtain professional **definitions** from other papers in the area or textbooks, and there are also available dictionaries of psychological terms. You must always cite the source of the definition. For definitions taken from papers or textbooks, provide also the page number (as with any quotation – Section 8.3).

If you wish to use **abbreviations**, make sure that you define these on their first appearance – by writing the term to be abbreviated out fully, together with the abbreviation in brackets. For example, "the galvanic skin response (GSR)"; "increasingly on the World Wide Web (WWW)". After this you can simply use the abbreviated form. Use abbreviations sparingly, however. Do *not* make up your own and use abbreviations *only* where the full term would have appeared frequently in the text.

Summary of Sections 8.1–8.2

1 Get into good writing habits from the outset: develop your arguments logically and write simply, clearly, precisely and concisely.

2 Define all critical terms, using a definition obtained from the literature.

3 Use abbreviations sparingly and only where the full term would have appeared frequently in the text.

8.3   References in the text

Not only is it important to reference in the text, but it is important to do so *properly*. Do *not* be slapdash about this! There are clear and detailed rules in psychology about *precisely* how you should reference in the text and you ignore these at your peril. Be warned: few things can incite the ire of a tired marker more easily than a failure to reference properly in the text. (Believe me.) Here are the basic rules. Abide by these and you should be fine.

The basic requirement is to provide the names of the authors whose work you are citing or quoting and the date on which the work was published. These references can either be *direct* or *indirect*. In **direct references** only the date is placed in parentheses:

Daft and Twit (1999) found that people typically prefer holidays to working.

Alternatively, you can recast the sentence and omit the parentheses:

In 1999, Daft and Twit found that people typically prefer holidays to working.

In **indirect references** both the names and date are placed in parentheses:

People typically prefer holidays to working (Daft & Twit, 1999).

Note also that the "and" in the direct reference changes to "&" in the indirect reference.

The next rule is that it must be clear to which authors and to which of their publications you are referring at all times. If there is no ambiguity – such as sometimes occurs when you are citing the same publication more than once on the same page – then you need not repeat the date. However, if there is potential for ambiguity, include the date as well.

> Daft and Twit (1999) found that people typically prefer holidays to working. They developed *holiday preference theory* (HPT) in the light of this finding. In a review of HPT, Daft, Twit, and Total-Idiot (2002) found little or no work on the theory by authors other than themselves. They concluded the review by stating that "it is time for more researchers to take up the challenges posed by HPT" (p. 32).

In the rare event that two authors of different articles share the same surname, to differentiate them put their initials before their surname each time you cite them in the same report.

The more prolific authors may publish more than one article in a given year. If you cite more than one publication by the same *single* author in the same year, then assign the different articles lower-case letters to distinguish them. Use these letters in the remainder of the report and in the REFERENCES section too (Section 7.3). You also need to do this for multiple authors *if* the same list of names appears in the same order on different articles in the same year.

> Smug and Prolific (2000a) dismissed HPT as "having no evidential basis whatsoever" (p. 15). They based this claim in part on their own finding that people spent considerably more of their lives working than on holiday (Prolific & Smug, 2000; Smug & Prolific, 2000b).

Don't make the mistake of copying lower-case letters over mindlessly from a reference in a published article or book and using them in your report when they're not needed.

Where a publication has more than two authors, include all the names the first time that you cite it. Subsequently, cite only the first author followed by "et al." to indicate that there are additional authors:

> In further work, Prolific, Smart and Verbose (2001) used focus groups to explore the meaning of work for workers in holiday settings, such as coastal resorts. The workers were often confused by having to work when other people were on holiday. Prolific et al. found that students working on the island of Ibiza for the summer were "particularly confused" (2001, p. 27).

If there are six or more authors, use the et al. version even for the first citation. If two different publications shorten to the same form, do not use the et al. at all when citing these references. *Never* use et al. in the REFERENCES.

Where you wish to use a number of references to support the same assertion then put these in *alphabetical* order. The rule is that the citations appear in the same sequence as they do in the REFERENCES section (Chapter 7). Use semicolons to separate publications by different authors.

> Since then, researchers have found confused students working in coastal towns and villages throughout the Mediterranean (Beano, 2002a, 2002b, 2003; Chancer, Luck, & Happy, 2002; Happy, Luck, & Mainchance, 2002; Nicejob & Gottit, 2001, 2002, in press; Smashing, 2001).

When you wish to **quote** what someone has written, you must quote *exactly* what he or she wrote (including any spelling or grammatical mistakes). You must also state on which page of which of his or her publications the quoted material appeared. Put the quote in double inverted commas. Do this every time you quote. The above examples include several illustrations of how this should be done.

If you want to quote a sizeable chunk of an author's text (40 or more words) then put this material as a **block quotation**. This starts on a new line and forms a block of indented text that stands out from the rest of your paragraph. You can see how this has been done in journal articles and textbooks. Because the text stands out as an extract from somewhere else, you do not use inverted commas for block quotations. In general, however, try to avoid using long extracts if you can. Ask yourself why you feel it is necessary to use such a big chunk of someone else's words.

Don't go overboard, however. It is unusual to need to quote extensively. Quote verbatim when it is essential to report the exact words used by another author (e.g., when using a definition or citing a key part of their instructions). Otherwise paraphrase rather than quote. When you paraphrase it must be clear whose work or ideas you are citing. However, there is no need to provide the page number for the paraphrased material.

Make sure that you *never* wittingly or unwittingly give the impression that other people's ideas or writings are your own. To do so is to commit the heinous crime of **plagiarism**. Sensible use of the rules described here will help you to avoid this problem. Make sure that your reader can readily identify the sources of the ideas, arguments and findings that you include in your report.

? **SAQ 23**   Correct the following references:

> Blake, Perry & Griffith, 1994, found that performance on the
> experimental task improved considerably when participants
> were in the presence of a group of peers. This contradicted
> previous findings in the area. (Bennett and Bennett, 1981, 1981:
> Scoular, 1973, 1964: Buchanan & Livermore, 1976, Pike, 1992).
> As Blake, Perry & Griffith put it "it is not clear why this
> happened."

You must make sure (a) that the reference exists, (b) that it says
what you claim it says, and (c) that you have referenced it correctly.
Do not be tempted to invent references: the chances of being caught
are high and the consequences serious.

Summary of Section 8.3

1 There are rules in psychology governing the way in which you make
   citations in text to references.

2 The basic requirement is to provide the names of the authors whose
   work you are citing or quoting and the date on which the work was
   published.

3 The rules are designed to make it clear to which authors and to
   which of their publications you are referring at all times.

4 You must make sure that the reference exists, that it says what you
   claim it says, and that you have referenced it correctly.

8.4   Tables and figures

You will certainly need to put **tables** in your report. Tables can convey
information more succinctly than can text. Likewise, a good **diagram**
or **figure** can save, if not exactly a thousand words, at least quite a
few. I'm often struck by how reluctant students can be to include
useful diagrams in their reports and essays, even where the verbal
descriptions that they have to use instead are convoluted and hard to
follow. So, consider the use of a figure whenever you are having
trouble describing something in text and if you think that including it
will add to your report without detracting from the flow. Do not
overdo this, of course. Too many figures can disrupt the flow of the
report.

Keep the format of tables simple and clear. There are rules and guidelines governing the production of tables for papers in journals, such as those in the *APA Publication Manual* (APA, 2001). I have based the tables in the example RESULTS on these guidelines. These rules are useful as they produce clean and well-spaced tables that are easier to read than fussier layouts. Things to notice and emulate include the extensive use of white space rather than vertical lines to separate the elements of the table and the limited use of horizontal lines. You should *never* use vertical lines in the tables in your report. Produce tables that look like the ones in this book or those that you see in the better psychology journals. Do not be fooled by your word-processing package into producing tables that look fancy but are more appropriate for a sale's talk than for reporting scientific material.

Make sure that your reader can readily interpret the entries in a table or a table heading. Do not, for example, use terms that are hard to decipher, such as "C1" or "Group A", unless you provide the key to them in a note beneath the tables and figures in which they appear.

Where you use them, think carefully about the balance between tables and figures and what you put in the text. It is easy to get confused over what should appear in tables and what should appear in the text. Tables and figures supplement but do not duplicate the text. Your task in text is to discuss their highlights. Think of yourself as somewhat like a tour guide to a new city or gallery of modern art. Your task is to help the visitor (your reader) to know where to look and something of what they should note when they do. So, you draw the reader's attention to a building or exhibit. ("The data are in Table 1"; "Figure 1 shows the interaction between . . .".) Then tell the reader something about what to note about this interesting object. ("Those receiving auditory warning signals performed significantly better on the monitoring task than those receiving visual warning signals, except when the visual displays were superimposed on the windscreen . . ."; "Participants attributed significantly more positive items than negative items to themselves, but significantly fewer positive items than negative items to their assigned partners . . .".) However, no guide is ever going to be able to say absolutely everything that there is to say about each and every exhibit. Similarly, you do not need to discuss every item of the table or every feature of the figure in the text. If you do, then they are redundant and should be omitted. Your goal is to draw your reader's attention to the main points of interest.

Likewise, it would be an odd guide who drew attention to one exhibit, but told the audience what to note in something else. So, put tables, figures and text together in coherent units, just as you would with exhibits in the gallery.

Where you use tables or diagrams, you must observe the following rules:

1 Label all tables consecutively, using arabic numerals (e.g., Table 1, Table 2, etc.).
2 Call everything else that is not a table a *figure*. This includes graphs (see Section 4.6).
3 Label all figures consecutively, also using arabic numerals (e.g., Figure 1, Figure 2, Figure 3, etc.).
4 *Always* use these labels when referring to them in the text (e.g., "Figure 1 illustrates the precise layout of the equipment"; "Figure 4 displays the interaction").
5 Give *every* table and *every* figure an informative title.
6 Put notes beneath the table or figure to explain any entries or features that are not self-explanatory.

Summary of Section 8.4

1 Do not be averse to including diagrams or other illustrations if these will add to your reader's understanding of what you did.

2 Keep the format of tables simple and clear. Use horizontal lines sparingly and *never* use vertical lines. Model your tables on those in the example sections of this book and in the better psychology journals.

3 Make sure that all entries in tables are self-explanatory or are otherwise explained in a note beneath the table.

4 Tables and figures supplement but do not duplicate the text. Your task in text is to discuss their *highlights*.

5 Where you use tables and figures, observe the rules for their use.

8.5   Graphing data

While I'm talking about figures, a few words about **graphs** are in order.[1] These days graphing your data is pretty easy and it can be very tempting to throw in a graph or two to make it look like you know what you're talking about, to camouflage the fact that you don't, and to dazzle your marker with your command of the software. Needless to say, this is a dangerous practice.

Graphs are useful things. They can display information succinctly. Used well, they enhance your report both in terms of conveying the information and the impression that you are on top of the material and good at the job. Be warned, however. In the wrong hands these useful tools can become little monsters. They can make the marker's heart sink. Avoid creating the impression that your report has been written by someone who knows how to use a graphing package, and how to cut and paste from one computer application to another, but has not really given a moment's thought to the purpose of the graph. Remember that graphs serve to convey information that is not so clear from a table of data. Bear this in mind at all times.

Before including a graph, always ask yourself what it is going to *add* to the story. Graphs should not be redundant with the text and tables. As with all figures, the best graphs enable you to reduce or eliminate lengthy bits of text. If the graph will add nothing, omit it.

Graphs can convey two aspects of your data that can be harder to communicate in text or glean from tables. First, they can convey information about the *pattern* of differences in summary statistics, such as a set of means. That is, a graph can make it easy to see which conditions tended to differ on the DV overall. Graphs are most commonly used in everyday life to display patterns of differences in this way. However, graphs can also convey information about the *shape* or *distribution* of the data. That is, they can also be used to indicate such things as how the scores were spread about the means in the different conditions. Providing this information *in addition* to information about the pattern of differences can be extremely useful. I will talk shortly about a feature that you can readily add when graphing your data – the inclusion of *error bars*.

8.5.1   One IV with two levels

Early on you can get away with graphing data from experiments with two conditions. However, recognize that this is mainly to start gaining experience of the graphing package and to illustrate to your marker that you're learning how to use it.

Use a **bar graph** (as in Figure 8.1). Keep it simple – for example, a straightforward light or dark fill for the bars. *Above all*, choose the scale wisely.

Let me explain why you have to be cautious. Once your inferential analysis shows you that a difference between two groups is statistically significant, even an average buffoon can look at two numbers and work out which is higher. There is thus little to be gained from graphing such data, beyond getting valuable experience with the graphing package, and much to lose. First, you run the risk of insulting your reader, who thinks, "hey, this person thinks I'm stupider than your average buffoon". Second, by using too small a scale you can make a

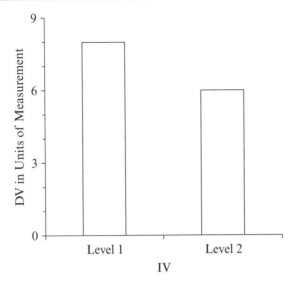

Figure 8.1.   Bar graph for a two-level independent variable.

small difference look huge, and by using too big a scale make the same difference look minute. (Politicians, advertisers and other propagandists use this fact to great effect.) So, only graph two-condition effects early on in your career and when you're sure that your marker will be suitably impressed by your capacity to use the graphing package.

However, things are different if you are able to add error bars to your graphs. If you do this as well, then the graph will be conveying useful information succinctly and its inclusion is more justifiable.

8.5.2   Error bars

Once you have mastered the software, you should get into the habit of adding error bars to your graphs. **Error bars** are lines in a graph that tell us something about the margin of error in the data.[2] There are a variety of error bars that you could use. For some purposes you might add bars that display the points that lie one standard deviation or one standard error above and below the mean. These enable us to see whether the data tend to be spread out or bunched closely around the mean. Alternatively, you might add bars that indicate confidence intervals for the mean in the population. We can then see whether these intervals are wide or narrow and whether those for the different conditions overlap (see Section 12.3).

For example, Figure 8.2 is the same as Figure 8.1 but includes also error bars showing the 95% confidence intervals about the mean.

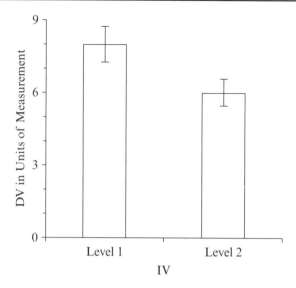

Figure 8.2.   Bar graph for a two-level independent variable.
Vertical lines depict the 95% confidence intervals about the mean in
each condition.

Looking at the graph, we can not only see that the means in the
two conditions are quite different, but also that the 95% confidence
intervals are relatively narrow and do not overlap. We can see that
for level 1 of the IV there is a 95% probability that the mean in the
population lies between about 7.2 and 8.9; whereas for level 2, there is
a 95% probability that the mean in the population lies between about
5.4 and 6.7. The graph thus conveys a lot of information succinctly
and has the potential to add to the reader's understanding of the
findings. (You can find out more about confidence intervals in your
statistics textbook).

Don't be daunted by this: you can certainly include graphs without
error bars, especially when there are enough conditions in the experiment to warrant a graph. However, if you know how to add error
bars as well, then this enhances the usefulness of the figure.

8.5.3 One IV with more than two levels

The same caveats and cautions apply here as for the two-condition
experiment: if there are not many levels you run the risk of insulting
the reader's intelligence; if you choose the wrong scale you run the
risk of exaggerating or downplaying the size of the difference. Having
said this, for IVs with four levels or beyond, a well-designed graph

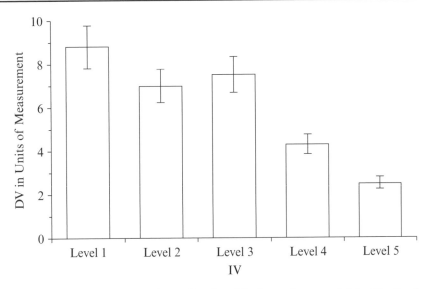

Figure 8.3. Bar graph for a five-level independent variable. Vertical lines depict the 95% confidence intervals about the mean in each condition.

can provide a useful indication of the relative impact of the different levels of the IV on the DV (Figure 8.3).

8.5.4 More than one IV

Once you start to run experiments with two or more IVs, graphs of effects can become pretty much essential tools to help you and your reader to better understand what you have found. Even the effects in a *two by two* design can be better appreciated from a well-constructed graph. You can find several examples of graphs of the effects in such designs in Section 13.7.

The same concerns about the size of the scale apply here as elsewhere. Do not use a scale that unduly accentuates or reduces the differences between the bars. Where the IV is categorical, use a bar graph to display the interaction. Where it is quantitative, use a line graph. (This issue is discussed in Section 13.7.) Where you have different graphs of equivalent data, use the same scale for *all* these graphs. If this is not possible, make it *very* clear in the text that the scale varies, otherwise you may mislead the reader.

You should be alert to a potential problem when using graphing packages that are attached to statistical software packages. The package may not take notice of the fact that you have more than one IV

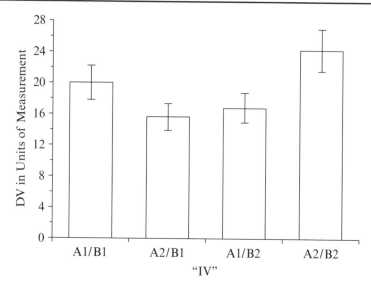

Figure 8.4. A design with two independent variables, with two levels on each, displayed erroneously as if it were a design with one independent variable with four levels. A1 = independent variable A, level 1, A2 = independent variable A, level 2; B1 = independent variable B, level 1, B2 = independent variable B, level 2. Vertical lines depict the 95% confidence intervals about the mean in each condition.

and may trot out a graph that simply represents the data as if they were from a single IV. This has happened in Figure 8.4. Here a 2 × 2 design is displayed wrongly as a single IV with four levels. The data are graphed correctly in Figure 8.5.

With all graphs:

- keep it simple. In a report (as opposed to an oral presentation) don't overdo the whizz bangs, 3-D, fills, use of colour.
- choose the scale appropriately. The vertical axis should be about three quarters of the length of the horixontal axis.
- label the axes.
- put the DV on the vertical axis and an IV on the horizontal axis.
- once you know how to, include error bars or graphical indices of dispersion.

Don't put too much information in one graph. Can your reader make sense of it without detailed explanation? Show it to a fellow student and see if they can explain it back to you.

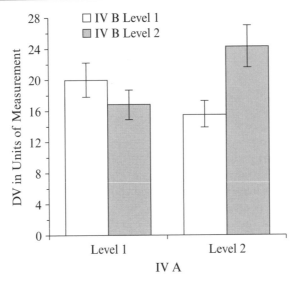

Figure 8.5. The same data as in Figure 8.4, this time correctly graphed as a design with two independent variables with two levels on each. Vertical lines depict the 95% confidence intervals about the mean in each condition.

Summary of Section 8.5

1 Use graphs sensibly to add to the reader's ability to understand the findings.

2 Graphs can be used to convey information about the shape or distribution of data *as well* as information about patterns of differences.

3 Be careful when graphing data from studies with one IV with only two or three levels.

4 Once you have mastered the software, get into the habit of adding relevant error bars to your graphs.

5 In graphs in reports keep it simple and clear. Do not put too much information in the one graph.

8.6　Drafting the report

The next sentence is one of the most important and also perhaps the most useless in the entire book: *Allow enough time to produce the report*. It is important because it is undeniably true that many reports are written too quickly and receive poorer marks than they would have done. It is useless because nothing I say here will make any difference if you are inclined to start work on your report the day before it is due in. For those of you who *do* allow yourself enough time, here are some tips that will help you to clarify and organize your ideas and express them clearly and economically:

- Write from an outline. Don't just bash out the first draft willy-nilly on the computer.
- Put aside the first draft and reread it after a delay. A fresh look can be a revelation.
- Read the draft out loud. You'll be amazed by what this tells you about the organization and clarity of the writing.
- Get a friend or your partner to read it, preferably one who is not a psychologist. Encourage them to be frank. Get them to tell you which bits they do not understand. They will *need* encouraging – the norm among friends is to lie and to tell you that it's all just fine when it is not. Be warned: markers do *not* adhere to this norm!

8.7   Producing the final version

In report writing, as in most things, appearance matters. Good production can enhance a good report, just as icing can enhance a good cake. However, a professional-looking layout cannot completely conceal a poor report any more than icing can mask a bad cake. Indeed, you can detract from a perfectly decent report by overdoing the frills. So, use the facilities of your word processor and other software packages sensibly and sensitively.

Always, *always* use the **spell checker**. It is frankly amazing how often this is not done. Spell-check before you print. Also use the grammar checking facility on the word-processing package. This can reveal things that you did not even realize were mistakes.

Spell-checking does not remove the need for **proofreading**, for spell-checking software cannot detect wrong but correctly spelled versions of words – such as *there* instead of their, *casual* instead of causal, *dependant* instead of dependent, and so on. So, proofread for additional spelling mistakes as well as (separately) for meaning.

Make sensible use of the other features of the software packages that you are using to produce the report: lay out the report clearly and elegantly. Produce a layout that is clear and uncluttered and that helps you to get your message across. Avoid features that distract or are irrelevant, and resist the temptation to show off your prowess with the software just for the sake of showing off your prowess with the software. Here are some tips:

- Choose a sensible, readable, **typeface**, such as Times, Palatino or Courier.
- Use a large enough typeface, not less than 12 point. (*Top tip*: this will go down especially well if your marker is getting on a bit.) Do not, however, try to mask a lack of material by using a big typeface or too much material by using a small one. We're not *that* stupid.
- Be consistent in your use of **headings**. Use the same style of heading for *all* the principal sections of the report. Use a different style of heading from this for the subsections of the METHOD, but the same one for each subsection. I recommend that you layout your headings exactly as I have done in the example sections of this book. (You can find these heading styles summarized on the Web site that accompanies this book.)
- Use *italic*, **bold** or underlining sparingly. Again, I recommend that you do so only as I have done in the example sections of this book.
- Leave reasonable **margins** for your tutor to put comments: 1 inch or 2 cm at minimum, preferably larger.
- Do not 'right adjust' your text. (**Right-adjusted text** is text as laid out in this book – where the right-hand margin is straight. Unless it is done professionally, however, it is harder to read than text that is left-adjusted only.)

If you're a postgraduate writing your thesis or an article for publication, there will be precise rules about features such as those above, so find out what they are – preferably before starting. If you are considering attempting to get something published in a journal, the latest edition of the *Publication Manual of the American Psychological Association* is indispensable. For the record, I have based the example sections in this book on the *APA Publication Manual* (APA, 2001). Unless your tutor tells you differently, these should suffice for you. Note that these produce quite plain-looking text. This is how those of us who try to get our ideas into print are required to produce our papers. It is a good idea to get into the habit of working with this format from the outset.

Finally, I recommend that you:

- Do not use exclamation marks!!
- Think twice before trying to be funny. Does your marker have a sense of humour? Is it the same sense of humour as your own?

Summary of Sections 8.6–8.7

1 Write from an outline and allow yourself enough time to reread drafts after a delay.

2 Read the draft out loud to get a sense of the report's organization and clarity. Get a friend to read it too.

3 Use the spell-checking and grammar-checking facilities of your word-processing package. However, also proofread for spelling as well as meaning.

4 Produce a report that is clear and uncluttered. I recommend following the layout used in the examples in this guide. These will make your reports look like the manuscripts that psychologists, such as your tutor, submit to journals for publication.

Check list for report writing

- Avoid mentioning things "in passing" – if they are worth mentioning at all, then give them the amount of space that they deserve.
- Make your points *explicitly* – do not leave it to your reader to work out what you mean. Be precise *at all times*. Never assume that the reader knows something, or expect readers to work something important out for themselves.
- Do not use note form at *any* stage of the report: *prose* is always required.
- Omit extraneous details: always look for ways of condensing the information that you give, within the limits imposed by comprehension.
- *Do not waffle* – unnecessary repetition is both tedious and obvious and is unlikely to impress the person marking your report (quite the opposite).
- Tell the truth!

What the marker is looking for

One of the most daunting things about report and essay writing is the fact that you're often not at all clear exactly what the marker is expecting of you. Of course, this book is an attempt to help you with this problem. In addition, here is a summary of *some* of the questions with which the marker might address your report. Note, however, that some of these requirements are rather more important than are others.

TITLE

- Does this convey a clear and accurate idea of what the study was about?
- Does it mention the major variables investigated?

ABSTRACT

- Does this convey a clear and accurate idea of what the study was about?
- Is it clear what the findings were?
- Is intelligible reference made to the contents of the DISCUSSION? Is a conclusion mentioned, and is this the one actually arrived at?
- Can you understand the ABSTRACT without referring to the report itself?
- Is it concise enough, or does it include unnecessary detail?

INTRODUCTION

Part 1

- Is the study introduced adequately, given the student's background? In particular, is there an adequate review of the relevant background literature? Is it to the point and neither too short nor too long?
- Is there a logical progression to the INTRODUCTION? Does it *build up* to an account of the study undertaken?
- Does the study have sufficient research justification? (Where applicable.)
- Does it have a good mix of classic and up-to-date material? (Where applicable.)

Part 2

- Is the study described adequately and accurately?
- Is there a clear statement of the hypotheses and predictions, and has the rationale for these been clearly expressed?

METHOD

Design

- Is the design described clearly and accurately?
- Are the IVs described clearly and accurately, including a clear description of the levels?
- Are the DVs described thoroughly and accurately, including a clear account of the units of measurement?
- Has the design been labelled correctly using appropriate terminology?
- Is the experiment well designed?

Participants

- Are the participants described adequately?
- Are there sufficient?
- Are they appropriate for this type of study?
- Have they been allocated to groups properly?
- Were they selected reasonably?

Apparatus; Materials; Apparatus and Materials

- Is this section properly labelled?
- Is the equipment used described in the kind of detail that would enable an *exact* replication to be undertaken?
- Are figures used appropriately and do they make things clearer?

Procedure

- Is this described in enough detail to allow for an exact replication?
- Is it clear how the procedure differed for the different conditions?
- Are the instructions reported adequately, with the gist where appropriate, verbatim where necessary? Were they standardized? Were they suitable?
- Was sufficient attempt made to ensure that the participants understood the instructions?
- Is a clear account provided of the randomization procedure?
- Is the experiment free of confounding variables? Was it run well?
- Was the experiment conducted ethically? Were participants debriefed?
- Does the procedure have flaws that render interpretation of the data difficult?

RESULTS

- Is it clear what data were analysed and how the numbers presented in the tables of data were arrived at?
- Are the data adequately described and clearly presented? Are tables labelled appropriately and readily intelligible? Has the student resisted the temptation to dump over unedited output from a statistical software package?
- Is it clear what inferential statistics were used in any given instance? Is it clear what was found?
- Is the necessary information provided for each inferential test? Has the significance level been adhered to? Have the data been used to good effect?
- Have the data been presented intelligently and well? Are the results presented in a logical order?
- Are graphs used sensibly? Are they correctly formatted and appropriately labelled?
- Has the student resisted the temptation to *interpret* the findings at this stage?

DISCUSSION

- Are the findings summarized intelligently and accurately? Have they been interpreted sensibly?
- Are the obvious interpretations of these findings discussed? Are any other interpretations discussed?
- Is the discussion sensible and balanced?
- Have any inconsistencies or contradictions in the findings been addressed?

- Has enough attempt been made to assess the implications of the findings for the material reviewed in the INTRODUCTION?
- Does the DISCUSSION include an account of any flaws in the design that might have affected the data?
- Have the broader implications of the findings been mentioned, and are these sensible?
- Is there any discussion of the implications for future research? Are any conclusions drawn? Are these sensible?

REFERENCE

- Is this section properly laid out, and does it contain the appropriate references?

MISCELLANEOUS

- Has the basis for the sample size been given? (Where applicable.)
- Have the conventions of report writing been properly observed? Does the material appear in the proper sections?
- Are references made for factual assertions, and is this properly done? Are any tables, figures, quotations, etc., properly constructed and referenced?
- Would the report be comprehensible to someone who had no knowledge of the study, or the area of psychology in which it took place?

Part 2 Designing experiments

9 Experimenting in psychology

The practical report as described in Part 1 is designed well for the reporting of *experiments*. Experiments are widely used in scientific psychology. However, there are other techniques available, such as the *correlation* or simple *description*. In this chapter I will introduce you to the key features of experimenting and also discuss correlation and description.

9.1 Experimenting

The first term that you must learn here is the term **variable**. In the language of design we tend to use this as a noun – that is we talk of "a variable" or "the variable". To us, a variable is quite simply something – anything – that *varies* or can come in *different forms*. All around us there are variables: people come in *different* shapes and sizes, belong to *different* groups and classes, have *different* abilities and tastes. As researchers we can ask the participants in our experiments to do *different* things – to learn different lists of words for a memory test, to do boring or interesting tasks, to do press-ups for 3 minutes or to spend the same amount of time relaxing. All of these things – from social class through to whether our participants did press-ups or relaxed – are *variables*. So, in the above example social class is a variable because there are *different* social classes; doing different tasks is also a variable because the task varies – it can be *either* interesting *or* boring. As our world is full of changing events, therefore, it is no surprise to find that almost anything in it is – or can be – a variable.

A variable, then, is something that can come in different forms or, as we say in design terms, that can take different *values* or *levels*. In practice, it can be anything from the number of white blood cells in a cubic centimetre of blood to whether or not someone voted Labour at the last general election or for the Democrat presidential candidate. With our scientific hats on we are extremely interested in variables, especially in finding out something about relationships *between* them.

Our ultimate aim is to find out which variables are responsible for *causing* the events that take place around us. We see a world full of variables and we want to know what factors are responsible for producing or causing them. Why is it that some people react with depression to events that others take in their stride? Why is it that some public speakers are more persuasive than others? What makes one list of words easier to recall than another? We believe that we live in a universe of causes and effects and our adopted task is to try to determine, as far as is possible, which are the causes and what are the effects they produce. That is, ideally we want to be able to infer cause and effect relationships, to make what are known as **causal inferences**. Our principal weapon in this battle is the psychological experiment.

9.1.1 The experiment

The principles of basic experimenting are dead easy. In an **experiment** what we do – quite simply – is play around with one variable (the one that we suspect to be the **causal variable**), and see what happens to another variable (the one that is the **effect variable**). That is, as experimenters we deliberately alter the values or levels of the causal variable – or, as we say in experimental design parlance, we **manipulate** this variable – and look to see if this produces corresponding changes in the other – the effect – variable. If it does, and we cannot see any other variable in the situation that may have produced this effect, we assume that the variable that we have manipulated has indeed produced the change that we observed. That is, we infer a cause–effect relationship between the two variables (i.e., make a causal inference). This is the logic of experimental design.

For instance, if we suspected that eating foods that contained particular additives was responsible for causing certain types of depression, we would *vary* the intake of these additives among our participants and see whether this produced any corresponding changes in the incidence of depression. That is, we would *manipulate* the variable food additives and *measure* the variable depression. Similarly, if we wanted to find out whether physical exercise affected mental alertness, we would *manipulate* the variable physical exercise and *measure* the variable mental alertness. In the above examples, food additives and physical exercise are the variables that we suspect to be causal; depression and mental alertness (respectively) the variables that we think they influence.

However, because they are both variables, and yet play quite distinctive roles in an experiment, we give these critical variables different names. The one that we play around with – the variable that we manipulate – we call the **independent variable** (IV). The IV, therefore, is the variable that we suspect is the *causal* variable. The variable that we look at to see if there are any changes produced by our manipulation of the causal variable – that is, the variable that we *measure* – we call the **dependent variable** (DV). The DV, therefore, is the variable that shows us whether there is any effect of changing the values of the independent variable. If there is such an effect, then the values that the dependent variable takes will *depend* on the values that we, as experimenters, set *independently* on our independent variable.

It is important that you get this straight. These terms are critical and you will need to apply them properly in your report. So read back through the last paragraph carefully, and then answer the following questions.

? SAQ 24   In an experiment, what is the name of the variable that we *manipulate*? What is the name of the variable that we *measure*?

For each of the following experiments, write down what the *independent variable* is and what the *dependent variable* is:

(a) An experimenter is interested in the effect of word frequency upon the time taken to decide whether a stimulus is a *word* or a *non-word* (a meaningless combination of vowels and consonants). She exposes the same set of participants to three sets of words which vary in their frequency (high, medium, or low) and measures the time that it takes them to decide whether they have seen a word or a non-word in milliseconds.

(b) A researcher is interested in the effect of the sex hormone oestrogen on the feeding behaviour of female rats. He injects one group with a suitable concentration of oestrogen and another group with an equivalent volume of saline solution. After 3 days he measures the changes that have taken place in their body weights in grams.

(c) A social psychologist is interested in the role that anxiety plays in persuasion. She develops three separate public information programmes on dental care. These programmes vary in the extent to which they arouse anxiety in their viewers: one provokes a comparatively high level of anxiety, another a moderate degree of anxiety, and the third comparatively little anxiety. She exposes three separate groups of participants to these programmes and then assesses how many of those in each of the three groups subsequently take up the opportunity to make a dental appointment.

(d) An experimenter is interested in the effects of television violence upon the level of aggression it induces in its viewers. He exposes three separate groups of participants to three different kinds of television programme: one in which the violence is "realistic" (i.e., the blows cause obvious damage to the recipients); one in which the violence is "unrealistic" (i.e., the blows do not appear to damage the recipient, or hinder his ability to continue fighting); and one in which no violence is portrayed. The participants are subsequently allowed to administer electric shocks to their own victims during the course of a simulated teaching exercise (although, unbeknown to them, no actual shocks are delivered). The experimenter measures the mean level of shock (in volts) administered by those in each of the three groups.

(e) An occupational psychologist wishes to examine the impact of working with others on the productivity of a group of factory workers. She measures the number of packets of breakfast cereal this group pack into boxes in a 20-minute period when: working alone; working with one other worker; working with two others; working with four others; and working with eight others.

As experimenters we only control the values of the *independent* variable; we have no control over the precise values taken by the *dependent* variable. You will obtain the latter values from your participants – reaction times (in milliseconds), number of errors made, scores on a scale (e.g., for extraversion on a personality scale), blood glucose level (e.g., in milligrams per 100 millilitres), and so on. Note that you must *always* mention the units in which your dependent variable was measured.

Summary

1 A variable is anything that can come in different forms.

2 In experiments we manipulate variables in order to see what effects this has on other variables – in other words, which variables *cause* changes in other variables.

3 The variable that we *manipulate* in an experiment is known as the *independent variable*.

4 The variable that we *measure* in an experiment to see if our manipulation of the independent variable has caused any changes is known as the *dependent variable*.

9.1.2 Experimental and control conditions

When we manipulate an IV, therefore, what we do is alter the values or **levels** that it takes. We then look to see if altering these values or levels produces any corresponding changes in the participants' scores on the DV. Where our experiment has a single IV, the different values or levels of this variable are the *conditions* of our experiment. What we are interested in doing is *comparing* these conditions to see if there is any difference between them in the participants' scores. This, in a nutshell, is the logic of experimental design. Now let's see how it all looks in a real experiment.

Suppose that you and I are interested in "folk wisdom" – and, in particular, in the old adage that eating cheese shortly before going to bed gives people nightmares. One basic way that we might test this proposition experimentally would be to take two groups of people, give one group a measured quantity of cheese (say, in proportion to their body weight) a standard time before going to bed (say, 3 hours) and ensure that those in the other group consumed no cheese during the same period. We could then count the number of nightmares reported by the two groups.

? SAQ 25   What are the independent and dependent variables in this experiment?

In this case we have manipulated our IV (cheese consumption) by forming two *conditions*: one in which the participants eat cheese (Condition 1), and one in which they do not eat cheese (Condition 2). We are interested in the consequences of this – in the effect that this will have on the number of nightmares experienced by the participants in the two conditions.

This is a very basic experimental design. Our manipulation of the IV in this case involves comparing what happens when the suspected causal variable (cheese) is *present* (Condition 1) with what happens when it is *absent* (Condition 2). If cheese *does* cause nightmares, then we would expect those in Condition 1 to experience more nightmares than those in Condition 2. If cheese does *not* cause nightmares, then we should expect no such difference.

There are particular names for the conditions in an experiment where the IV is manipulated by comparing its *presence* with its *absence*. The condition in which the suspected causal variable is *present* is called the **experimental condition**. The condition in which the suspected causal variable is *absent* is called the **control condition**.

SAQ 26   Which is the *control* condition in the above experiment?

Experiments in which we simply compare an experimental with a control condition can be simple and effective ways of finding things out in psychology. However, such a design does not exhaust the possibilities. We may, for instance, be more interested in comparing the effects of two different *levels* of the IV, than in comparing its presence with its absence. For instance, we might be interested in finding out whether different *types* of cheese produce different numbers of nightmares. We might therefore wish to compare a group of participants that ate Cheddar cheese with a group that ate Caerphilly cheese. In such an experiment, cheese would be present in *both* conditions. We would therefore have an experiment with two *experimental* conditions, rather than a *control* and *experimental* condition.

Such a design is perfectly acceptable in psychology. In fact, we don't even need to restrict ourselves to comparing only *two* experimental conditions – we can compare three or even more in one experiment. Moreover, one of these can be a *control* condition if we wish – that is, a condition in which the suspected causal variable is absent. So, for instance, we might expand our cheese and nightmare experiment to one in which we had a group of participants who ate Cheddar cheese, a group who ate Caerphilly cheese, a group who ate Red Leicester, a group who ate Cheshire cheese, and a group who ate no cheese at all.

 SAQ 27   How many conditions are there *overall* in this version of the cheese experiment? How many of these are *experimental* conditions?

 SAQ 28   Go back through the experiments described in SAQ 24, and state how many conditions each independent variable has. Do any of these have a control condition? If so, which ones?

I will discuss designs involving more than two levels of the IV in Chapter 13.

9.1.3   Control: eliminating confounding variables

What we do in an experiment, therefore, is manipulate the variable that we suspect to be causal – what we have learned to call the independent variable – and examine what impact this manipulation has upon the effect variable – what we have learned to call the dependent variable. If we subsequently find that there are indeed changes in the DV, this strengthens our suspicion that there is a causal link between them.

However, in order to make this causal inference we have to ensure that the IV really is the only thing that we are changing in the experiment. Thus, in our cheese and nightmare experiment, for example, we don't want more people who are suffering life crises, or taking sleeping pills, or who are otherwise prone to experience nightmares, to end up in the one condition rather than the other. If they did, we would no longer be sure that any differences that we observed in our DV (incidence of nightmares) would be due to our manipulation of the cheese variable, or to these other variables. For if our groups of participants indeed varied in their intake of sleeping pills, it might be that the variable *sleeping-pill consumption* is responsible for any differences between the groups in the extent to which they experience nightmares, rather than our IV (cheese consumption).

A variable that changes along with our IV is always an alternative possible cause of any differences that we observe in our DV. It represents a rival explanation for these effects, and is consequently an unwelcome intruder. We must, therefore, attempt to eliminate such variables, and we do this by *controlling* them.

The most effective way of achieving **control** is to hold the other main candidates for the causal variable *constant* throughout our experiment, while changing the IV alone. Thus, in our cheese and nightmare experiment we would attempt to ensure that the only important difference between our groups of participants was whether or not they ate cheese before going to bed. Consequently, we would do our best to make sure that the groups really did not differ in their sleeping-pill consumption, or life crises, or any other variable that might make them prone to experience nightmares.

Uncontrolled variables that change along with our independent variable are known in the trade as **confounding variables** (to confound = to confuse), for they confound the effects of the independent variable. Confounding variables are not just any old variables that happen to exist in an experiment over and above the IV(s) and DV(s). Confounding variables are special – they are variables that themselves have different levels that coincide with the different levels of the IV – things like finding that more people with sleep problems are in the experimental than in the control condition (or vice versa). Confounding variables are spanners in the works of the experiment, fundamental flaws in the design or execution that undermine the capacity to draw causal inferences.

You will find that much of the time that you spend on the design of your experiments will involve spotting and controlling potential confounding variables. For confounding variables prevent us from unequivocally attributing the changes that we find in the DV to our manipulation of the IV. This is because they provide possible alternative explanations – for example, that any difference in the occurrence of nightmares is caused by sleeping pills, rather than by cheese consumption.

To recap, then, in an experiment what we do is take a variable, the variable that we suspect or are led to believe may be causal (the independent variable) and manipulate this variable (e.g., by varying whether it is absent or present). We then look for associated changes on the effect or outcome variable (the dependent variable). If we find that the effect is present when the suspected cause is present, but is absent when the suspected cause is absent, *and if* we have held everything else *constant* across the two conditions of our experiment, then we can conclude that the variable is indeed causal. There can be no other explanation for the measured variation in the effect variable, because the only thing that changes across the two conditions is the presence or absence of the causal variable. If, however, we find that the effect occurs, even though the suspected cause is not present, then we can safely conclude that it is not the causal variable after all.

Summary of Sections 9.1.2–9.1.3

1 In order to design an effective experiment we have to isolate the variables that we are interested in and hold other variables constant across our experimental conditions. This is known as *controlling* these other variables.

2 Variables that change along with (*covary* with) our independent variable are *confounding* variables.

3 An effective experiment does not have confounding variables.

9.1.4 Experimental and null hypotheses

In an experiment, then, we *manipulate* an independent variable by altering the *values* that it takes. Simultaneously, we *control* other candidates for the causal variable by holding them *constant* across the conditions. We then look to see if the changes that we make to the IV result in changes to the DV – that is, whether there are differences in the DV between our conditions. In particular, if our IV really is the causal variable, then we can anticipate, or *hypothesize*, what the actual outcome will be. This is a fundamental feature of experimenting. It is time to consider it in some detail.

Think back to the cheese experiment. If folk wisdom is correct, then what would we expect to happen in this experiment? Wisdom has it that eating cheese shortly before going to sleep will result in nightmares. Therefore, we should expect those in the cheese condition to experience more nightmares than those in the control condition. That is, if cheese really does cause nightmares then we would expect more of those eating cheese before going to bed to experience nightmares than do those not eating cheese before going to bed.

? SAQ 29   However, is this the only possible outcome? What else might happen? Put the book down for a while and think about this clearly.

In fact our experiment can have one of *three* possible outcomes. We might find that those in the experimental condition experience *more* nightmares than do those in the control condition. On the other hand, we might find that those in the experimental condition experience *fewer* nightmares than do those in the control condition. Finally, we might find that there is essentially *no difference* between the conditions in the number of nightmares that the participants experience. This will be true of *all* experiments in which we test for differences between two conditions; between them, these three options exhaust the possibilities. So – and this is important – we can specify *in advance* what the outcome of our experiment might be.

However, there is an important distinction to be made between these three potential outcomes. Two of them predict that there will be a *difference* between our conditions in the incidence of nightmares. These happen to be the outcomes that we would anticipate *if* cheese affects nightmares in some way (either by stimulating or suppressing them). The third outcome, however, is that there will be no noteworthy difference between them. This is what we would expect if cheese has no influence upon nightmares.

Thus, if we assume that cheese *does* affect the occurrence of nightmares in some way, we would predict a different outcome to our experiment than if we assume that cheese has no effect upon the incidence of nightmares. That is, if we assume that cheese in some way changes the likelihood of experiencing nightmares, we would predict that there will be a difference of some sort between our groups in the frequency with which they report nightmares. Of course, the assumption that cheese influences the occurrence of nightmares is the very assumption that led us to design our experiment in the first place. So, under the assumption that led to the experiment, we would predict a difference of some sort between our two groups. For this reason we call this assumption the **experimental hypothesis**. In fact:

1 *All* experiments have experimental hypotheses.
2 This hypothesis leads us to predict that there will be a difference between conditions. That is, from the experimental hypothesis we derive the prediction that there will be a difference as a result of manipulating the levels of the IV.

 SAQ 30   Go back to SAQ 24 and work through the examples there, stating for each what you think the prediction might be under the experimental hypothesis.

Now, the predictions derived from the experimental hypotheses come in one of two forms. The **nondirectional** prediction states that there will be a difference somewhere between the conditions in your experiment, but says nothing about the *direction* of this difference (i.e., does not state which condition will exceed the other on the dependent variable). In contrast, the **directional** prediction not only leads us to expect a difference, but also says something about the direction that the difference will take. (Alternative names that you might come across for these are **bidirectional** for the nondirectional prediction and **unidirectional** for the directional prediction.)

Thus, in our cheese and nightmare experiment, the nondirectional prediction simply states that the experimental and control group will experience *different* numbers of nightmares. A directional prediction, on the other hand, would state for example that our cheese group will experience *more* nightmares than our no cheese group.

However, what of the third possible outcome – the prediction that there will be *no difference* between the two conditions? This is a very important prediction and is derived from a hypothesis called the **null hypothesis**. You will find that the null hypothesis plays a crucial role in the process by which you come to analyse your data. In fact:

1 *All* experiments have a null hypothesis.
2 The null hypothesis is that the independent variable does not affect the dependent variable. It therefore leads us to predict that there will be little or no difference on the dependent variable between the conditions in the experiment.[1]

Under this null hypothesis we assume, therefore, that the IV does *not* cause changes in the DV. It is called the null hypothesis because it is capable of being tested and thus of being *nullified*. As you will discover in Chapter 11, we use the null hypothesis to help us to calculate the statistics that we need to make sense of our data. Despite its name, the null hypothesis is thus a very important hypothesis.

It is very important that you learn to distinguish clearly between the predictions derived from the null hypothesis and those derived from the experimental hypothesis. The experimental hypothesis leads us to predict a difference between the conditions. In contrast, the null hypothesis leads us to predict that there will be no such difference. Do not confuse these! Design your experiments so that the *experimental* hypothesis leads to predictions of a difference *somewhere* between your conditions. Otherwise you will actually be failing to test your theoretical ideas (because you will be confusing the predictions derived from the experimental hypothesis with those derived from the null hypothesis – see Appendix 1).

This is why it is important not to think of the experimental hypothesis as the *experimenter's* own personal hypothesis. It is perfectly conceivable that you might design and run an experiment in which you don't really expect there to be a difference between your conditions (e.g., if you're testing a theory that you don't agree with). Nevertheless, the experimental hypothesis would still lead you to predict a difference, even if this wasn't the hypothesis that you favoured or expected. For instance, you might be sceptical about the validity of folk wisdom and thus expect (privately) to find no difference in the incidence of nightmares in the two conditions (eating or not eating cheese). Nevertheless, the *experimental* hypothesis will still lead you to predict such a difference. For this is the proposition under test in the experiment.

Summary of Section 9.1.4

1 All experiments have one null hypothesis and at least one experimental hypothesis.

2 The experimental hypothesis involves the assumption that the IV affects the DV. It leads to the prediction that there will be a *difference* on the DV somewhere among the conditions in the experiment.

3 The prediction derived from the experimental hypothesis can either lead us to expect a difference between conditions in one direction (*directional*) or in either direction (*nondirectional*).

4 The null hypothesis involves the assumption that the IV does *not* affect the DV. It therefore leads to the prediction that there will be *no difference* among the conditions in the experiment.

9.1.5 More on controlling variables

As budding experimenters, you will come to appreciate not only that the world is full of variables, but that when you have on your experimenter's hat, most of them, most of the time, are at best irrelevant and at worst a downright nuisance. When we are interested in whether cheese causes nightmares, as well as consuming or not consuming our measured amount of Cheddar at a standard time before retiring for the night, our experimental and control participants will also vary in what they had for their evening meal, how long they take to drop off to sleep, what they wear in bed, what colour the bedroom wallpaper is, what TV they watched and for how long that evening, whether they drank any alcohol, how many in-laws they have, whether and how they voted in the last election, how recently they last went swimming and whether they believe in God. Some of these variables may be obviously relevant to the issue at hand, the relationship between the IV and the DV, and others will not. For example, drinking alcohol is likely to influence a person's quality and depth of sleep and may, therefore, influence whether or not they experience nightmares. For this reason we would not want to discover that too many more of our participants in one of the conditions drank alcohol over the course of the experiment than did participants in the other condition.

 SAQ 31   Why not?

Indeed, we may well be concerned enough about the possibility that alcohol would nullify or otherwise distort the relationship between our IV and DV that we would want to make this one of the variables that we held constant across our experimental conditions. Unpopular though it might make us, we might therefore outlaw alcohol consumption for our participants during the period in which they participated in the experiment.

However, what about everything else? Should we attempt to control for the number of in-laws? The colour of the bedroom wallpaper? Whether our participants believe in God? Well, whereas in theory we would control absolutely everything if we could, so that the *only* difference between our conditions was the IV, in reality – in human work at least – this is not possible. Instead, we use our judgement and discretion to decide which of the millions of irrelevant or **extraneous variables** (extraneous = not belonging to the matter in hand) swishing around in the psychological universe we need to control by holding them constant. Other variables we control for, not by holding them at a constant level, but by attempting to ensure that they will vary roughly equally across the conditions of our experiment and thus not represent confounding variables. We will talk more about this in the next chapter, when we consider *randomization*. For now, however, you need to recognize that you cannot control for absolutely everything. Instead, you have to decide on the priorities for control. That is, you have to decide which of the variables in the situation you will be able to control by holding them constant across conditions.

Although this may sound pretty confusing, in fact it is relatively straightforward. With the cheese and nightmare experiment, we have already sketched a basic design: One group of people will consume a measured amount of cheese a standard time before going to bed. The control group will not eat cheese before going to bed. (However, really they should eat a standard amount of something that looked like cheese, but contained none of the ingredients of cheese, an equivalent time before going to bed.)

? SAQ 32   Why?

We have already mentioned some of the other key variables that we would wish to control by holding them constant: we would probably exclude from the study anyone on medication likely to influence sleep quality (thus holding this variable at the level *no relevant medication* across both conditions). We would also probably not allow alcohol consumption (thus holding this variable at the level *no alcohol* across both conditions). We might also investigate the sleep history of our participants and exclude from the study anyone with a pattern of sleep problems (thus holding this variable at the level *no sleep problem history* across both conditions). In doing this you can see that, if we do find more nightmares in our experimental condition, we can rule out explanations that these are caused by more people in the experimental group having their sleep disturbed by medication, alcohol, or just being more prone to sleep problems in the first place.

There may be other variables that we'd control for in this way, but we'd have to stop somewhere. For instance, our participants will sleep in rooms with different coloured walls. We'd be unlikely to demand that for the purposes of our experiment they all had their rooms painted a standard shade of a restful pastel colour. Thus, participants in both conditions will sleep in rooms of different colours and the variable *colour of bedroom walls* will be left to vary rather than being held constant. However, we would hope that there was no consistent or *systematic* difference in the colours in the bedrooms of the experimental group when compared with the control group.

Of course, if we were very concerned that an environmental factor like the colour of the room slept in by the participants was likely to make a difference then we might well take active steps to control for it. One way in which we could rule out such environmental factors would be to have the experiment take place not at home but in a sleep laboratory. There we could ensure that a whole range of additional factors was held constant across our experimental and control conditions. Laboratories offer opportunities for controlling a whole range of extraneous variables, which is one of the reasons for their appeal in psychology.

Summary of Section 9.1.5

1 In reality there are usually too many variables in the situation that are irrelevant or *extraneous* to our experiment for us to control them all by holding them constant.

2 We thus select the more important of these to be controlled for by holding them constant, such that each participant has the same value or score on this variable.

3 The remaining variables we allow to vary among the participants *within* our conditions, but try to ensure that the overall or average scores or values for this variable do not differ *systematically* between conditions (i.e., that if calculated, the average score would be roughly equal for each of the conditions).

4 However, this control at the level of the group or condition, rather than at the level of the participant, does not *guarantee* that there will be no systematic differences between the conditions.

9.2   Correlation

Most of this book is concerned with designing and reporting experiments. However, there are other types of study that you might undertake and have to report. Indeed, it is not always possible to conduct experiments. There may, for instance, be practical or ethical factors that prevent us from actually *manipulating* variables in the way that we need to for our studies to qualify as true experiments. Under such circumstances we can turn to a rather less powerful, but still informative, technique – the **correlation**.

The critical difference between the experiment and the correlation is that, with a correlation, we are unable to distinguish between *independent* and *dependent* variables. This is because we do not *manipulate* variables when we undertake correlational work. Instead, we rely on *natural* changes or differences to tell us something about which variables are related in some way to each other.

To illustrate this, imagine that you and I are interested in whether living close to the transmitters that relay messages to and from mobile phones is a cause of behavioural problems in children. An experimental approach to this question would involve assigning individuals from birth randomly to live either close to or far away from such transmitters and then comparing the numbers in each group that eventually developed behavioural problems. This is not only profoundly unethical but also clearly impractical. Under these circumstances, if we wish to gather data on humans, then we are restricted to *correlational* data. In this instance we rely on differences that already exist in the population. That is, we would look to see if there were any correspondence between the distance existing groups of people lived from the transmitters and the incidence of behavioural problems. However, this has profound implications for our ability to say whether there is a *causal* relationship between the variables "distance from transmitter" and "behavioural problems".

For instance, suppose that we find that there is a relationship between these variables and that this is indeed the one that we suspect: that, as the transmitters get closer, so there is an increase in the incidence of behavioural problems. This would be an example of what we call a **positive correlation** (because *increases* in proximity to the transmitters are accompanied by *increases* in the incidence of behavioural problems). Such a relationship is depicted graphically in Figure 9.1.

Now, at first glance it may seem obvious to conclude that the transmitters are responsible for *causing* the behavioural problems. However, we actually have no grounds for drawing this conclusion. For, with correlational data, all we know is that there is an *association* between these variables – that as one varies (goes up, goes down), so does the other. It could be that the transmitters do indeed *cause* the problems. However, it could also be that something else is responsible for the relationship. Perhaps the transmitters are placed in poorer areas of towns and cities, where people need the money from the telephone companies or feel too powerless to object to them placing transmitters in their communities. In which case the association may not be between the transmitters and the behavioural problems, but a third variable, such as poor diet or unsatisfactory schooling, may be responsible for the behavioural problems and the relationship between transmitters and behavioural problems is more apparent than real. Such a relationship is described in the trade as **spurious** (spurious = not genuine).

An illustration might reveal this more clearly. There is, in fact, a positive correlation between the consumption of ice cream and the

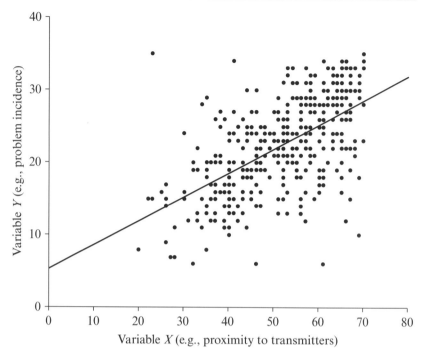

Figure 9.1.   A scatter plot showing a positive correlation between variables X and Y.

incidence of deaths by drowning. That is, as people tend to eat more ice cream, so more people tend to die in drowning accidents.

 SAQ 33

Does this mean that there must be some kind of causal relationship between them (even if we can't say which way it goes)?

Now the relationship between ice cream consumption and deaths by drowning is sufficiently bizarre for us to suspect that something strange is going on. Nevertheless, *even where the direction of causality seems obvious* it is still not permissible to assume that one of the two variables is responsible for causing the changes that we observe. For, in relying upon natural changes, rather than manipulating variables, we are unable to control variables that *covary* with (i.e., vary along with) the ones that we are interested in. That is, we are unable to control for *confounding* variables (for, as you know, a confounding variable is an extraneous variable that covaries with the one that we are investigating).

Correlational data are thus *inevitably* confounded. So, be aware of this problem – it applies to many issues within and outside psychology, even those – such as smoking and lung cancer, or the consumption of saturated fats and heart disease – in which the direction of causality seems "obvious". With such data we cannot rule out the possibility that the causal relationship is the reverse of the one that we believe or even spurious. (Thus, although the experimental data on animals and other data suggest it is highly probable that smoking causes lung cancer and excessive consumption of saturated fat contributes to heart disease, it remains possible that those who are prone to lung cancer are those who for some reason choose to smoke, or that those who are prone to heart disease are those who for some reason tend also to eat diets high in saturated fat.)

As you can see, it's no surprise that the biggest debates in our scientific and public lives often centre around issues for which the data, concerning humans at least, are *correlational*. Moreover, as you can see from the above examples, this is certainly not an issue that is restricted to psychology.

9.3 Description

Rather than concerning ourselves with relationships *between* variables, we may be content simply to *describe* particular variables. For instance, we might wish to examine the nature of people's attitudes towards genetically modified crops, or to find out what they can tell us about some aspect of their social behaviour. Such studies are neither experimental nor correlational. They are *descriptive*.

A classic example of such an approach is the public opinion poll. Opinion polls tell us things like the percentage of the sample questioned who stated that they would be prepared to vote for particular parties if an election were held immediately, or who they thought would make the best prime minister or president. This is **description.** It is simply an attempt to make a statement about the characteristics of the variable "the voting public". However, there is no attempt to *explain* these findings. That is, the data themselves are not used to explain *why* the individuals sampled intend to vote the way that they do. Data of this nature are usually generated by *questionnaire* or *interview*, take the form of what is called a *survey*, and are described solely in terms of *descriptive statistics*, such as percentages and means (Section 4.1). It is highly unlikely that as a student you will generate numerical data that are simply descriptive. If not experimental, your quantitative data are likely to be correlational.

Now there's no need to worry about telling these techniques apart at this stage. The important thing is to bear in mind that the report as illustrated in Figure 1.1 is designed principally for the reporting of *experiments*. The format illustrated there may require some degree of modification for the reporting of other types of study, particularly *surveys*. (There is advice about reporting such studies on the Web site that accompanies this book.)

Summary of Sections 9.2–9.3

1 The critical difference between the correlation and the experiment is that in the correlation we are unable to distinguish between *independent* and *dependent* variables. This is because we do not *manipulate* any variables in a correlation. Instead, we rely upon differences that already exist to discover which variables are related to each other.

2 The consequence of this is that we are unable to draw *causal inferences* from correlational data. That is, correlations reveal *associations* between variables, rather than causes and effects.

3 The structured sequence of the report's sections shown in Figures 1.1–1.4 is designed primarily for writing up reports of *experiments* and *may* need some modification when reporting other types of study.

10 Experimental design I

Although experiments have a universal *basic* logic, they vary in design and complexity. For instance, they may have one or more than one independent variable, any or all of which may employ *unrelated* or *related* samples. It is time to find out what this means.

10.1 Unrelated and related samples independent variables

Suppose that you and I have been approached to undertake some research into the effect of listening to music in the car on driving performance. There are lots of ways that we could go about doing this. For instance, we might examine actual driving performance on the road, or on a test track, or perhaps we could gain access to a driving simulator and test people's performance on that. Similarly, we might examine only certain aspects of driving performance: for example, manual control (things like gear changing, driving in the right lane, etc.) or average speed. Or we could assess the number of mistakes made over a standard course, or monitor the participants' eye movements as they drive to discover whether there are any differences in the way that they monitor the situation unfolding outside as a consequence of having music on or off.

On the other hand, we might wish to refine the question that we explore – examine whether different materials (e.g., different types of music or different types of radio programme) affect performance in different ways or to a different extent. Similarly, we might examine whether the volume at which people listen is important and whether this differs with the material being listened to. Or we might want to find out whether teenagers are affected more than older drivers, or men more than women.

All of these possibilities hold different implications for the experiment that we would eventually design and the conclusions that we would ultimately draw. Essentially, we have here a whole series of decisions that we have to make about the IV(s) and DV(s) in our experiment. However, there's one fundamental feature of our design that we would still have to decide upon, even after we have decided on the precise question that we wish to examine, chosen our IV and DV, and set the levels on the IV. This is how we will *distribute the participants* in our experiment.

For instance, suppose that we decided to run the above experiment on a driving simulator, using a computer to display a standard set of hazards and problems in a random sequence. We could then measure driving performance on a range of *relevant* measures, from average speed through manual control to number of (virtual!) pedestrians knocked over. Participants would be free to choose their own listening material and to set the volume and adjust it whenever they desired.

So far, so good. However, we have yet to decide how we are going to distribute our participants across the different conditions (music on versus music off). We could, for example, have one group of participants performing in the music on condition and another (different) group in the music off condition. If we did this, we would have *different* samples in the two conditions. The scores on our DV would therefore be from different groups of people and thus would be *unrelated* to each other. Our IV would thus be an **unrelated samples** IV.

However, instead of assessing the driving performance of different participants, we could compare the driving performance of the *same* participants. That is, we could measure each participant's performance when driving with music off and his or her performance when driving with music on. In this experiment we have the *same* sample of participants performing in each of our conditions. In this case, the scores on our DV would be from the same set of participants and the scores under the two conditions would be related to each other. In this case, therefore, our IV employs **related samples**.

 SAQ 34

What type of IV did we have in our original, two-condition cheese experiment? How else could we have run this experiment, and what type of IV would we have then employed?

These, then, are the two basic IVs used by psychologists: the *unrelated* samples IV, in which we take a different batch of participants for each of the conditions or levels on the IV, and the *related* samples

Table 10.1   An Unrelated Samples IV with Two Conditions: Allocation of Participants

Condition 1	Condition 2
p02	p01
p04	p03
p09	p05
p10	p06
p11	p07
p13	p08
p14	p12
p19	p15
p21	p16
p24	p17
p25	p18
p26	p20
p28	p22
p29	p23
p30	p27
p32	p31

Note: Participants have been allocated to conditions randomly. p = participant

IV, in which we use the same batch of participants for the conditions or levels on that IV.

? SAQ 35   Now go back through the experiments outlined in SAQ 24 and state what type of IVs the experimenters employed in each.

Designs involving these IVs are illustrated in Tables 10.1 and 10.2. You can see that for our experiment involving unrelated samples we need 32 participants to obtain 16 participants per condition. For the related samples version, however, we need only 16 participants to achieve this.

Those of you who are not expected to contribute to the design of your experiment will still need to be able to state which type of IV(s) you employed. So you must learn to make the above distinction. However, those of you who are expected to contribute at the design stage will also need to be able to decide which type to employ. So we'll turn to a consideration of the factors to bear in mind when deciding which types of IV to use in your experiment. First, however, we need a brief word about terminology.

Table 10.2   A Related Samples IV with Two Conditions

Participant	Condition 1	Condition 2
p01	2nd	1st
p02	1st	2nd
p03	1st	2nd
p04	2nd	1st
p05	2nd	1st
p06	1st	2nd
p07	2nd	1st
p08	1st	2nd
p09	2nd	1st
p10	1st	2nd
p11	2nd	1st
p12	2nd	1st
p13	1st	2nd
p14	2nd	1st
p15	1st	2nd
p16	1st	2nd

Note: Orders have been counterbalanced and allocated randomly. p = participant

Summary of Section 10.1

1 Two basic independent variables employed in psychology are the *unrelated* samples IV and the *related* samples IV.

2 In the unrelated samples IV, a *different* set of participants is assigned to the conditions or levels on the IV.

3 In the related samples IV, the *same* set of participants appear in the conditions or levels on the IV.

10.2   Other names for unrelated and related samples independent variables

Sometimes when you are learning about methodology and statistics in psychology you can feel that you are spending almost as much time learning terminology as you are learning concepts. Moreover, just when you get to grips with one term for something you find that there is another term for the same thing (perhaps more than one additional term, which is about the last thing that you need). Sadly, this is especially true of names for this basic distinction between types of IV.

Until quite recently psychologists referred to the participants in their experiments as **subjects**. This usage is no longer acceptable, primarily because it is thought to be inconsistent with the fact that those who take part in our experiments are first and foremost our fellow human beings and not simply "subjects" of experimental enquiry. However, some important terms in statistics and methodology retain the old-fashioned terminology and you may well come across this terminology in some of the other textbooks that you use, such as your statistics textbook, and when you are using certain statistical software packages.

A traditional term for unrelated samples IVs is **between-subjects**. This is because when we use *unrelated* samples, our comparisons are *between* different participants. Other terms that you may come across for the same thing are **independent** or **uncorrelated samples** or **measures** or **between-participants**.

A traditional term for related samples IVs is **within-subjects**. This is because when we use *related* samples, our comparisons are *within* the same participants. (That is, we are comparing the performance of the same person across the different conditions and thus making comparisons *within* the person.) Other terms that you may come across for the same thing are **dependent** or **correlated samples** or **measures**, **repeated measures** or **within-participants**.

Unfortunately, the problem is compounded by the fact that people can become surprisingly worked up about what label should be used. Throughout this book I use "unrelated samples" to denote IVs where the data in the different levels come from different participants. I use "related samples" to denote IVs where the data in the different levels come from the same participants. Given the strength of feeling that this issue can evoke, however, it is a good idea to find out whether your tutor favours other labels for these IVs and, if so, to use these instead. The important thing (of course) is to make sure that you can recognize these different types of IV and understand the distinction between them. What you choose to call them is secondary. (However, you should be consistent in your use of terminology in a report.)

Summary of Section 10.2

1 There are a number of different terms available to make the same basic distinction between IVs where the data in the different levels come from different participants and IVs where the data in the different levels come from the same participants.

2 The important thing is to understand the distinction underlying these types of IV and to be able to recognize which is which.

10.3   Deciding between related and unrelated samples

In order to consider how you might choose between these types of IV, we must think back to the logic of experimental design discussed in Chapter 9. The aim is to manipulate the variable that we suspect to be causal (the IV) and examine what impact this manipulation has upon the effect variable (the DV). If we find that, when we alter the IV, there are changes in the DV as well, this strengthens our suspicion that there is a causal link between them.

However, as we pointed out earlier, in order to make this causal inference we have to ensure that the IV really is the only thing that we are changing in the situation – that is, we do not want any *confounding* variables. One source of confounding can be our particular sample of participants. Thus, in our driving and music experiment, for example, we don't want too many more of the better drivers to end up in the one condition rather than the other. For, if they did, we could no longer be sure that any differences that we observed in our DV (e.g., number of errors made over a standard course) would be due to our manipulation of the music variable or to basic differences in driving ability. Confounding variables, remember, prevent us from unequivocally attributing the changes that we find in the DV to our manipulation of the IV. This is because they provide possible rival explanations for any effects that we find (e.g., that any difference in driving performance between the conditions is due to basic differences in ability to drive rather than to the effect of having music on or off). Essentially, related and unrelated samples IVs differ in the nature and extent of their potentially confounding variables.

Let's illustrate this with an example. Suppose that we ran our driving and music experiment using *unrelated* samples and found that those who drove without music performed better than those who drove with music on. This could of course be because listening to music affects concentration and impairs ability to drive. However, it could also be simply because more of the better drivers were put into the "music off" condition. For there are pronounced *individual differences* in driving ability. Any differences in driving performance between groups of *different* people, therefore, might well stem from this basic fact of life, rather than from any manipulation of the independent variable. When we use *unrelated* samples, of course, we are inevitably comparing the performances of *different* people.

There are ways in which we can attempt to *minimize* the impact of individual differences upon our experiment. However, there is only one way in which we can actually *eliminate* this source of *extraneous* variation. This is by employing *related* samples.

When we use related samples, we do not compare the performances of different people. Instead, we compare the performances of the *same* people on different occasions. So, in the case of our music experiment, we would assess the driving performances of any given individual both when driving with music on and when driving with music off. We can safely assume that any differences in performance under the two conditions cannot stem from individual differences in driving ability because it's the same person in both conditions.

If you are still confused by this, imagine that we developed a revolutionary kind of running shoe that we suspected would improve the running performance of those who wore it. Using *unrelated* samples would be like giving the shoes to half of the runners in a race and comparing their finishing positions with the runners who didn't have the new shoes. Using *related* samples would be like getting the runners to run at least once with the new shoes and once with their normal running shoes. In the first race it is possible that our runners with the new shoes might find themselves up against people who were simply much better than them anyway. In the latter race, however, you can see that this wouldn't matter, because we wouldn't be interested in where our runners came in *absolute* terms, but simply in how well they fared in comparison with their performance without the new shoes (e.g., in time taken to complete the course). That is, in the first instance it would make a great deal of difference if they found themselves running against a team of Olympic athletes; in the latter case it wouldn't matter at all (provided, of course, that they ran against the same athletes on both occasions and that they were not too demoralized by the first drubbing).

Using related samples, therefore, eliminates from the experimental equation permanent or chronic **individual differences** in ability at the experimental task – the things that make people *generally* better or worse at the task regardless of the IV. We know that some people will simply be better than others on the driving simulator regardless of whether they are listening to music or not. Using unrelated samples, we trust that the variation due to such individual differences in ability will be spread roughly equally between the two conditions. With related samples, however, differences in performance arising from such individual differences in ability are constant across the two conditions and can be removed from the equation.

In eliminating chronic individual differences from our experiment, related samples reduce the amount of background or **extraneous variation** that we have to cope with – variation *other than* that arising from our manipulation of the IV. From our point of view, this is a good thing. For this reason, using related samples is, at least in principle, to be preferred to using unrelated samples. As you have to start somewhere, therefore, a good rule of thumb when designing experiments is to start by exploring the possibility of using related samples IVs, and only turn to the alternatives when you discover obstacles that prevent you from doing so.

Summary of Section 10.3

1 In all experiments the effects of the IV on the DV are assessed against a background of *inherent* or *extraneous* variation.

2 Permanent or chronic *individual differences* in ability at the experimental task are a considerable source of such extraneous variation.

3 Related samples, in eliminating such *individual differences*, thereby remove a large part of this extraneous variation. Related samples IVs should, therefore, be used in preference to unrelated samples IVs when there are no insurmountable obstacles to having related samples.

10.4   Related samples

Related samples are preferable *in principle* to unrelated samples. However, this does not mean that using related samples is without problems and difficulties.

10.4.1   Advantages

The major advantage of using related samples is that doing so reduces the background variation against which we have to assess the impact of the IV upon the DV. It does this by *eliminating permanent* or *chronic individual differences*. There is also a practical advantage that, as students, you will probably find extremely useful – you need fewer participants.

10.4.2   Disadvantages

If using related samples eliminates one source of variation, it unfortunately introduces another – *order* effects. When we run an experiment using related samples, by definition, we will obtain more than one score from each participant (see Table 10.2). This means, of course, that we will have to present our conditions one after the other. This produces problems of its own – problems that do not exist when we use unrelated samples.

For example, suppose that we ran our music experiment using related samples, testing all of our participants first with the music off and then with the music on. Suppose that we found that driving actually improved when the drivers had the music on. Can you think of an alternative explanation for this finding, other than the suggestion that listening to music led to the improvement in performance?

Well, the improvement in driving performance might simply be due to the fact that the participants in our experiment got better at the task as they became more familiar with the driving simulator. That is, they might have got better because they became more *practised* and, because they all did the music on condition second, this **practice effect** contributed more to performance with the music on than to performance with the music off. In other words, we have here a *confounding* variable arising from the *order* in which we ran the conditions. Moreover, the same argument would apply even if we'd found the opposite: that is, if we'd found that the performance of our drivers had *deteriorated* from the first condition to the second. In this case, it could simply be that our participants had become *bored* with the task or were *fatigued* and started to make more mistakes because of this.

Order effects are the price that we pay for eliminating individual differences with related samples. Order effects come in two forms. There are those that lead to an *improvement* in the participant's performance – things like practice, increasing familiarity with the experimental task and equipment, increasing awareness of the task demands. In contrast, there are those that lead to a *deterioration* in performance – things like loss of concentration, due to fatigue or boredom. Both types of effect occur simultaneously, but have opposite effects on the DV. Both types of effect need to be controlled for.

10.4.3 Controlling for order effects

The best way of controlling for order effects is to employ a technique known as **counterbalancing**.

When we counterbalance we ensure that each condition in our experiment follows and is preceded by every other condition an equal number of times. Thus, for each participant who does one particular sequence of conditions, there are other participants who perform the conditions in all the other possible combinations of orders. Although in the abstract this sounds horrendously complicated, generally it can be achieved comparatively easily. So, for instance, in our driving experiment a very simple control for order effects would be to ensure that half of the participants drove with the music on *before* they drove with the music off, whereas the other half drove with the music on *after* they

Table 10.3   A Counterbalanced Design Using Related Samples to Examine the Effects of Having Music Off or On upon Driving Performance

Participant	Music on	Music off
p02	1st	2nd
p03	1st	2nd
p06	1st	2nd
p08	1st	2nd
p10	1st	2nd
p13	1st	2nd
p15	1st	2nd
p16	1st	2nd
p01	2nd	1st
p04	2nd	1st
p05	2nd	1st
p07	2nd	1st
p09	2nd	1st
p11	2nd	1st
p12	2nd	1st
p14	2nd	1st

Note: Participants have been randomly allocated to orders. p = participant

had driven with it off (see Table 10.3). This way, although we would not have *eliminated* order effects (our participants are still likely to get better or worse as they go along) we will have rendered these effects *unsystematic*. That is, practice, fatigue and boredom should affect the music on condition about as much as they affect the music off condition.

We will talk more about counterbalancing when we consider extending the number of levels on an IV (Section 13.1.2). Sometimes, however, there are too many conditions to counterbalance. Under these circumstances there are a number of alternatives. One of these is to **randomize** the order of the conditions.

For example, if we had an experiment with six conditions, this would give us 720 different orders. If we wished to counterbalance these orders, we would need a minimum of 720 participants (one for each different sequence of the six conditions). Although there are alternatives that you may come across later on in your statistics course (e.g., the *Latin square*), under these circumstances you will most probably find yourselves *randomizing* the orders undertaken by your participants.

When we randomize the order of our conditions we don't actually ensure that all the conditions are followed by and preceded by every other condition an equal number of times. Instead, we trust a *random*

*Table 10.4   Randomized Orders of Conditions for the First
10 Participants in a Six-Condition Experiment Employing
Related Samples*

Participant	Sequence
p01	C D A E F B
p02	B D F A C E
p03	F D B A E C
p04	A C B F D E
p05	F A D E B C
p06	A B F C E D
p07	E D B F A C
p08	C D B F E A
p09	D A E B F C
p10	E F C D B A

Note: Each sequence of conditions has been created randomly and separately for each
participant. p = participant

sequence to spread the order effects more or less equally around the
various conditions. So, for instance, if we randomized the orders in
which our participants performed in an experiment with six experimental conditions, we would hope that each of the conditions would
appear in each of the ordinal positions (first, second, third, etc.) just
about as often as the others. The more participants that we have, the
likelier it is that this will be the case.

This is because the critical feature of a random sequence is that the
items in the sequence all have an equal chance of being selected for
any of the positions in that sequence. In the case of orders, what this
means is that any of the conditions can appear first, second, third,
etc., for any of the participants. So, for example, in a six-condition
experiment, Condition A has the same chance as Conditions B, C, D,
E and F of being the first condition undertaken by Participant 1. If
Condition C is the one actually chosen by the random process then
Conditions A, B, D, E and F all have an equal chance of being the
second condition undertaken by Participant 1. (See Appendix 2 for
the details of how to go about making such choices.) If Condition D
is chosen as the second condition, then Conditions A, B, E and F all
have an equal chance of being the third condition undertaken by
Participant 1, and so on until all the conditions have been assigned to
this participant by the random process. Moreover, the same applies to
Participant 2, and indeed to *all* of the participants in the experiment
(Table 10.4). (For the record, this is randomization *without* replacement
– see Appendix 2.)

When used to control for order effects, however, both counterbalancing and randomization have one thing in common. They are based upon the assumption that our participants are *not much more* fatigued or bored or practised when the music off condition comes after the music on condition, than they are when the music off condition comes first. If they are, then we have what we call a significant **carry-over effect** among the conditions in our experiment. Neither counterbalancing nor randomization can control for carry-over effects.

When you suspect that the conditions of your experiment will have a carry-over effect, therefore, you should not use a related samples design. An extreme example of such a case would be, for instance, if we were attempting to compare two different techniques of teaching a particular task. Once participants have learned the task once, it is not possible to make them unlearn it in order to learn it once again by the different method. Similarly, if we were undertaking research into the effects of alcohol upon risk perception, it would be a mistake to have our no alcohol condition following immediately upon our alcohol condition. So you must watch out for treatment conditions in your experiments that tend to markedly alter the state of your participant. Such conditions will have a lingering effect and will consequently influence performance in subsequent conditions, thus having a carry-over effect.

If these effects are only temporary, one way around them is to introduce a longer than usual time delay between conditions (e.g., hours, days, or even weeks). However, if the effects are more or less permanent (e.g., teaching methods) or if this strategy is not feasible (e.g., lack of time, lack of co-operation on the part of your participants) then it would be better to employ one of the alternative designs.

So, when designing any experiment involving related samples IVs, think sensibly and carefully about whether there are likely to be any significant carry-over effects between conditions and, if there are, about whether it is possible to modify your design to cope with them. If not, then you need to abandon the idea of using related samples on the offending IV.

Another problem that arises with related samples is the need to duplicate and *match* materials. For example, suppose that you and I were interested in establishing whether scores on a test of reasoning are influenced by the ways in which the questions are phrased – in particular, whether the problems are couched in *abstract* terms (e.g., using algebraic expressions like $A > R$) or in *concrete* terms (e.g., by using examples drawn from everyday life to express the same relationships – things like "Antony is older than Richard"). There are profound individual differences in people's ability to reason, so ideally we would like to run this experiment using related samples. We could do this by giving participants *both* concrete and abstract problems

*Table 10.5   A Design Using Related Samples with Matched
Materials to Examine the Effects of the Phrasing of the Questions
(Concrete or Abstract) on Reasoning Performance*

Group	Test A	Test B
1	Concrete	Abstract
2	Abstract	Concrete

and comparing their performances on the two types of item. However, we would need to make sure that any differences in performance between the two conditions arose from the ways in which the problems were expressed and not from the fact that one of the sets of problems was simply easier to solve. That is, we would need to *match* our materials so that they were equivalent in all respects other than the IV – whether they were couched in concrete or abstract terms. In this case, this is not all that difficult to do. If you imagine two sets of problems, Test A and Test B, we can give one group of participants Test A couched in concrete terms and Test B couched in abstract terms, and the other group of participants Test A couched in abstract terms and Test B couched in concrete terms (Table 10.5). Thus, any differences that we find in overall performance on the concrete and abstract items cannot be due to differences in the ease of the items themselves – because the two sets of items have appeared equally as often under the concrete and the abstract conditions.

Summary of Section 10.4

1 The cost of eliminating individual differences when we use related samples is the introduction of another source of extraneous variation – *order effects*.

2 Order effects are of two kinds: those that lead to an *improvement* and those that lead to a *deterioration* in the participant's performance on the experimental task.

3 These order effects must be *controlled* for – for example, by *counterbalancing* or by *randomizing* the order of the conditions.

4 These methods do not *eliminate* the variation introduced by order. They simply *transform* it into unsystematic variation.

5 These methods will not work when there are significant *carry-over* effects. Under these circumstances, related samples must not be used.

6 With related samples you are likely to need to duplicate and *match* the materials.

10.5   Principal alternatives to related samples

Where there are insurmountable order effects, or it is difficult to match materials, or when the participants simply *have* to be different (e.g. in personality research, studies involving differences in intelligence, culture, gender, etc.) then related samples are not suitable. Under these circumstances, you should turn to one of the alternatives. The principal alternative is to use unrelated samples. However, you might also consider matching your participants in some ways (Section 10.7). If you have more than one IV, then you may be able to use a combination of related and unrelated samples IVs (see Chapter 13).

10.6   Unrelated samples

The principal alternative to the use of related samples is to use unrelated samples on your IV. As pointed out earlier, however, the biggest disadvantage of unrelated samples is the presence of *individual differences*. However, there are ways in which we can attempt to minimize their impact on our experiment.

10.6.1   Advantages

It just so happens that the advantages of unrelated samples correspond to the weaknesses of related samples. That is, there are no problems with order effects and we do not need to duplicate and match our materials.

10.6.2   Disadvantages

However, the reverse is also true. If there are no problems with order effects, this is more than offset by the intrusion of individual differences. Likewise, if we do not have problems with materials, we have to find a lot more participants.

10.6.3   Ways around these disadvantages

With respect to the bigger disadvantage, individual differences, we must attempt to rule out any *systematic bias* stemming from such differences between participants. We cannot eliminate individual differences; we can, however, try to ensure that they are equally distributed across conditions (e.g., that as many good drivers are assigned to the music on as to the music off groups). One possibility would be to try to *match* our participants, assessing them on driving performance and making sure that equal numbers of good and bad drivers are assigned to each group (Section 10.7). In order to do this we would need to assess the performances of our participants *before* running the experiment (i.e., run a *pretest*).

Often, however, we have neither the resources nor the time to collect and act upon this information. Under these circumstances, the alternative we turn to is again *randomization* – in this case the *random assignment* of participants to their conditions (see Appendix 2). To do this, we go to our pool of participants and assign them randomly to conditions, trusting the random sequence to spread individuals who differ in basic ability at the experimental task more or less equally among the conditions. So, for instance, in our music and driving experiment we might assign our participants to either the music on or the music off condition using random number tables (Appendix 2). We would hope that this procedure would give us a fairly even split of good, poor and indifferent drivers between the conditions. The more participants we use, the more effective this procedure is likely to be.

Random assignment of participants to the conditions of an unrelated samples IV (or, conversely, to the different orders of conditions on a related samples IV) is the critical feature that makes an experiment a true experiment. Random *assignment* of participants to conditions should not, however, be confused with the random *selection* of participants from a population. Ideally you should do both. In practice, as students, you will probably only do the former (see Sections 10.8 and 10.9). Moreover, unless you check, you can never really be sure that your randomization has been effective. That is, you will be unable to state categorically that differences in ability among your participants did *not* lead to the differences that you observed on your DV. The same is true of randomizing to control for order effects. It may be that there were systematic differences in the orders in which your conditions appeared, even though these were randomized. So, you should bear this in mind when you come to interpret your findings. (Once you have become experienced enough, you should consider checking the effectiveness of your randomization. You can find advice on this on the Web site that accompanies this book.)

With regard to the problem of having to obtain larger numbers of participants with unrelated samples than with the related samples equivalent, like the problems with materials in related samples designs, this is simply something that you have to live with. However, where you have more than one IV you may be able to reduce the number of these that require different participants – that is, employ what we call a *mixed* design (Section 13.3) – and thereby reduce the number of participants that you need overall.

Summary of Sections 10.5–10.6

1 Using *unrelated* samples *eliminates* order effects and the need to duplicate materials.

2 It *introduces* individual differences and requires larger numbers of participants than the equivalent related samples design.

3 We can attempt to control for individual differences by assigning our participants to conditions randomly.

4 This does not *eliminate* the variation introduced by individual differences; it is simply an attempt to render it *unsystematic*.

5 As with controlling for order effects by randomization, it is possible that assigning participants randomly to conditions does not completely transform the systematic variation. You should bear this in mind when interpreting your findings (and check the randomization if you know how – see the Web site).

10.7 Matching participants

If you have the time and the resources to collect the relevant information, then *matching* your participants can give you a good half-way house between the unrelated and related samples designs. **Matching** involves finding groups or even pairs of participants who are similar on some variable that you think is related to the IV. With the music and driving experiment, for instance, we might assess each participant's driving ability *before* assigning them to experimental conditions and then attempt to make sure that equal numbers of good and poor drivers are assigned to each group. Similarly, we might run the reasoning experiment by assigning equal numbers of good, poor and indifferent reasoners to the concrete and abstract conditions. This way we don't trust to a random sequence to spread individual differences equally between conditions – we attempt to ensure ourselves that this is done.

Where possible, therefore, it is a good idea to match the participants in an experiment in which you have different participants in conditions, as this will reduce the possibility of individual differences *confounding* the effects of your independent variable. However, you will of course still have to assign matched participants to the experimental conditions *randomly*. That is, which particular condition any one of the better drivers or reasoners or any one of the less able drivers or reasoners is to go in must be decided at random in exactly the same way as you would do with a sample of unmatched participants.

? SAQ 36   Why?

Where you have *matched* participants, therefore, you will still need to assign them to experimental conditions randomly. You do this by randomly assigning the members of each group of matched particip-ants separately. So, for instance, you would assign the *better* drivers to their conditions using the sort of methods described in Appendix 2. Separately, you would do the equivalent with the *less* able drivers. This way you would end up with the same spread of ability in each condition but within any level of ability participants would have been assigned randomly to their conditions.

In effect, in doing this, you will have introduced an additional IV into your experiment – an unrelated samples IV comprising the better and poorer drivers. This is not a problem (in fact, usually quite the reverse): I will talk in Chapter 13 about such designs.

When you have matched *pairs* of participants, it is sometimes argued that the data can be analysed statistically as if it were from a *related* sample. As a student, however, it is extremely unlikely that in human work you will achieve the necessary level of matching for this, so usually you should consider data from matched pairs of partici-pants to be *unrelated* when analysing them.

Summary of Section 10.7

1 A good half-way house between the related and the unrelated samples design is to use unrelated samples in which the participants have been matched and assigned to conditions such that there is an equal spread of ability on the experimental task between the conditions.

2 Such designs reduce the possibility of individual differences *con-founding* the effects of the independent variable.

10.8   **The external validity of your experiment**

With this knowledge about unrelated and related samples IVs and about matching participants you are already well on the way towards being able to design interesting experiments in psychology. In theory there is no limit either to the number of levels that you can have on an IV or to the number of IVs that you can have in an experiment. In practice, however, there are important issues that you need to con-sider when using IVs with many levels or more than one IV. I will introduce you to these in the final chapter, once you have learnt about significance testing and have been introduced to the important issue of the power of your experiments. Now, however, I want us to turn to two other issues that you need to be aware of when experimenting: external and internal validity (the subject of this section and the next) and ethics (the subject of Section 10.10).

In the previous chapter we considered how the capacity of the experiment to allow causal inferences stems from the *control* that is achieved. Control involves holding other factors constant across the conditions so that they cannot account for any changes observed in the DV. Remember, we can make unequivocal causal inferences – that the IV causes the changes we see in the DV – only if we have held everything else constant.

Of course, this is a condition that can never be realistically achieved. There are just too many variables in the world. In practice, we aspire to holding constant those variables that plausibly may be rival explanations for the observed changes in the effect variable and others that can be held constant without too much effort or too much distortion of the situation. Others we allow to vary in the hope that they will not turn out to differ systematically across the conditions. Yet others – the vast majority – we assume are irrelevant (perhaps wrongly) and disregard. Often we take it one step at a time, controlling for different variables across a series of separate experimental studies.

There is however an inevitable tension between experimental control and *generalizability*. **Generalizability** is the extent to which the findings generated by your experiment can be extrapolated. For example, are they relevant to everybody, regardless of race, class, gender, age? Or are they circumscribed in some way – for example, relevant only to middle-class, white youngsters of above average intelligence?

The worst state of affairs is that the findings cannot be generalized to any people or circumstances beyond those used in the particular experiment that you ran. This is very unusual. However, it can be the case that the findings are of limited applicability because of some of the variables that you had to hold constant for control purposes. An obvious example would be if you choose to use only male participants (i.e., hold the variable *sex* constant across conditions); then there would be question marks over the extent to which the findings could be generalized to females.

The generalizability of the findings is also called the **external validity** of your experiment: *external* validity because it concerns the relevance of your findings to situations beyond or *external* to those used in the experiment. Experiments high in external validity have highly generalizable findings – that is, the findings apply to a range of people, times and situations beyond those assessed in the experiment.

One threat to external validity comes from the conditions that you imposed on the time, setting and task for the purposes of control.

? SAQ 37 For instance, for some years I helped to run a class experiment at an Open University summer school to test whether people can taste the difference between mineral water and tap water. We found that most people cannot. In this experiment, the variable *temperature* was controlled by keeping the water at room temperature. Does this mean that we can conclude that people in general cannot taste the difference between mineral water and tap water?

Another potential limit to external validity stems from your participants. Are they representative of the group from which you took them (e.g., students)? Are they representative of a wider range of people? Many studies in psychology, for example, use undergraduate psychology students as participants. Yet students, of course, tend to come from a restricted sector of the population. They are almost invariably young, supposedly intelligent, and predominantly middle-class. Add to this the probability that those interested in psychology may also have peculiarities of their own, and it could be that the findings of studies based on samples of undergraduate psychologists cannot be generalized to other populations.

However, the validity of this criticism depends on the IV being investigated. If the variables that *differentiate* such participants from the general public (e.g., age, intelligence, class) are thought to have some impact on the DV (e.g., reasoning, attitudes) then the criticism may be valid. However, other variables may not be so influenced (e.g., motor skills, visual perception). So, don't *automatically* assume that having a student sample seriously limits the extent to which you can generalize your findings. Always bear in mind that – if your study is in other respects well designed – the results should be generalizable to at least some subgroup in the population. After all, in some respects at least, students are still members of the human race and, believe it or not, there are young, middle-class, intelligent people who are not students.

At first, many of you are concerned that you should always have a random sample of people from the general population in your experiments and doubt the usefulness of experiments lacking such samples. We will consider this issue below once I've introduced you to the concept of internal validity. For now, remember that this is a concern with **random selection** and it relates to the *external* validity of the experiment.

Summary of Section 10.8

1 There is often a tension between the demands of experimental control and the extent to which you can generalize your findings to people, times, and situations not directly assessed in the experiment.

2 Experiments with highly generalizable findings are high in *external* validity.

3 Threats to external validity can come from constraints on the time, setting, task, and the participants used.

4 Concerns about the failure to randomly select a sample from a population relate to the external validity of the experiment.

10.9 The internal validity of your experiment

For practical reasons, most of the experiments that you run as a student are unlikely to be very high in external validity. They must, however, be high in *internal* validity. **Internal validity** refers to the extent to which we can relate changes in the DV to the manipulation of the IV. That is, a well-designed experiment with no confounding variables is an experiment very high in internal validity. This is an experiment in which we can make the unequivocal causal inferences that we desire.

However, high internal validity is often paid for by holding many extraneous variables constant and thus sacrificing external validity. For example, in our cheese and nightmare experiment, the more we introduce controls for variables that might also produce nightmares, the more we run the risk that the generalizability of our findings will be limited by the values at which we hold those variables constant. For example, if we require people to eat cheese 3 hours before they go to bed the findings may not apply to cheese eaten 10 minutes before going to bed. Likewise, if we restrict ourselves to one type of cheese (say, Cheddar), the findings may be limited to that type of cheese, or only to hard cheeses, or only to cheeses made with milk from UK cattle, and so on.

Internal validity represents the degree of control that we exercise in the experiment. One of the key elements in achieving high internal validity (but by no means the sole one) is that we randomly assign participants to conditions (or orders of conditions to participants) in order to maximize our chances of rendering the variation on extraneous variables unsystematic between conditions. This is the issue of **random assignment** and it relates to the *internal* validity of the experiment.

Thus, *random assignment* of participants to conditions should not be confused with *random sampling* of participants from a population. At the start of your careers in psychology most of you tend to be much more concerned about the latter than you are about the former, whereas at this stage the reverse should be the case! This is because, whereas both of the types of validity described above are important, internal validity is the more important. It is of little consolation to be able to generalize a set of equivocal findings to a lot of people and many situations, when you run an experiment high in external but low in internal validity. In contrast, an experiment high in internal validity usually has at least a modicum of generalizability. Of course, ideally in our studies we should aim for both. However, as students, most of the time you should concentrate your time and energies on ensuring that your experiments are at least high in internal validity. You know how to do this: by selecting carefully the variables to hold constant across conditions, standardizing your procedures and materials, and using *truly* random procedures to attempt to ensure that other important sources of variation do not differ systematically between the conditions. Random assignment of participants to conditions (or orders of conditions to participants) is a key element in striving to achieve this.

Summary of Section 10.9

1 The experiments that you run as a student are unlikely to be very high in external validity.

2 They must, however, be high in *internal* validity.

3 An experiment high in internal validity is one in which we can relate changes in the DV unequivocally to the manipulation of the IV.

4 One of the key elements in achieving high internal validity is to randomly assign participants to conditions or orders of conditions to participants.

5 Random assignment of participants to conditions should not be confused with random sampling of participants from a population. The former relates to the internal validity of the experiment, the latter to the external validity of the experiment.

10.10   Ethics: the self-esteem and welfare of your participants

A concern with variables and control is not the only element of experimental design in psychology. Regard for the welfare, rights and

dignity of your participants is as essential to good experimental practice as is the pursuit of experimental rigour and elegance. Never underestimate the impact that being in a psychological experiment can
have on your participant. We live in a competitive society, and the
experiment has all the trappings of a test. Those of you who have
participated in a psychological experiment will probably have been
struck by just how difficult it can be to shake off the feeling that
somehow you are under scrutiny. You can feel that you have to do
your best, even though you know that an experimenter's interest is
rarely in particular individuals, but invariably in making statements
about the influence of the IV on *groups* of people. Those of you who
haven't participated in one should try to if possible. It gives you an
invaluable insight into the sorts of factors that can influence a participant's performance in an experiment.

When designing experiments it is important to have clearly in mind
the participants' welfare, self-respect and dignity. You must not put
people through an experience that undermines their welfare or self-
regard. So, think about the impact that your experiment will have
on your participant when you think about designs that you might
employ, measures that you might use, and issues that you might address
by experimenting. For example, look closely at your procedures, the
wording of your instructions, the items on any questionnaires or other
measures that you are thinking about using. Is it really appropriate
and sensitive to use the depression inventory that you are considering? Could some of the questions on the anxiety scale that you are
thinking of using cause embarrassment or distress? If so, are there
better alternatives? If not, is your use of these measures really justified
and ethically acceptable? (While we're on the topic of published measures, such as scales and tests, make sure that you have permission to
copy and use any published measures that you want to use in your
study. See your tutor for advice on this.)

Even as students, your conduct is expected to adhere to ethical
principles. In your early work in practical classes the tutors running
the course will have primary responsibility for ensuring that the things
that they ask you to do are ethically acceptable. However, when you
undertake your own project work (e.g., in the UK in the final year of
an undergraduate degree) the likelihood is that you will be expected
to submit details of your proposed study to an ethics committee for
prior assessment. You will be allowed to run your study only once
you have received approval from that ethics committee.

It is important, therefore, that you get hold of a copy of the ethical
principles or code that is used in your department or school. You
must familiarize yourself with these from the outset. When the time
comes you should also make sure that you know when and how to

submit your studies to the relevant ethical committee and that you do not undertake work that needs prior ethical approval without having that approval. If in any doubt, check with your tutor.

In the unlikely event that your department or school does not have a set of **ethical principles** then you can obtain some from the professional body that oversees the conduct of properly qualified psychologists in your country. These are organizations such as the British Psychological Society and the American Psychological Association. You can usually download these principles from the organization's Web site. Failing that, you can ask them to send you a copy.

The principles deal with a number of aspects of conducting yourself ethically with participants. These include:

- approaching people and encouraging them to take part in your study;
- what you do to them and how you interact with them during the study;
- how you respond if they decline to take part or wish to withdraw once they've started;
- what you say to them after they've finished;
- how you look after and report the data that you've obtained from them.

You must make sure that you have read the most relevant set of principles and that you abide by them.

10.10.1 Informed consent

A key feature of all principles is that of *informed consent*. **Informed consent** is what it sounds like – telling people enough about your experiment to enable them to make an *informed* decision about whether or not to take part. For example, the *APA Publication Manual* (APA, 2001, p. 391) states that psychologists should "use language that is reasonably understandable to research participants" to:

- inform them of the nature of the research;
- inform them that they are free to participate or to decline to participate or to withdraw from the research;
- explain the foreseeable consequences of declining or withdrawing;
- inform participants of significant factors that may be expected to influence their willingness to participate (such as risks, discomfort, adverse effects);
- explain other aspects about which the prospective participants inquire.

Principle 3.1 of the British Psychological Society's *Ethical Principles* is similar (British Psychological Society [BPS], 2000).

The principle of informed consent is very important. However, respond to it sensibly. It is not a directive to spell out *everything* about the study to prospective participants. Given that people would respond very differently in many studies if they knew *precisely* what the experiment was about, you must think carefully about what you need to tell them about your study. It is important to give your participants a general idea about what you will ask them to do, how long it will take (honestly!), and so on. It is *essential* that you tell them about risks, discomfort, or any other aspects that might affect their willingness to take part. (Indeed, the ethics committee will insist on this as a condition of approval.) However, think carefully about what you tell potential recruits about what the study is *about*. Tell them the things that they need to know in order to make an informed decision. Do not jeopardize the study unnecessarily by telling them things that are important to interpreting the experiment and yet *not* key to whether or not they will agree to take part. (As ever, take your tutor's advice on this.)

Do not confuse *masking* or *concealing* or *withholding* the hypothesis with *deception*. **Withholding the hypothesis** involves encouraging participants to suspend judgement about what you are investigating until after the experiment has finished and you are ready to debrief them. **Deception** involves deliberately misleading participants into believing that the study is about something it is not about. Participants generally are quite willing to do the former and can be pretty aggrieved by the latter. As a student you must not run an experiment involving deception without prior ethical approval and *extremely* close supervision by a tutor.

10.10.2   Debriefing your participants

You must make time available for those who want it at the end of the experiment to discuss any questions that they may have regarding what you have asked them to do. This is known in the trade as **debriefing** your participant, and it is an integral part of good experimenting. At this stage, answer their questions informatively, honestly, and willingly, discussing the thinking behind your ideas, and the purpose of the experiment if that interests them. If you cannot tell them precisely what the experiment is about, for fear that word will get about and future participants will no longer be naive about the experiment, then see if they are prepared to wait for full debriefing until all the participants have taken part. If so, you should take contact details and send them an account of the experiment and the findings as soon as these are available. Debriefing is for the *participant's* benefit, not yours.

10.10.3 Data confidentiality

Ethical considerations do not finish with the completion of the study. Most countries now have rules and regulations regarding how data on human beings are stored, and professional guidelines also cover this aspect of conduct. You must keep the data safe, secure and confidential, no matter how dull, boring and uninteresting they may seem to you to be. This includes both the original measures (such as a set of questionnaires or response sheets) and the data that you have on computer. Consult the relevant guidelines to learn more.

Summary of Section 10.10

1 Regard for the welfare and comfort of the participants in your experiment is an integral part of good experimental design. You have no right to put your participants through an experience that undermines their welfare, self-respect or dignity, and you must bear this in mind when thinking about procedures that you might employ and issues that you might address in experiments.

2 You should be aware of the contents of the most relevant set of ethical principles before you start designing and running your own experiments. Even as students, your conduct must adhere to ethical principles.

3 If you go on to do project work you may need to submit your proposed study to an ethics committee for approval. If so, you must not start the study before receiving ethical approval.

4 A key feature of all ethical principles for research with human beings is the principle of informed consent. Make sure that you understand this principle and abide by it.

5 Make time available at the end of your experiment to discuss any questions that your participants have regarding what you asked them to do. You should answer their questions honestly, openly and willingly. This is known in the trade as debriefing your participant, and it is an essential feature of any well-run experiment.

6 Keep the data safe, secure and confidential and in accordance with the laws governing the storage of information about humans.

11 Statistics: significance testing

So far in this guide I have talked rather glibly about *differences* between conditions and *correlations* between variables. However, what I have really meant here is what you will come to understand as differences and correlations that are **reliable**. For there is something special about the differences and correlations that interest us. We are not interested simply in, say, a difference in the numbers between two conditions; we are interested in those differences (and correlations) that would usually be repeated if we were to run the experiment (or other study) again.

Thinking back to our driving and music experiment, if we were to measure the performance of any given participant on the driving simulator on a number of occasions, we would not expect him or her to make an *identical* number of errors on each occasion. We would not even expect this when s/he was fully accustomed to the apparatus. Similarly, I have already pointed out that one of the problems with *unrelated* samples is that there are generally differences between people in their basic abilities on experimental tasks. This means, of course, that even when we assign participants to experimental conditions randomly, we would hardly expect our different groups to obtain identical mean values on the dependent variable.

If you have any doubts about this, then try the following exercise. Try balancing a book on your head. (Make sure that it isn't too heavy, and keep away from breakable objects!) See how long you can keep it there (a) in silence and (b) with the radio on. Do it five times under each condition. (Make sure that you set up a *random* sequence *in advance*.) Record your times, and then work out the *mean* time for balancing under both conditions. Are they identical? I bet they're not! Does this mean that having the radio on has affected your ability to balance a book on your head? (I trust that you've controlled adequately for the effects of practice and fatigue.)

The point of this is that you will more or less inevitably find differences between conditions on the DV, *even when the IV does not in fact cause changes in the DV*. So, for example, even if listening to music had absolutely no impact whatsoever on the ability to drive, we would still expect to find our participants apparently driving better in one of the experimental conditions than in the other. That is, we will always have to assess the effects of our IV against a background of *inherent* variation.

We need, therefore, to find a way of being able to distinguish a difference that *has* been influenced by our IV (a *reliable* difference) from one that has *not* been so influenced – a difference that would be there anyway. That is, we need to be able to detect the sort of difference that would occur simply if we took a group of participants and measured their performances on repeated occasions *without* exposing them to the IV. This is why we turn to *inferential statistics*.

Summary

1 We will invariably find that there are differences between the conditions on the DV even when the IV does not cause changes in the DV.

2 We therefore have to find some way of distinguishing a difference that has been caused by the IV (a *reliable* difference) from one that is simply the product of chance variation.

3 We employ *inferential* statistics to assist us with this task.

11.1 Inferential statistics

Think back to our cheese and nightmare experiment. Imagine that we actually ran this experiment one night and obtained the data in Table 11.1. (There are 50 participants in each condition.) You can see from Table 11.1 that 11 more of those in the cheese condition reported nightmares than did those in the no cheese condition. Thus, *more* people reported nightmares in the cheese condition than in the no cheese condition. This is a difference, but as yet we don't know whether it is the sort of difference that we would be likely to find anyway. The question is, if eating cheese actually has *no effect* upon the incidence of nightmares, how likely would we be to obtain a difference of 11 between our conditions?

To understand this, imagine that we took 100 table tennis balls and stamped "nightmare" on half of them and "no nightmare" on the remainder. We then placed these in a large black plastic bag, shook them up, and drew them out one by one. Imagine also that we simply

Table 11.1   Numbers of Participants Reporting Nightmares and Reporting No Nightmares in the Cheese and No Cheese Conditions

	Nightmare	
Condition	*Yes*	*No*
Cheese	33	17
No cheese	22	28

decided to assign the first 50 table tennis balls that we drew out to a hypothetical *cheese* condition and the remainder to a hypothetical *no cheese* condition. The question is, doing this, how likely would we be to get the sorts of values that we have in Table 11.1?

Ideally we need some way of assessing this. This is precisely where **inferential statistics** come in. These statistics enable us to assess the likelihood that we would obtain results like ours *if* we assume that our IV did *not* cause changes in our DV. That is, using such statistics we can assess whether we would have been likely to get data like ours *if* we assume that there isn't a genuine effect of eating cheese on the incidence of nightmares.

You may have spotted that the assumption that the IV does *not* cause changes in the DV is one that we have met before. It is, of course, the *null hypothesis* (Section 9.14). Essentially, therefore, inferential statistics tell us the probability that we would obtain results like ours *if we assume that the null hypothesis is true*. This is what we call the probability *under the null hypothesis*.[1]

There are inferential statistical tests available to assess this probability for all kinds of data (see Section 11.4 and the Web site for more on how to go about choosing an appropriate test). For all of these, however, at the end of the calculations you should end up with a single score. This score is the value of the statistic that "belongs" to your data. Associated with this statistic is a *probability*. This is the probability that we are interested in. It tells us how likely you would be to obtain your value – and, by implication, these data – if we assume the null hypothesis to be true. Statistical software packages usually print out this probability for you, along with the statistic. If you've calculated the statistic by hand, however, you can look up the probability associated with your calculated statistic in the appropriate tables of *critical values* (to be found at the rear of most textbooks of statistics – see Appendix 3).

For instance, as we have only one observation from each participant (nightmare or no nightmare), an appropriate statistic for the above example is chi-square (Section 4.6.1). Chi-square tests for an *association*

Table 11.2   Probabilities Under the Null Hypothesis Associated with Particular Values of Chi-Square with One Degree of Freedom

Chi-square	Probability
0.016	.90
0.15	.70
0.46	.50
1.64	.20
3.84	.05
5.02	.025
10.83	.001

between two variables – in this case whether there is any association between eating cheese and the numbers of nightmares that are reported. So, you can see that it is eminently suited for the question that we wish to ask of our data.

Table 11.2 contains a range of values of chi-square, together with their associated probability if we assume the null hypothesis to be true. You can see that, under this assumption, a value of $\chi^2 = 0.15$ has a probability of occurring of $p = .7$, which is quite high. A value of $\chi^2 = 3.84$, however, has an associated probability of only $p = .05$, which is quite low.

For those new to the idea of **probability**, it is measured conventionally from one to zero. An event with a probability of one is *inevitable*. An event with a probability of zero is *impossible*. Most events in our universe tend to lie somewhere between these two extremes.

If you enter the data in Table 11.1 into your statistics package it will calculate for you the value of chi-square that belongs to these data. Alternatively, you can find details of how to calculate chi-square by hand in almost any textbook of statistics. Either way, you should obtain a value of $\chi^2 = 4.89$. What you need to establish next is whether this value is *likely* or *unlikely* to have occurred under the null hypothesis – that is, even if cheese does not cause nightmares.

If you calculated chi-square using a statistical software package, the package will give you the *exact* probability associated with the statistic. This value is $p = .03$ (to 2 decimal places). Those who worked out the value of chi-square by hand can establish from Table 11.2 that the value of $\chi^2 = 4.89$, with 1 degree of freedom, has a probability under the null hypothesis of somewhere between $p = .05$ and $p = .025$. For the value of chi-square that has a probability of $p = .05$ is 3.84, which is *less* than our obtained value of chi-square. However, the value of chi-square that has a probability of $p = .025$ is 5.02, which is *greater* than our obtained value. So, our value lies somewhere in between these and consequently the probability associated with it must lie somewhere between $p = .05$ and $p = .025$. This agrees with the $p = .03$ that we obtained from our statistics package but is less exact. (See Appendix 3 for more on how to work out the probability associated with your statistic if you are not using a statistics package.)

The probability of obtaining a value of chi-square as *large* as 4.89 under the null hypothesis, therefore, is three times in 100 (this is just another way of expressing $p = .03$). Essentially, therefore, if we were to draw our table tennis balls randomly from our big black plastic bag we would expect, *on average*, to obtain data similar to ours three times for every 100 times that we did it.

? SAQ 38   Our obtained value of chi-square has an associated probability of $p = .03$. Is this nearer the inevitable or the impossible end of the continuum? (That is, is this nearer one or zero?)

Let's recap. We've run our experiment and generated the data in Table 11.1. We then realized that in order to make any sense of it – in order to find out what it tells us about the relationship between eating cheese and experiencing nightmares – we needed to discover how likely we would have been to obtain results like these anyway. So, we employed a statistical test appropriate for our data (chi-square) and we discovered that the value of chi-square that we obtained (4.89) has a low probability of having occurred *if* we assume that eating cheese *does not* induce nightmares. Does this mean, therefore, that we can safely conclude that eating cheese *does* induce nightmares?

Well, the simple and rather unsettling answer to that question is – no. For the problem is that we still don't know whether the IV does or does not affect the DV. All we know is that the probability of getting data like ours is relatively low *if* we assume that the IV does *not* affect the DV. Thus, under the null hypothesis, data like ours are *unlikely*. However, they are still *possible*. We know, therefore, that on any given occasion we would be unlikely to draw a similar distribution of values to those in Table 11.1 from our big black plastic bag of table tennis balls. Nevertheless, we might actually do so. We have, in fact, about a 33–1 chance of doing so. Moreover, as some of us know to our (very!) occasional benefit, long shots, though infrequently, still win races.

In fact we will *never* know whether the null hypothesis is true or false. Inferential statistics don't provide us with sudden insights into the laws of the universe. They simply tell us the probability that we would get values like those that we have obtained on our DV *if* the null hypothesis *were* true.

So how do we get around this problem? Well, all is not lost. The procedure that we traditionally adopt to resolve this dilemma is described next.

11.2   Testing for statistical significance

In this procedure, what we do is set up a criterion probability for our statistic. We do this before we even begin collecting the data. We decide subsequently to obey a simple rule. The rule is as follows. If we find that the *probability* associated with our obtained statistic falls *at* or *below* the criterion (i.e., is the same value as the criterion probability, or nearer zero) then we will *reject* the assumption that the null hypothesis is true (see Figure 11.1). If, however, we find that the probability associated with the statistic falls *above* this criterion (i.e., is nearer one) then we will *not* reject the assumption that the null hypothesis is true.

This is the principle of **statistical significance** testing. Using this approach, we *always* do this when we test our data for differences

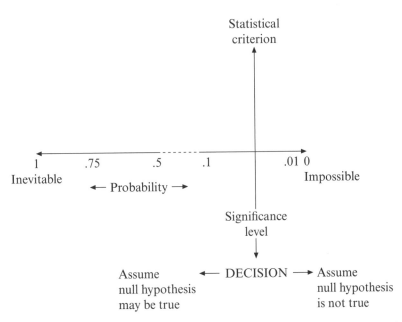

Figure 11.1. Statistical inference. If the probability associated with the obtained statistic falls to the left of the statistical criterion (i.e., nearer $p = 1$), then assume that the null hypothesis may be true. If it is the same as the criterion probability or falls to the right (i.e., nearer $p = 0$), then assume that the null hypothesis is not true.

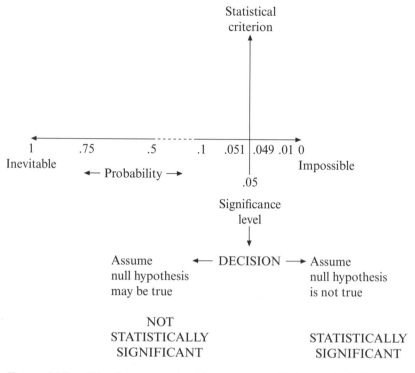

Figure 11.2. The 5 percent significance level. If the probability
associated with the obtained statistic is greater than $p = .05$, do not
reject the null hypothesis. The data are not statistically significant.
If this probability is equal to or less than $p = .05$, then reject the
null hypothesis. The data are statistically significant.

between conditions. The criterion is referred to as the **significance
level** or **alpha level**. Although we are free to vary it, this level is often
set at a probability of less than or equal to .05 (in other words five
times in 100 or one in 20). This is known as the **5 percent significance
level** (Figure 11.2).

What we do, therefore, is compare the probability associated with
the obtained value of the statistic with our chosen significance level.
If this probability *equals* or is *less* than the significance level (i.e.,
is nearer zero, a less probable event) then we decide that we have
sufficient evidence to **reject the null hypothesis**. Such data we describe
as **statistically significant**. Under these circumstances we would talk of
a "statistically significant difference" between our conditions. If, however, the obtained statistic has a probability *greater* than our significance level (i.e., is nearer one, a more probable event) then we decide
that we have insufficient evidence to reject the null hypothesis. We

thus **fail to reject the null hypothesis**. Findings such as these we describe as **not statistically significant**.

This terminology, though widely used, is nevertheless unfortunate. To call our results *statistically* significant does not necessarily mean that they have much *psychological* importance. Likewise, results that are not *statistically* significant may yet be *psychologically* informative. Significance, in this context, is a *statistical* concept. It merely tells us something about the statistical nature of our data. The *psychological* importance of a set of findings, whether statistically significant or not, remains to be established. When working with inferential statistics it is important, therefore, to differentiate in your mind the concepts of *statistical significance* and *psychological importance*. Do *not* assume that the former implies the latter. I will have more to say about this in Chapter 12.

In the strict application of this procedure, once you have set up the significance level, you are compelled to abide by the outcome. So, if the probability associated with your obtained statistic turns out to be *greater* than the significance level (even if only by a minute amount) then you must assume that there is insufficient evidence to reject the null hypothesis. I will have more to say about this in the next section.

In the case of our cheese and nightmare experiment, we calculated a value of $\chi^2 = 4.89$. We now need to find out whether this is *statistically* significant at the 5 percent significance level. (This is the significance level that I chose on our behalf before collecting the data.) This means that we need to work out whether the probability associated with $\chi^2 = 4.89$ is less than or equal to $p = .05$.

? SAQ 39

Earlier we established that the probability associated with $\chi^2 = 4.89$ with 1 degree of freedom is $p = .03$. Is our value of χ^2, therefore, statistically significant at the 5 percent significance level?

In effect, therefore, at the end of our experiment, having analysed the data, we find ourselves in a position to make a decision regarding the null hypothesis – that is, whether to reject it or not to reject it. We do this on the basis of whether or not the probability associated with our obtained statistic is less than or equal to the significance level that we set before running the experiment.

Summary of Sections 11.1–11.2

1 *Inferential* statistics tell us how likely we would be to have obtained our data *if* the IV did *not* cause changes in the DV. That is, they tell

us this probability *assuming the null hypothesis to be true*. Such statistics do not, however, tell us whether or not the null hypothesis *is* true.

2   In fact, we can never know for certain whether the null hypothesis is or is not true.

3   One way around this problem is to adopt a criterion probability. We call this the *significance level* or *alpha level*.

4   Although we are at liberty to alter the significance level, it is set conventionally at $p = .05$. This is known as the "5 percent significance level".

5   If the *probability* associated with our obtained statistic is *less than* or *equal to* our significance level, we decide to *reject* the assumption that the null hypothesis is true. Such results we describe as *statistically significant*.

6   If the probability associated with our obtained statistic is *greater than* our significance level, we decide *not to reject* the assumption that the null hypothesis is true. Such results we describe as *not statistically significant*.

7   In this context, significance is a *statistical* concept. To say that a difference is *statistically* significant does not mean that *psychologically* the difference has much theoretical or practical importance. Likewise, the absence of a statistically significant difference may be of theoretical or practical importance.

11.3   Type I and type II errors

At the end of our experiment, therefore, we will have decided whether or not to reject the null hypothesis. However, the simple fact is – *we could always be wrong*. That is, we may find ourselves *rejecting* the null hypothesis when – had we seen the tablets of stone on which are written The Laws of The Universe – we would find that the null hypothesis should, in fact, *not* have been rejected. For instance, in the case of our cheese and nightmare experiment, our obtained value of chi-square is 4.89, which has an associated probability that is less than the conventional significance level of $p = .05$. Using this significance level, therefore, we would have to reject the null hypothesis. However, suppose that you receive a visitation from the powers that run the universe, who reveal to you that actually the null hypothesis is in this case correct. Under these circumstances we would have *rejected* the null hypothesis when we should not have done. This is known as a **type I error**. Moreover, not only is this error an integral feature of the process of statistical inference – of acting as if we know something for certain when we do not – but, in this world at least, we never know whether we have made it (visitations from the powers that run the universe aside). However, we do know the *probability* that we have.

> What is the probability of making a type I error (i.e., of incorrectly rejecting the null hypothesis)?

The probability of making a type I error (if the null hypothesis is true) is, in fact, the significance level. We decide to reject the null hypothesis when the probability associated with our obtained statistic reaches the significance level. Under these circumstances we *always* reject the null hypothesis. On some of these occasions, however, un-beknown to us, the null hypothesis will be true. With the 5 percent significance level, therefore, because we reject the null hypothesis *every* time that our data reaches this level, we will make a mistake, on average, once in every 20 times that we do it.

So, what can we do about this? After all, we would like to minimize our mistakes. We don't want *too* many of the factual assertions that we make about the psychological universe to be wrong. Well, if our significance level is a measure of our type I error rate, then one thing that we might do is to reduce the probability of making this error by *making our significance level more stringent* (Figure 11.3). We make our significance level more stringent by choosing to use a *lower* probability under the null hypothesis to be the significance level. For a significance level of $p = .01$ has a type I error rate of only 1 in 100, rather than the 5 in 100 (or 1 in 20) of the $p = .05$ significance level.

Now, doing this isn't necessarily wrong. However, although we can get the probability of making a type I error *closer* to zero, the only way that we can actually *make* it zero is by saying nothing at all about the existence or non-existence of a reliable difference between the conditions in our experiment. If we wish to say anything at all, there-fore, we will have to accept some probability of making a type I error.

Making the significance level more stringent is a cautious or, as we say in the trade, a *conservative* thing to do. Sometimes it may be the appropriate step to take. For example, those who undertake research into extrasensory perception tend routinely to employ more stringent significance levels in order to reduce their chances of making a type I error. However, our job as scientists is essentially to make the best guesses we can about the existence of causal relationships. Making the significance level more stringent may well reduce our tendency to make mistakes, but it does so at the cost of reducing our ability to say

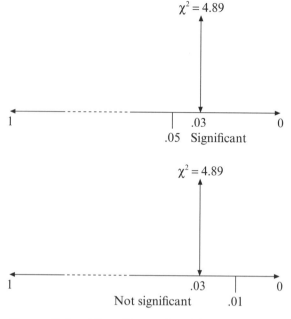

Figure 11.3. The effects of making the significance level more stringent. A chi-square of 4.89 with one degree of freedom is statistically significant at the 5 percent significance level but is not statistically significant at the 1 percent significance level.

anything. Take it too far and we are in danger of throwing the scientific baby out with the statistical bathwater.

To put it another way, in making the significance level more stringent, we are indeed reducing the probability of making a *type I* error. That is, we reduce our chances of thinking that there is a reliable difference when there isn't one. However, at the same time, we are *increasing* the probability of making another type of error – that is, of *not rejecting* the null hypothesis when we should have done. This is known as a **type II error**. When we make a type II error, we *fail* to detect a reliable difference that *is* there.

For instance, suppose that we had adopted the $p = .01$ level of significance for our cheese and nightmare experiment. With $\chi^2 = 4.89$ (our obtained value) we would not have achieved statistical significance, and so would have been compelled not to reject the null hypothesis (Figure 11.3). However, suppose that on the tablets of stone containing the laws of the universe was written that eating cheese will induce nightmares in humans. By making our criterion too stringent, we would therefore have missed the opportunity to make a correct statement about the universe in which we live. I will have more to say about type II errors in Chapter 12.

Summary of Section 11.3

1 Sometimes we will reject the null hypothesis when it is in fact true. This is known as a *type I error*. We cannot avoid making such errors if we wish to say anything positive about the psychological universe.

2 If the null hypothesis is true, then the probability of making a *type I error* is the *significance level*.

3 We can, therefore, reduce the likelihood of making a type I error by using a more stringent significance level. However, this *increases* the probability of making a *type II error* – the error of *not* rejecting the null hypothesis when it is in fact false.

4 The conventional significance levels ($p = .05$ and $p = .01$) are compromises between the rates for these two types of error.

11.4　Choosing a statistical test

This, then, is the procedure in principle. It is the same for all tests of statistical significance. However, how you realize the procedure for testing for statistical significance in practice depends on the precise test that you need to employ to analyse your data. You will have to employ different tests of significance under different circumstances if you wish to arrive at a meaningful answer to the same question: should I reject the null hypothesis in my experiment? Even if you are not using the test for the purposes of significance testing, you still need to know what is the most appropriate procedure for obtaining the statistics that you require.

　Choosing the appropriate statistical test is the key to the whole process of finding out exactly what your data have to tell you. However, it is nowhere near as daunting a process as it may seem. (I know, we all say this, but believe me it *is* true.) If you keep a clear head and take things *step by step*, most of the time you should have few problems in arriving at an appropriate test for your data. Indeed, your problems will be reduced in this respect if you get into the habit of thinking about how you are going to analyse your data *before* you start running your study. You can then modify the design if you foresee any problems.

In order to decide which test to employ, you need to be able to answer a number of questions about the *type of study* that you conducted, the *nature of the data* that you obtained, and the *precise questions that you wish to ask* of these data. Below is a list of the key questions that you should consider:

1 Do you want to (a) *compare conditions* or (b) *correlate variables*?
2 What type of *data* do you have? Are they (a) *nominal*, (b) *ordinal* or (c) at least *interval*?
3 If at least *interval*, can you assume that the data come from a population of scores that is *normally distributed*?
4 If you wish to *compare conditions*, did you manipulate more than one IV in your study?
5 If you wish to *compare conditions*, how many do you wish to compare *at any one time*?
6 Do you have the *same* or *different* participants in these conditions?

You can find more about each of these issues (including the distinction between parametric and non-parametric tests) on the Web site that accompanies this book. Most textbooks of statistics also contain useful flow charts to help you choose an appropriate test.

One problem to watch out for when writing your report is that there can sometimes be more than one way of analysing the same set of data. That is, it is not uncommon to find that you can test the *same* prediction using the *same* dependent variable but with *different* statistical tests. For example, the independent *t* test and the Mann–Whitney U test are alternative tests for data from an unrelated samples IV with two conditions. For the purposes of your report, however, you should not *duplicate* tests. That is, under these circumstances you should use and report only *one* of the comparable tests. (For example, *either* the independent *t* test *or* the Mann–Whitney U test.)

Summary of Section 11.4

1 Choosing the appropriate statistical test is the key to the whole process of arriving at a meaningful answer to the question: should I *reject* or should I *not reject* the null hypothesis in my experiment?

2 In order to decide which test to employ, you will need to address a number of questions about the type of study, the nature of the data, and the precise questions that you wish to ask. Advice on this can be found on the Web site that accompanies this book and in your statistics textbook.

3 Often there may be more than one way of testing statistically the same prediction using the same dependent variable. Under these circumstances, however, you should report the outcome of only *one* of the tests.

11.5   Two-tailed and one-tailed tests

With some statistics you need to decide whether to use a **two-tailed** or a **one-tailed** test of significance. This relates to whether or not you consider the predictions derived from your experimental hypothesis to be directional or nondirectional and it introduces us to another controversy.

Earlier I said that you should consider your predictions to be directional if you were able (for sound theoretical reasons) to specify the *direction* in which the difference between your conditions should occur. Some authors argue that this translates directly into whether or not you should employ a one- or a two-tailed test of significance.

The difference between a one- and a two-tailed test of significance has to do with the way in which you use the tails of the distributions of whichever statistic you are employing. (If you want to know precisely what it involves you will need to turn to your statistics textbook.) What it means in practice is that you can obtain significance with data using a one-tailed test that would fail to reach significance with a two-tailed test. This is the reward for specifying the direction in which the postulated difference will occur.

Now, you may read elsewhere that whether or not you choose to employ a one-tailed or a two-tailed test depends on whether the predictions are directional or nondirectional. That is, on whether or not you have reasonable grounds for specifying in advance (*a priori*) that one of the conditions will exceed another on the DV. Unfortunately, however, it is not quite as simple as that.

I recommend that you employ the one-tailed test *only* when you have asked a "whether or not" question of the data. That is, a question of the form "whether or not" a particular teaching method improves the rate at which people learn a particular task, or "whether or not" a particular set of work conditions improves output. Under these circumstances, if you find a difference between the conditions that is opposite to the one that you expected this would mean the same to you as if you had found *no difference* between the conditions. That is, if you found that the teaching method actually *impairs* the rate at which people learn the task, or the work conditions actually *decrease* output, this would be the same to you as finding that the new teaching method was no quicker than the old one, or that production was similar under the usual working conditions.

In practice, such questions generally concern those attempting to solve an *applied* problem. As students, however, most of the time you will be running studies in which findings that *contradict* the predictions will be every bit as important as findings that are *consistent* with the predictions. So, most of the time you will also be interested in findings that go in the *opposite* direction to the one that you specified and your test should therefore be two-tailed. Only when your experimental question can simply be either confirmed or refuted – when it is open to a simple yes or no answer – should you employ the one-tailed test of significance.

If you have to use tables of statistics, most contain the probability values for two-tailed comparisons. For many of the tests that you are likely to use as a student, you can derive the one-tailed value simply by halving the significance level. So, if the value that you obtain is significant at the 5 percent level (two-tailed), then the significance for a one-tailed test is actually 2.5 percent. Check in your textbook of statistics whether this is the case for the statistic that you are using.

? SAQ 40   The value of $t = 1.73$ is the critical value of t with 20 degrees of freedom at the 5 percent significance level for a one-tailed test. What is its associated probability for a two-tailed test?

One final thing to bear in mind about your analyses is that statistics only deal with the numbers fed into them. A statistical package will churn around any set of numbers that you feed into it in a suitable format. Just because the data were analysed doesn't mean either that the analysis itself or its outcome was necessarily meaningful. For instance, the value of chi-square for the cheese and nightmare experiment is perfectly reasonable, given the numbers that I fed into the analysis. Nevertheless, this doesn't tell us *anything* about the relationship between eating cheese and experiencing nightmares – I made the numbers up (sorry!). Bear in mind also that rejecting the null hypothesis doesn't automatically entail that the results went in the direction that you predicted. I am constantly amazed how few students actually *look at* their data once they've analysed them, or think much at all about what the results really mean. Get into the habit of going back to your data and thinking about what the outcome of your analyses might mean. (This is particularly a problem when you reject the null hypothesis and yet the direction of the difference is in fact *opposite* to the one that you predicted with a directional hypothesis.)

Summary of Section 11.5

1 Tests of significance can be one-tailed or two-tailed. The difference in practice between these versions of the same test is that you can obtain statistical significance using the one-tailed version, with data that would fail to reach statistical significance using the two-tailed version.

2 You can use one-tailed tests when you are prepared to *ignore* any differences that occur in the direction *opposite* to the one predicted from the experimental hypothesis. When you will *not* ignore such differences (even though these would contradict the experimental hypothesis) the test is two-tailed. Most of you, most of the time, will therefore be undertaking two-tailed tests.

3 Just because the data have been analysed statistically doesn't mean that the analysis or its outcome is necessarily meaningful. Get into the habit of going back to the data to interpret the outcomes of the analyses and to ensure that these outcomes appear to make sense. In particular, watch out for occasions when you've been compelled to *reject* the null hypothesis and yet the differences between the conditions are in fact *opposite* in direction to the ones that you predicted.

11.6   Testing for statistical significance: summary of the procedure

1 Decide whether the *inferential* question involves *comparing* conditions or *correlating* variables.
2 Choose a test that asks this question and that is appropriate for the type of data gathered in the study.
3 Recall what significance level you decided to adopt and (where appropriate) whether the test was to be one- or two-tailed.
4 Calculate the *obtained* value of the above statistic, whether using a statistical package or by hand.
5 With statistical packages the software will print out for you the exact probability associated with the obtained value. Check whether this probability is equal to or less than the significance level that you decided to use before the experiment (commonly $p = .05$). If it is, then the data are statistically significant. If it is not, then the data are not statistically significant.
6 If calculating by hand, look in the appropriate set of tables for the statistic used, at the significance level that you have adopted, to find the relevant *critical* value of the statistic (Appendix 3). If

the *obtained* value of the statistic differs from the *critical* value in the direction required for statistical significance, or if it is *equal* to the critical value, then the data are statistically significant. Under these circumstances, *reject* the null hypothesis. If not, then the data are not statistically significant. Under these circumstances, *do not reject* the null hypothesis.

7 Look again at the descriptive statistics and think about why the data have compelled you to reject the null hypothesis or not to reject it. What, if anything, does this tell you about the relationship between the IVs and DVs?[2]

12 Statistics: effect size and power

When we test for statistical significance, therefore, we end up either rejecting the null hypothesis or not rejecting it. Following this, we critically examine our experiment, looking for any flaws that might be rival explanations for our findings (see Chapter 5). The ultimate goal of this procedure is to be able to determine whether or not the IV has a causal effect on the DV. This is the traditional procedure by which psychological experimentation has worked.

Recently, however, people have argued that we should be asking a subtly different question of the data. That is, instead of asking whether there is or is not a causal effect of the IV on the DV, why not ask *how big* an effect there is? Does the evidence suggest that the IV affects the DV not at all, a small amount, a medium amount, or a large amount? For example, in our driving and music experiment, it would be useful to know that listening to music makes a big difference to driving performance rather than a small one. We might conclude very different things if we found that it makes driving much worse than if we found that it made driving only slightly worse.

The difference between the questions is subtle, but the implications are quite profound. For example, some of those who promote asking the "how big" question also advocate abandoning significance testing altogether. Some of the reasons for this may become clearer as you work through this chapter. For now, however, I want you to focus on two issues that arise from the "how big" question that are important to think about even when testing for statistical significance: the *effect size* of our IVs and the *power* of our experiments.

12.1   Effect size

There are statistics available to help us to answer the "how big" question. These statistics use the data to form estimates of the difference that the IV makes to scores on the DV. They are called statistics of *effect size*. For many years psychologists tended to ignore the issue of effect size and concentrated on whether or not an effect or a relationship was statistically significant. One psychologist in particular – Jacob Cohen – has been especially influential in making psychologists think more about the size of the effects that we report.

Put loosely, **effect size** is the magnitude of the difference between the conditions in an experiment. (With correlations, effect size refers to the strength of the relationship between the variables.) In a well-designed experiment effect size is the difference that the IV makes to the scores on the DV. So, for example, in a well-designed, two-condition experiment of the sort discussed in Chapter 10, it is the difference between the scores when not exposed to the IV (the control condition) and when exposed to the IV (the experimental condition). Thus, everything else being equal, the bigger the impact that the IV has, the bigger will be the difference between the scores and the bigger will be the effect size.

Effect size can be measured in standard deviations. One of the advantages of this is that we can then compare effect sizes across different experiments. In order to help us to describe and compare effect sizes, Cohen (1988) suggested some guidelines for determining whether an effect is large, medium or small. He suggested that we consider an effect of at least 0.8 standard deviations to be a large effect size and one of around 0.5 standard deviations to be a medium effect size. An effect of 0.2 standard deviations he suggested we regard as a small effect size.

You will learn more about effect size in your statistics course. The important thing to note for now, however, is that Cohen argued that in psychology effect sizes are typically small or medium, rather than large. This has important implications for the way that we should design our experiments and other studies. For if many of the effects that we are interested in are likely to be small or at best medium, then we need to make sure that our experiments (and other studies) have the *power* to detect them.

Summary of Section 12.1

1 Instead of asking whether there is or is not a causal effect of the IV on the DV, some authors suggest that we should ask how big an effect there is.

2 There are statistics available to help us to answer the "how big" question. These are called statistics of effect size.

3 Effect size is the relative magnitude of the difference between the conditions in an experiment. It is often expressed in standard deviations.

4 Cohen has argued that in psychology effect sizes are typically small or medium, rather than large.

5 If the effects that we are interested in are likely to be small or medium then we need to make sure that our studies have the power to detect small or medium effects.

12.2   Power

In this context, **power** is the capacity of an experiment to detect a genuine effect of the IV on the DV. The power of a statistical test is thus its capacity to *correctly* reject the null hypothesis. In other words, power is the probability of *not* making a type II error, of *not* failing to find a difference that is actually out there in the psychological universe.

Experiments vary in power. The more powerful the experiment is, the smaller are the effects that it can detect. In this way, experiments to psychologists are rather like telescopes are to astronomers. Very powerful telescopes can see even dim and distant stars. Likewise, very powerful experiments can detect even tiny effects of the IV on the DV. Low-power experiments are like low-power telescopes. Telescopes lacking in power may be unable to detect even fairly close and bright stars. Similarly, experiments lacking in power may be unable to detect even quite strong and important effects of the IV on the DV.

Power is measured on a scale from zero to one. With a power of zero there is no chance of detecting any effect of the IV on the DV, even if one exists. With a power of .25 there is a 25 percent chance of detecting an effect of the IV on the DV if the effect exists. This is not very likely and thus not very powerful. With a power of .70 there is a 70 percent chance of detecting the effect of the IV on the DV, and we are beginning to be in business. We need our designs to have at least this level of power if they are going to be worth running (and preferably higher than this). So, how do we go about assessing and improving the power of our experiments?

12.2.1   Estimating power

Fortunately, we can estimate the power of our studies – including our experiments – before we run them. This enables us to check whether they will be powerful enough to detect the effects that we are interested in. If they look like they will not be powerful enough we can then take steps to increase their power.[1]

Power is influenced by a number of factors:

- the effect size;
- the significance level;
- whether the test is one- or two-tailed;
- the type of statistical test;
- the number of participants;
- whether the IV uses related or unrelated measures.

Perhaps you can see that the only one of these factors that we do not know for certain *before* running the experiment is the *effect size*. If we can make a reasonable guess about the likely effect size in our experiment, therefore, we can estimate the power of our experiment before running it. If necessary, we can then think about ways of increasing power.

There are two basic ways of estimating the likely effect size in advance of running the experiment. The best way is to base the calculations on other experiments that have investigated the effects of this particular IV. This enables us to estimate the *likely* effect size of our IV.[2] If such research is not available, however, we can still estimate how powerful our experiment would be *if* the IV had a given effect size. That is, we can assume that the effect size will be small or medium or large and calculate how likely our experiment would be to detect the effect under each of these circumstances. Again, we can then think about ways of increasing power if we find that the current design will be unlikely to detect a small or medium effect. On the other hand, if we find that it has the power to detect a small effect, we know that it will also be able to detect a medium or a large effect.

These calculations, not surprisingly, are called **power calculations**. Typically, we use them to help us to estimate how many participants we will need for our experiments to have enough power (say, .80) to stand a reasonable chance of detecting the effect that we are interested in. Alternatively, we can save some effort by looking up power in relevant *power tables* or by using one of the many Web sites that are available to calculate power for us. You may learn more about power and even about how to calculate it in your statistics course. If so, you will find that the results are salutary: it can be surprising to find out quite how many participants we need to stand, say, an 80% chance of rejecting a false null hypothesis with an unrelated samples IV.

This leads us to the next question. How can we go about *increasing* the power of our experiments if we need to?

12.2.2   Increasing the power of our experiments

In theory, we could increase power in any of the following ways: by increasing the effect size; making the significance level less stringent; using a one-tailed test; employing a parametric test; increasing the number of participants; and using a related samples IV. In practice, however, some of these are more practical and desirable ways of increasing power than are others.

Changing the effect size is, of course, beyond the powers of us mere mortals. As we have seen from the previous discussion, making the significance level less stringent (e.g., using the 10 percent significance level instead of the 5 percent one) means that there is greater chance of rejecting the null hypothesis. However, it increases our chances of doing so when we should not (i.e., of making a type I error). We should therefore be cautious about altering this. Likewise, you should be cautious about using one-tailed tests as these limit the inferences that you can draw from your experiment (Section 11.5). You should use the most powerful statistical technique that your data allow (e.g., parametric rather than nonparametric tests where appropriate; see the Web site or your statistics textbook for more on this distinction). The remaining routes of increasing the power of our experiments, therefore, are to run enough participants and to use related samples IVs whenever possible. Let's consider these.

One relatively straightforward way of increasing power is to run more participants, especially with unrelated samples IVs. You need as many as will enable you to detect an effect of the size that you suspect that the IV may have on the DV. For example, if listening to music has only a small effect on driving performance you will need more participants to detect this small causal effect than if listening to music has a medium effect on driving performance. With too few participants you would fail to detect the effect and conclude (erroneously) that listening to music makes no difference to driving performance.

? SAQ 41   What type of error would you have made?

So, with unrelated samples in particular, increasing the number of participants can be an effective way of increasing the power of your experiment to the level that you need. The larger the sample size, the greater the power (other things being equal). We will discuss this further in Section 13.1.1.

Using related samples increases power by reducing the background variation against which we have to assess the effect of the IV on the

DV (Section 10.4). This is a very efficient way of increasing power. It is a bit like using a radio telescope that has a filter that cuts out a lot of the background "noise" – the irrelevant signals that can mask the signals from the less powerful stars. Filter this out and you can "see" the signals from these weaker stars more clearly. This is one of the reasons why I suggested earlier that you should try to use related samples IVs whenever possible. However, as you know, it is not always possible to use related samples for an IV (Section 10.4).

Summary of Section 12.2

1 Power, in this context, is the capacity of an experiment to detect a genuine effect of the IV on the DV. It is thus the capacity to *correctly* reject the null hypothesis.

2 Experiments vary in power. The more powerful the experiment is, the smaller are the effects that it can detect.

3 Experiments that lack power may be unable to detect even quite strong and important effects of the IV on the DV.

4 Power is measured on a scale from zero to one. The closer to one, the greater the power of the design and the better its chance of correctly rejecting the null hypothesis.

5 We can estimate the power of our studies before we run them. If we need to, we can then take steps to increase their power. Doing this in advance helps us to avoid wasting time by running an experiment that has too little power to detect the effects that we are interested in.

6 The principal ways in which we increase power are to run enough participants and to use related samples IVs whenever possible.

12.3   Effect size and power: reporting and interpreting findings

Let's recap. The more powerful the experiment, the smaller the effect sizes that it can detect. If the design lacks power, however, we may not be able to detect even quite large effects. Therefore, our experimental designs can be insufficiently powerful to detect effects of our IV on our DV, even if such effects exist and even if the effect size is quite large. This is just like using a weak telescope to look for stars: if the telescope is weak, we will not be able to see even quite strong stars.

Of course, we would not conclude that the only stars that exist are those which we can see through a weak telescope! Likewise, it is important to make sure that our experiments are powerful enough for the effects that we are investigating. Estimating the effect size of our differences *in addition* to statistical significance assists us with this problem. Doing so helps us to assess whether the lack of statistical significance is a result of the IV having little or no effect on the DV (the question that the experiment was designed to answer) or because the experiment lacked sufficient power.

As you can see, these issues have important implications for the studies that we run and the ways in which we report and interpret our findings. In terms of design, it obviously helps to consider power from the outset, to think carefully about the size of the effect that we are expecting and to adjust the design accordingly. However, what about the implications of effect size and power for reporting and interpreting our findings? The rest of this chapter has advice on this. (If you know how to calculate power or effect size statistics, you can go straight to Section 12.3.2.)

12.3.1 Reporting for those who do not know how to calculate power or effect size statistics

Courses vary greatly in when they teach you about these issues. Some of you will be introduced to them from the very start of your careers as students of psychology. Others of you may find that you are taught about power and effect size only quite late on in your studies. Some of you will be taught how to calculate effect size statistics and even power. Others of you will be taught about these things conceptually but not taught the calculations. Nevertheless, most of you should have at least some awareness of these issues by the time that you come to undertake project work (e.g., in the UK in the final year of a degree course). If you have not been taught how to calculate power or to obtain effect size statistics by that stage, you should at least be aware of how these issues affect the inferences that you can draw from and about statistically significant and statistically nonsignificant findings.

Here is some advice about what you can do in your reports if you have been taught about these things conceptually but not taught how to calculate effect size statistics or power.

In the RESULTS you can do the following, as I advised in Chapter 4:

1 Whenever possible, report the exact probabilities associated with the obtained values of your statistic, whether these are statistically significant or not.
2 Where appropriate, report standard deviations as well as means in tables of descriptive statistics.

3 If you know how, report appropriate confidence intervals such as the 95 percent confidence intervals around the mean, or for a difference between two means. You can do this regardless of whether or not the effects are statistically significant.

Reporting relevant confidence intervals is increasingly being encouraged in psychological research. There are a variety of reasons for this. Among them is the insight that such confidence intervals offer about the power of your experiment. To put it simply, the more powerful the study (other things being equal) the narrower will be the confidence interval. This will help you to interpret results in which the null hypothesis has not been rejected. With a low-power study, the confidence interval will be wide and will encompass everything from zero effects to quite large effects of the IV. With a high-power study, the same confidence interval will be narrow and will encompass zero to very small effects only.

Those of you using and reporting the correlation coefficient Pearson's r might also consider reporting and commenting on an easily computed statistic of effect size. If you *square* the value of r (i.e., calculate the statistic called r^2) this will tell you how much of the variance is shared between the two variables in the correlation. This is a measure of effect size. It is useful to do this, as it will help you to avoid giving precedence to the statistical significance of the coefficient rather than to the size of the relationship. For, with enough participants, even correlations as small as $r = .2$ or even $r = .1$, can become statistically significant at the 5 percent significance level. Yet these are very small relationships. An $r = .2$, for instance, gives $r^2 = .04$, which indicates that only 4 percent of the variance is shared.[3] So, think about calculating r^2 when you use Pearson's r.

One thing to avoid at all costs – especially in the DISCUSSION – is to confuse statistical significance with the size of the effect. If you have been able to follow the drift of this discussion in this chapter you will perhaps see how the problem arises. If the experiment or study is powerful enough, *any* difference between your conditions will be statistically significant, no matter how small it is numerically and how trivial it is psychologically. (Many of you realize this intuitively when you write in your reports that "our findings would have been significant if we'd had more participants". It is precisely because this is *inevitably* true that – unless you defend it sensibly – this remark tends to evoke the scorn and wrath of your marker.) A very powerful experiment may well tell you that an effect is statistically significant even if the IV has only a relatively trivial effect on the DV. Thinking about effect size *in addition* to statistical significance helps you to avoid this problem. Doing so helps you to assess whether the effect is large enough to be potentially interesting psychologically. Remember that with a very powerful experiment it is possible for an effect to be highly significant *statistically* but for the effect size to be so small that the effect of the IV on the DV is trivial, both numerically and psychologically.

Don't panic if you don't yet know how to produce or calculate confidence intervals or statistics of effect size! Even without them you can still make some efforts to address effect size in your report. *Look at the sample size.* If the experiment has been well designed in other respects, the sample size is small and yet the effect is statistically significant (especially on an unrelated samples IV) then this suggests that the IV has a pretty large effect size. However, if the sample is large, then the results are ambiguous, for even trivial effects may be statistically significant with large samples. If the experiment has been well designed in other respects, the sample size is small and the effect is not statistically significant (especially on an unrelated samples IV) then the results are ambiguous, for even large effects may not be statistically significant with small samples. However, if the sample is large, then the failure to reject the null hypothesis suggests the absence of an effect of much size or psychological importance. (Of course, this depends on just how large the sample size is.)

It is very easy to confuse statistical significance and effect size, and people often do. So, don't worry if this discussion doesn't fall into place at once. These issues require thought and effort before they become clear. You may need to reread this chapter and also your statistics textbook several times before the penny even begins to drop.

12.3.2 Reporting for those who have been taught how to calculate power or effect size statistics

Obviously, if you are taught how to do even rudimentary power calculations or to use power tables or Web sites, then you should include these in the METHOD of your report. Advice on this is in Section 3.6.3.

If you know how to calculate confidence intervals or how to get a statistical software package to produce these, then include them in the RESULTS (see Section 4.6.9). Likewise, once you know how to calculate or produce effect size statistics and understand what they mean, you will be able to report relevant statistics of effect size *as well as* the obtained value of your statistic and its associated probability. To give you an idea of how you might do this, here is the paragraph describing the principal findings from the mnemonic experiment, this time with an effect size statistic added. This statistic is known as *partial eta squared* (η^2) and is one of the effect size statistics available when using ANOVA.[4]

The data in Table 1 were analysed using 2 × 2 ANOVA for mixed designs, with imageability (easily imaged or hard to image) as the related samples variable and instruction (mnemonic or no mnemonic) as the unrelated samples variable. There was a statistically significant main effect of instruction, $F(1, 38) = 7.20$, $p = .01$, with those in the mnemonic group recalling more items overall than did those in the no-mnemonic group ($M = 15.65$, $SD = 3.97$; $M = 12.40$, $SD = 3.74$, respectively). Partial $\eta^2 = .16$, indicating that 16% of the overall variance was attributable to this manipulation. There was also a statistically significant main effect of imageability, $F(1, 38) = 145.22$, $p < .001$, with more items from the easily imaged list being recalled than from the hard-to-image list ($M = 15.98$, $SD = 4.12$; $M = 12.08$, $SD = 4.48$, respectively). Partial $\eta^2 = .79$, indicating that 79% of the overall variance was attributable to this manipulation. However, these main effects were qualified by the significant Instruction × Imageability interaction, $F(1, 38) = 11.55$, $p = .002$. Partial $\eta^2 = .23$, indicating that 23% of the overall variance was attributable to the interaction between the variables. Figure 1 displays this interaction.

You should use these statistics in the DISCUSSION to help you to answer the following questions:

1 If an effect is statistically significant, what do the effect size statistics tell us about the likely size of the effect? Is the effect big enough to be of psychological interest and importance?
2 If an effect is not statistically significant, what do the confidence intervals tell us about power? Are the 95 percent confidence intervals broad (suggesting that the analysis lacked power) or narrow (suggesting that it did not)? What do the effect size statistics indicate about the likely size of the effect? If these indicate that the effect is not small, this suggests that the analysis lacked power. If you conclude that the experiment lacked the power to detect the effects, suggest what steps might be taken in future to run studies with sufficient power.

Perhaps now you can see why some researchers have called for the abandonment of significance testing altogether. If we report statistics of effect size together with the exact probability associated with the obtained value of our statistic, so the argument runs, then at best statistical significance is redundant and at worst it is downright mis-leading. Pursuing this debate is beyond the scope of this book. How-ever, you may well discuss these issues further in your statistics course.

Summary of Section 12.3

1 There are things that you can do about these issues in your reports even if you have not been taught how to calculate power or to obtain effect size statistics.

2 These include reporting the exact probability associated with your obtained statistic and, once you know how, reporting appropriate confidence intervals.

3 Whatever you do, make sure that you do not confuse statistical significance with effect size. A very powerful experiment may well tell you that an effect is statistically significant even if the IV has only a relatively trivial effect on the DV. On the other hand, a large effect may not be found to be statistically significant if the design lacks power.

4 Even without statistics of effect size, looking at the sample size can help you to make some inferences about effect size.

5 If you do any power calculations, report this in the METHOD. You may also be taught to generate other statistics indicative of effect size and power. If so, report these statistics in the RESULTS and use them to help you to interpret your findings in the DISCUSSION.

13 Experimental design II

Once you have mastered the basics, you can start to think about designing more complex experiments. There are two basic ways of extending experiments:

1 You can use an IV with more than two levels.
2 You can manipulate more than one IV simultaneously.

You can do either of these things or both at the same time.

13.1 Extending the number of levels on the independent variable

As you know, we need not restrict ourselves simply to manipulating the *presence* versus the *absence* of the suspected causal variable. Experiments using IVs with three or more levels are very common in psychology and are not hard to design. As with any IV, these can employ either unrelated or related samples. The principal design issues that arise have to do with using sufficient numbers of participants with unrelated samples to ensure sufficient power or being able to adequately control for order effects with related samples.

13.1.1 Unrelated samples IVs

Having adequate numbers of participants to ensure sufficient power is an issue for *all* experimental designs, but it is an especially pressing issue with unrelated samples because it is so easy to design a study that lacks power. As discussed in Section 12.2, power in this context refers to the capacity of your experiment to detect a genuine effect of the IV on the DV. The *more* participants you use, all things being equal, the *more* likely you will be to detect any impact of the IV on the DV. Indeed, unless the IV has a pretty dramatic impact on the DV (e.g., listening to music *massively* impairs or improves driving performance) designs using unrelated samples with small numbers of participants will be useless.

How many participants do you need? The number of participants that you need depends on a number of factors, including how strong you estimate that the effect of the IV will be on the DV (Section 12.2.2). Sadly, therefore, there is no simple answer to this question. (It really is just like asking how long is a piece of string.) Obviously, the ideal way of estimating this number is through *power calculations* (Section 12.2.1). However, this is of little help to those of you who have no idea how to carry out such calculations. For you, the only sensible answer that I can offer is that this number is almost certainly going to be much larger than the one that you first thought of! Thinking in terms of 10–15 participants *per condition* is unlikely to give you much chance of rejecting a false null hypothesis. Even double these numbers may be insufficient. As an incredibly rough rule of thumb, with a number plucked out of the sky, look to use no fewer than 20 per condition and try to use substantially more than this if you can. You therefore need to think very carefully when considering extending the number of levels on an IV with unrelated samples. Make sure that you have the time and the resources to get reasonable numbers of participants in each condition.

Particularly early on in your career, you may *have* to use fewer participants than this (e.g., for reasons of time or problems with access to people who can take part in the experiment). Under these circumstances, remember two things. First, if you are playing a role in the design of the experiment (as opposed to having it designed for you by a tutor) then make sure that the IV *has* to use unrelated samples. Moreover, think carefully *before* extending the levels on this unrelated samples IV beyond two or three. Second, if your findings are not statistically significant, bear in mind that a potential explanation for this is that the design was not powerful enough to detect the effect, rather than that there was no effect to detect.[1]

Later on (for UK students, especially in your final-year projects), this is likely to be one of the issues on which you are assessed. When using IVs with unrelated samples you need to have sufficient numbers of participants in each of the conditions, so bear in mind when designing the experiment the number of participants that is likely to be available to you. However, don't overreact to this problem by using *too many* participants. The number of participants that you run should be optimum, as determined either by power calculations or by reasonable guesswork.

Summary of Section 13.1.1

1 With unrelated samples the principal design issue arising from IVs with more than two levels is to use enough participants in each condition to ensure sufficient power.

2 This means that you will have to think carefully when considering extending the number of levels on an unrelated samples IV. Will you have the time and resources to get enough participants in each condition?

3 Do not overreact to this issue by using too many participants. The number of participants should be optimum – either as determined by power calculations (preferably) or by reasonable guesswork if you cannot do the calculations.

4 With findings that are not statistically significant, examine whether this is because the experiment lacked sufficient power to detect an effect.

13.1.2 Related samples IVs

As we discussed in Chapter 10, numbers of participants is much less of a problem when using *related* samples. This is because of the greater power of related samples (Section 12.2.2). Here, instead, the principal problem is usually *order effects*. Exactly the same issues arise as we considered in Section 10.4.3. You cannot eliminate order effects; you therefore need to ensure that the effects due to order contribute approximately equally to each of the experimental conditions. As before, the ideal way of achieving this is to *counterbalance* the design. With three conditions, there are six different combinations (given by three factorial, $3! = 3 \times 2 \times 1 = 6$). With four conditions, there are 24 different combinations ($4! = 4 \times 3 \times 2 \times 1 = 24$), as you can see in Table 13.1. (You can use this table to help you to counterbalance any experiment in which you have a four-level, related samples IV – it lists for you *all* of the possible combinations.)

With five conditions there are actually 120 different combinations. This means, in effect, that counterbalancing is possible for most of us only up to IVs with *four* levels. After that we need too many participants and will have to use alternative controls for order.

Table 13.1   All Possible Combinations of Four Conditions (A, B, C and D)

ABCD	BACD	CBAD	DBCA	ACDB	BCDA
CADB	DCAB	ACBD	BCAD	CABD	ABDC
DCBA	BADC	CBDA	DBAC	ADBC	CBDA
BDAC	DABC	ADCB	BDCA	CDAB	DACB

Note: Use this table to help you to counterbalance any experiment in which you have a four-level, related samples IV.

? SAQ 42

Suppose that you wanted to run an experiment with three conditions using related samples.

(a) Which, if any, of the following numbers of participants would you need to run to ensure that the design was counterbalanced?

    3 5 6 10 12 15 18 20 22 25

(b) Which, if any, of the numbers that you have chosen would it be better to use?

? SAQ 43

Suppose that you wanted to run an experiment with *four* conditions using related samples.

(a) What would be the minimum number of participants that you could run to ensure that this experiment was counterbalanced and why?

(b) If you considered that this minimum number was unlikely to be sufficient to detect the impact of the IV on the DV, what would be the next lowest number of participants that you could run to ensure that it was counterbalanced?

If for some reason you cannot counterbalance for the effects of order, then you might try partially controlling for these effects instead. For example, the first column in Table 13.1 contains four orders in which every condition appears in each ordinal position (first, second, third, fourth) and is followed by and preceded by every other condition once only. You could use this to partially control for order in an experiment involving fewer than 24 participants. (For example, you could take blocks of six participants and randomly assign one of the orders to each of them using randomization without replacement – see Appendix 2.)

When even this solution is not possible, then turn to that good old standby, *randomization*. Just as before, however, remember that randomization does *not* guarantee that the order effects will be spread around equally, and also that it is likely to be more successful in achieving this (though again not inevitably so) the more participants that you have.

Finally, remember that controls for order are *only* useful where there are no *carry-over* effects. Just as before, if you suspect that doing one of the conditions before another will have a permanent or disproportionate effect on performance, then do not use related samples for that IV.

? SAQ 44

Those among you who relish a challenge might now like to go back to SAQ 24 and work out how you could control for order effects in the two designs using related samples, (a) and (e). State what the minimum number of participants would be for these experiments, given the controls that you have chosen to employ.

Summary of Section 13.1.2

1 With related samples IVs the principal design issue arising from IVs with more than two levels is controlling for order effects.

2 With IVs with three or four levels it may be possible to control for order by counterbalancing. (Table 13.1 lists all the possible combinations of a four-level IV to help you counterbalance such a design.)

3 With more than four levels the alternatives are to control for order partially or to randomize.

4 Controls for order are only useful when there are no carry-over effects. If doing one of the conditions before another will have a lingering, permanent or disproportionate effect on performance, then related samples should not be used for that IV.

13.2　Experimental designs with two or more independent variables

Experiments involving more than one IV are very common in psychology. Such experiments enable us to test more sophisticated ideas about the variables in the psychological universe, such as whether the variables *interact* with each other.

*Table 13.2   An Experimental Design with Two Independent
Variables, Two Levels on Each*

| | *IV: music* | |
IV: alcohol	*Level 1: off*	*Level 2: on*
Level 1: no	Condition 1	Condition 2
Level 2: yes	Condition 3	Condition 4

For example, rather than simply concerning ourselves with the effects
of having the music on or off on driving performance, we might want
to find out whether this affects those who have been drinking alcohol
more than those who have not been drinking alcohol. In order to do
this we could design an experiment in which we simultaneously manipulated *both* the IV *music* and the IV *alcohol*. How would we do this?
Well, we could turn to our pool of participants and assign half of
them randomly to a music on condition, and half to a music off
condition. Of those in the music on condition, we could assign half
randomly to drink a standard amount of alcohol, with the remainder
remaining sober. Likewise with the music off condition, we could ask
half of our participants to drink the standard amount of alcohol, with
the other half remaining sober (Table 13.2). We would thus have
manipulated *two* independent variables, (music and alcohol) with two
levels on each (music on or music off, and alcohol or no alcohol).
This is quite a common design in psychology. It is sometimes referred
to as a **two by two** or **2 × 2** design.

Of course, we need not restrict ourselves to manipulating the *presence* versus the *absence* of the suspected causal variables. We could,
for instance, vary the *amount* of alcohol that our participants consumed, so that one group drank no alcohol, another drank the equivalent of one glass of wine, another the equivalent of two glasses of
wine, and another the equivalent of three glasses of wine. At the same
time we would have half of the participants driving with the music on,
the other half with the music off. Such a design appears in Table 13.3.
On the other hand, we could simultaneously vary the *volume* at which
the music was played – with one group listening to the music at low
volume, another at medium volume, and a third at high volume. Such
a design appears in Table 13.4.

In principle, there is no limit to the number of independent variables that you can manipulate simultaneously in an experiment.
Neither is there any restriction over whether these variables employ
related or unrelated samples. For example, in the first version of the
above experiment the variables could *both* be unrelated (with different

Table 13.3   An Experimental Design with Two Independent Variables, One with Two Levels, the Other with Four Levels

	IV: music	
IV: alcohol[a]	*Level 1: off*	*Level 2: on*
Level 1: 0 glass	Condition 1	Condition 2
Level 2: 1 glass	Condition 3	Condition 4
Level 3: 2 glasses	Condition 5	Condition 6
Level 4: 3 glasses	Condition 7	Condition 8

[a] Glasses of wine, where each glass equals 1 unit of alcohol.

participants in Conditions 1–4) or *both* related (with the same participants in Conditions 1–4, albeit with a suitable time lag between the alcohol and the no alcohol conditions). Or we could have a *combination* of related and unrelated samples (for instance, the music variable could employ *related* samples, the alcohol variable *unrelated* samples).

Given this flexibility, it is important to know how to design and run studies involving more than one IV. It is also important to know how to refer to such designs in the DESIGN and RESULTS. The next section deals with two ways of labelling such designs.

Table 13.4   An Experimental Design with Two Independent Variables, Four Levels on Each

	IV: music			
IV: alcohol[a]	*Level 1: off*	*Level 2: low volume*	*Level 3: medium volume*	*Level 4: high volume*
Level 1: 0 glass	Cond. 1	Cond. 2	Cond. 3	Cond. 4
Level 2: 1 glass	Cond. 5	Cond. 6	Cond. 7	Cond. 8
Level 3: 2 glasses	Cond. 9	Cond. 10	Cond. 11	Cond. 12
Level 4: 3 glasses	Cond. 13	Cond. 14	Cond. 15	Cond. 16

Note: Cond. = Condition.
[a] Glasses of wine, where each glass equals 1 unit of alcohol.

Summary of Section 13.2

1 It is perfectly possible to design experiments in which we manipulate more than one IV at the same time. Among other things, such designs enable us to assess whether there is an *interaction* between the IVs in our experiment.

2 In experiments involving more than one IV, each IV can have two or more levels. The IVs can be exclusively unrelated samples or exclusively related samples IVs or any combination of unrelated and related samples IVs.

13.3   Labelling designs that have two or more independent variables

One way of labelling these designs is to describe them in terms of a combination of the *number* and *nature* of their IVs. So, for instance, the experiment in Table 13.2 would be called a "two-way" experiment, because it has two IVs. If both the IVs used unrelated samples, the experiment would have a "two-way, unrelated samples" design. If both the IVs used related samples, it would have a "two-way, related samples" design. If one of the IVs used unrelated samples and one used related samples, the experiment would have a "two-way, mixed" design, for designs involving both types of IV are described as having **mixed designs**. Using this convention, the designs that we talked about in Chapter 10 were *one-way* designs.

So, to label your design correctly using this method, first count how many IVs there are in your design. If there is one IV, it will be a *one-way* design. If there are two, it will be a *two-way* design. With three it will be a *three-way* design, and so on. Once you have determined this, then work out for each IV whether it uses related samples or unrelated samples. If all the IVs use related samples, then it is a *related samples* design. If all the IVs use unrelated samples, then it is an *unrelated samples* design. If there is at least one of each type of IV, then it is a *mixed* design. The logic extends to "five-way" experiments, "six-way", and so on. However, my advice is that you restrict yourself to experiments with a maximum of three IVs (Section 13.6).

If you have been taught to use different labels for your IVs than the ones that I am using in this book, then use these to label the design. For example, you might call your design a "two-way, within-participants" or a "three-way, between-participants", and so on. If so, just substitute the label that you have been taught for the ones that I am using.

When writing your report you will need to specify the number of levels on each of the IVs and what these levels were. With mixed designs, you will need to be very clear about which of the IVs used related samples and which used unrelated samples. (See Chapter 3 for an example.)

Another way of labelling these designs is to refer to them by describing the number of levels on each of the IVs. For example, the design in Table 13.2 could be described as a "2 × 2 related samples" design if you had used only related samples IVs. If you had used only unrelated samples IVs, it could be described as a "2 × 2 unrelated samples" design. If you had used one of each type of IV it could be described as a "2 × 2 mixed" design. Likewise, a three-way design involving one unrelated samples IV and two related samples IVs with three, three and four levels respectively could be referred to as a "3 × 3 × 4 mixed" design, and so on.

Again, when writing your report you will need to make clear which IVs had which number of levels and what these levels were. With mixed designs, you will need to specify which of the IVs used related samples and which used unrelated samples.

? SAQ 45

Below you will find a list of experiments that have more than one IV. Go through each in turn and attempt to name these designs using *both* of the conventions outlined above.

(a) An accident researcher is interested in the effects of different levels of alcohol (0, 2, 4 or 8 units) on driving performance. Over the course of several weeks, she varies the quantity of alcohol given to a group of participants on different occasions. She then examines whether the impact of the alcohol varies with the person's sex and the length of time since they passed their driving test (passed in the previous 6 months, in the previous 7–18 months, or more than 18 months previously).

(b) An occupational psychologist is interested in the effects of different types of physical stressor (in this case heat, noise, or light) and the nature of the task (demanding or undemanding) on blood pressure. He exposes different groups of participants to the different types of stress, and measures the performance of all of them on both types of task.

(c) A psychologist interested in personality wishes to examine the effects of sex and extraversion (extravert or introvert) on public speaking performance.

(d) Another accident researcher is interested in the effect of listening to the car radio on driving performance. Using a driving simulator, she varies the driving conditions (easy, moderate, or difficult), the nature of the material listened to (talk or music), and the volume at which it is played (low, moderate or loud), on the driving performance of a group of experienced drivers.

Note that sometimes you will find designs with more than one IV referred to as *factorial designs*, and also come across references to *repeated measures* or to *split-plot designs*. **Factorial designs** are ones that use all the possible combinations of the levels of the different IVs. The designs in Tables 13.2–13.4 are all factorial designs. **Repeated measures** is another name given to designs employing (usually only) IVs with related samples. **Split-plot** is an alternative term for a mixed design that stems from the origins of this research design in agricultural research. Other names may also be used. However, you should never come across (or use) the term "one-way, mixed design".

? SAQ 46   Why not?

Summary of Section 13.3

1 You must be able to label accurately designs involving more than one IV.

2 The goal in writing your report is to make clear for each IV in your experiment whether it used a related or unrelated samples IV, how many levels it had and what these levels were.

3 You can do this succinctly with a basic design statement.

4 This section described two methods. One involves specifying the number of IVs in the basic design statement (e.g., two-way, three-way, and so on). The other involves specifying the number of levels on each IV in the basic design statement (e.g., 2×2, $2 \times 3 \times 3$, and so on).

5 Designs involving a combination of unrelated and related samples IVs are called mixed designs.

6 Although these methods have been illustrated using the labels for IVs employed in this book (unrelated and related samples IVs) other terms that you may use for these IVs can easily be substituted for these labels in the basic design statement.

13.4   Main effects of independent variables

With designs involving two or more IVs we can test for *interactions* between the different IVs as well as for *main effects* of each IV. Testing for interactions enables us to test more sophisticated ideas about the ways in which causal variables operate in the psychological universe.

The **main effect** of an IV is the effect of that IV on the DV, *ignoring* the other IVs in the experiment. For example, in the experiment in

Table 13.2, a significant main effect of alcohol would indicate that driving performance with alcohol differed from driving performance without alcohol. A significant main effect of music, on the other hand, would indicate that driving performance when listening to music differed from driving performance when not listening to music. You can potentially get significant main effects for each IV in your experiment, irrespective of whether it uses related or unrelated samples. Thus, you may find that any or all of the IVs in your experiment have significant main effects.

? SAQ 47   How many significant main effects could we find in each of the experiments in SAQ 45?

13.5   Statistical interactions

Often, however, we design experiments to test whether there is evidence that the IVs *interact*. When IVs **interact**, the effect of one IV is *different* at the levels of the other IV or IVs. For example, in Figure 13.1 you can see that drinking alcohol makes a bigger difference to performance when participants listen to music than it does when they do not listen to music. That is, the *difference* between driving performance

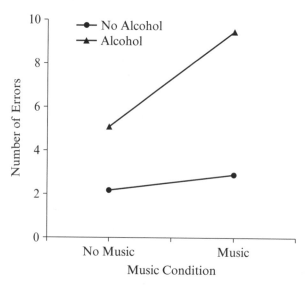

Figure 13.1.   Line graph displaying one type of interaction between two IVs.

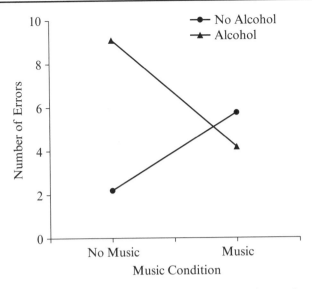

Figure 13.2. Line graph displaying an alternative type of interaction between two IVs.

with alcohol and with no alcohol is bigger at one level of the music IV (music) than at the other level of the music IV (no music). Therefore, the IVs interact.

Figure 13.2 contains another example of an interaction. Here you can see that the IVs interact to such an extent that the effects of alcohol are actually *opposite* in direction at the levels of the music IV. Here driving is worse among those who have drunk alcohol when they do not listen to music but better among those who have drunk alcohol when they *do* listen to music. (Obviously, I have made these effects up!) Again, the IVs interact. That is, the effect of one IV is *different* at the levels of the other.

Both of these are examples of interactions. Had the IVs *not* interacted then, when graphed, the data would have looked more like Figure 13.3. Here the difference between driving performance with alcohol and with no alcohol is more or less the same when participants listen to music as it is when they do not listen to music. Therefore, the IVs do *not* interact.

As a student you can sometimes struggle to understand statistical interactions. Yet, when you first start designing your own studies in psychology, you are in fact naturally very aware of the possibility that variables can interact. Remember those first studies in which you wanted to include all of the variables that you could think of? From ethnic background, social class, time of day, gender of participant, gender of experimenter, temperature in the room and what the

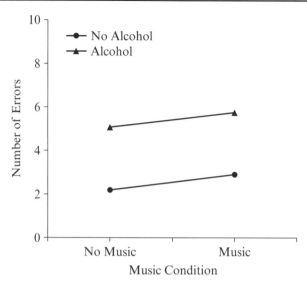

Figure 13.3. Line graph displaying no interaction between the two IVs.

participants had for breakfast, to how much coffee they had drunk? This reflects your natural, intuitive awareness that these variables may well make a difference to the effects. That is, you were concerned that the effect of the variables of interest may be changed – accentuated, reduced or even eliminated – in the presence of other variables. That's what an interaction tells us – that the effects of an IV are different – accentuated, reduced or even eliminated – at the levels of another IV.

You can find out more about both main effects and interactions on the Web site that accompanies this book. You will also hear more about these effects on your statistics course.

13.6   Analysing designs involving two or more IVs

Designs involving the simultaneous manipulation of two or more IVs are commonly analysed using the statistical test known as **analysis of variance** (ANOVA). You will certainly learn more about ANOVA on your statistics course. With ANOVA you can simultaneously test *all* of the main effects and interactions in your experiment for statistical significance. To help you with this, you will find on the Web site a table that lists all of the effects that you can find in designs using from one to four IVs. Use this table to check against your statistical output. It will help you to keep track of the effects that you can expect to find in the analysis. Any or all of the effects listed there can be found to be statistically significant in a particular analysis.

Note that you do not need to know the number of levels or whether the IVs use unrelated or related samples in order to be able to use that table. You *do*, however, need to know these things in order to analyse the data appropriately. For this reason it is important to specify *which* particular version of ANOVA you used in your analysis. So make sure that you include an accurate and sufficiently detailed statement about which ANOVA you used in the RESULTS (see Section 4.6.10).

Finally, be careful about how many IVs you use in an experiment. My advice is to restrict yourself to three at the most, unless you have lots of experience or will receive very close supervision from a tutor. One reason for this is that in such designs controlling for order, matching materials, or obtaining enough participants is difficult. The main reason, however, is that interpreting three-way interactions is hard and interpreting interactions above and beyond three-way interactions (e.g., four-way interactions) is *so* hard that it can make your brain start to feel like it is dissolving uncontrollably.

13.7 Graphing statistical interactions

Graphing significant interactions is a *very* useful aid to interpreting them. This has been clear for even the 2×2 designs that I discussed in Section 13.5. It is even more so when you have more levels on your IVs or more IVs involved in the interaction (or both).

I used **line graphs** in Figures 13.1–13.3 to illustrate the effects. The principal reason for this is that, because they represent inconsistencies in effects, interactions are revealed by deviations from the parallel. This is easy to see with a line graph. Technically, however, I should have used a *bar graph* for these examples, as the IV on the horizontal axis (music) is not quantitative. That is, the conditions *no music* and *music* are absolute, categorical states with no gradations between them. Yet there is a line on the horizontal axis for points between them and this is meaningless. Had I put alcohol on the horizontal axis this would have made sense, as there are sensible gradations between 0 units and 2 units of alcohol. Figure 13.4 is a *bar graph* showing the same interaction as in Figure 13.1. Take the advice of your tutor on which type of graph to use. Whichever you do use, get into the habit of graphing statistically significant interactions to help you to interpret them, and include figures displaying the key ones in your report (Section 8.5). (You can find on the Web site that accompanies this book advice on how to graph three-way interactions.)

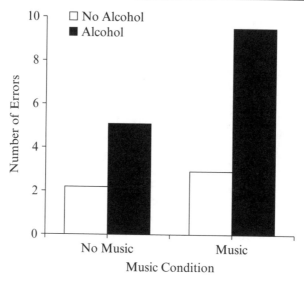

Figure 13.4. Bar graph displaying the same effects as in Figure 13.1.

Summary of Sections 13.4–13.7

1 In experiments involving more than one IV we can differentiate and test for the main effects of the different IVs and for interactions between the different IVs.

2 The main effect of an IV is the effect of that IV disregarding the other IVs in the experiment. There is a potential main effect for each IV in the experiment.

3 An interaction occurs when the effects of one IV are different at the different levels of another IV.

4 It is difficult to interpret interactions between three or more IVs. So, as a general rule you would be well advised to limit the number of IVs that you manipulate in an experiment.

5 You should get into the habit of graphing statistically significant interactions and include graphs of the key ones in your report.

13.8   Watch out for "IVs" that are not true independent variables

Sometimes you will include in your experiments variables that look like IVs but that are not actually truly independent variables. These are variables like sex, personality variables (e.g., optimists or pessimists; people who are high, medium or low in trait anxiety), or differences in attitudes or behaviour (e.g., being for or against abortion; being a smoker or a non-smoker). Variables such as these are not *truly* independent variables because we have not been able to assign participants randomly to the different levels of the variable. That is, participants arrive at our experiment *already* assigned to the levels of these variables. For example, they come to us *already* as women, or against abortion, or smokers. Thus their assignment to groups is not determined by us – it is predetermined.

This does not mean that we should avoid testing for sex differences or for differences in response between people classified in other ways that are predetermined. On the contrary, we often want to know a great deal about what other responses and variables are associated with being male or female, politically committed or apolitical, being of average or above average IQ, for or against genetic modification, and so on. The important point is that, even though these variables look like IVs, we must remember when reporting the study and interpreting the findings involving these variables that they are not IVs in the strict sense. You can find out more about this on the Web site that accompanies this book.

Because of this, some researchers suggest that we should replace the terms independent and dependent variables with ones that do not imply causality. One possibility is to refer instead to the **explanatory** variable and the **response** variable. Other possibilities include **classification** variable, **subject** variable or **predictor** variable instead of IV, and **measured** variable or **criterion** variable instead of DV. Your tutor may encourage you to use such alternative labels, so watch out for this issue.

One relevant term that you are very likely to come across in your reading is **quasi-experimental design**. A quasi-experimental design is one that looks like an experimental design but that lacks the critical ingredient – random assignment. Quasi-experimental variables are thus particular versions of these variables that look like IVs but that are not actually truly independent variables. Quasi-experimental designs are interesting and useful methods of attempting to conduct experiments in real-life settings where it is not possible to randomly assign participants to treatment conditions. You may learn more about such designs in your methods course.

Summary of Section 13.8

1 Sometimes you will include in your experiments variables that look like IVs but that are not truly independent variables.

2 For a variable to be a true independent variable you must be able to randomly assign participants to the levels or orders of conditions to participants.

3 Quasi-experimental variables are ones in which participants are in different conditions but have not been assigned to these conditions randomly. They are thus a particular class of variables that look like IVs but that are not true IVs.

13.9   Some final tips to help you to design better experiments and write better reports

This brings us almost to the end. I would just like to spend the final few pages giving you a few tips to help you to design better experiments and, I hope, also to write better reports. You can find on the Web site that accompanies this book some more tips for your later experiments – those that you design as you become more experienced (e.g., in the UK, in the second and third years of an undergraduate degree).

13.9.1   The basic rule

The rule to remember is that there is no such thing as *the* right way to design an experiment to test a given hypothesis. Although there will be lots of wrong ways, there will usually be several right ways, perhaps many. So, do not feel overawed by the task. Relax! Your task is to design a reasonable, meaningful experiment, free of confounding variables, not to find the "correct" way to design it.

13.9.2   Getting reliable measures of the dependent variable

Would it be fair if your degree classification or grade for any other major qualification were based on a single end-of-course exam? If I wanted to find out how good you were at something – say bowling – would it be a good idea to judge you after a single roll? In both cases the answer is, of course, no. A range of factors, not just ability, influences performance on any task. For any single performance, such as one exam, these factors may serve to make you perform below or above par. This is why you tend to be assessed many times on a course.

Well, exactly the same arguments apply to the performance of your participants in an experiment. A common weakness of many student experiments is to measure the performance of a participant once. This is unlikely to be *reliable*. If you can, you should take enough measures from each participant to be reasonably confident that you have a *reliable* estimate of their performance in each condition of the experiment in which they appear. Technically, **reliability** is the extent to which your measure of performance produces similar results on different occasions. A reliable measure of performance is essential if we are going to be able meaningfully to assess the effects of the IV.

Thus, wherever possible, experiments should have more than one *trial* per condition. A **trial** in this context is a basic unit of experimental time. It begins when you present something to the participant and ends when they give you back a response on your DV.

However, as with all aspects of good experimental design, you need to use your common sense. You should have as many trials (i.e., take as many separate measures) of the DV as you need, but not so many as *to induce fatigue or boredom*. (The optimum number of measures is one of the things that you can establish during the piloting phase of the study – see below.) You should also watch out for situations in which it is not possible to have more than one trial per condition (e.g., when doing so will ask too much of your participants, creates significant carry-over effects, or might reveal too much to your participant about the purpose of the study).

13.9.3   Pilot testing

Once you have designed your experiment, chosen the question that you wish to examine experimentally, the IV that you wish to manipulate, the DV that you think will best assess this manipulation, decided whether you would be better off comparing the same or different participants, prepared your materials, set up your random sequences, and standardized your instructions, you might think that you're finally ready for the off. However, a little more patience at this stage may well pay dividends later. For, rather than diving straight into running your study, a sensible procedure to adopt here is to **pilot test** your experiment. That is, to try it out on a few participants first to see whether it makes sense to them, to uncover any serious flaws or problems that might have been overlooked at the design stage and to generally "fine-tune" the procedure. Pilot testing also enables you to familiarize yourself with your role as experimenter so that you are practised and professional by the time that you encounter your first participant proper.

Pilot testing can save you a lot of wasted time and effort. It provides you with a golden opportunity to improve the design *before* you've wasted too many participants. It is, therefore, a good habit to get into. Indeed, it will become increasingly important as you take greater responsibility for designing your own experiments.

A pilot test can also reveal whether you have a potential *floor* or *ceiling* effect in your data. For instance, thinking back to the driving and music experiment, we need to set our participants a course on the driving simulator that is neither so difficult that few can do it (**floor effect**) nor so easy that more or less everyone can (**ceiling effect**). Otherwise, we will not be able to assess the effects of manipulating our IV on performance itself. However, it is often difficult to decide on the appropriate level of task difficulty in the abstract. A brief pilot test on participants who are *representative of those who will take part in the experiment proper*, however, can help with this problem (it is no good piloting on your relatives and their friends but running the experiment on a sample of students, for example).

Do do it – even one or two participants may tell you something useful about your study. (Of course, you should run more than this if you can.)

13.9.4   The post-experimental interview

Once you have finished collecting all the data that you need from a participant, it is often a good idea to spend a few minutes with him or her, before debriefing (Section 10.10.2), conducting a **post-experimental interview**. Set yourself up a little interview schedule with gently probing questions to try to find out more about what crossed participants' minds while they did your experiment. This may give you insights into factors controlling their behaviour and the extent to which they were aware of the hypotheses of the experiment. It may help you better to interpret your findings and even give you ideas for future research.

If possible, someone who is blind to condition should conduct the interview. Such interviews are an essential feature of pilot tests and can also be useful in the main experiment. Unlike the debriefing, the post-experimental interview is primarily for *your* benefit, not the participants'.

13.9.5   Check and screen your data before statistical analysis

After putting all the effort and time into designing the experiment, running it and collecting the data, an odd thing can happen. You can find yourself suddenly not caring about how accurately the data have been entered into the machine for analysis and just keen (desperate?) to get the analysis done and dusted. When you enter the data yourself this can be because you cannot imagine that you have made a mistake (as *if*). However, it happens even when someone else has entered the data for you. I suspect that it is because you are so close to completion and is part of the general need that we have for closure and for starting the next task on our list. It is important to guard against this tendency, of course.

Whenever you collect any data, whether from an experiment or any other study, you *must* ensure that you have entered them accurately prior to analysis. It is easy to make mistakes when doing something as dull as entering data into a computer. **Check the data** entry in at least two ways. First, get on your screen a frequency count, histogram or bar chart of the IV and the DV, just to check that all the values are ones that make sense (i.e., that they all fall in the right range of values). (Print this out only if you can be sure that it won't cost the earth in paper.) For example, if you find a value of 9 or 33 for a 7-point scale or of 222 for age, you *know* that this is outside the range of possible or legal values. It *must* be a mistake. However, this technique cannot help you spot values that are legal but wrong (for example, giving someone a score of 1 instead of 6 on the 7-point scale). So, second, **proofread** the data by checking that the numbers in the data window for a given participant match those on whatever source was used to input the data (e.g., the relevant coding sheet or questionnaire). If you have lots of participants, do this for about 25 percent of the sample in the first instance, making sure that you sample the data entered early, in the middle and late on. If you discover errors, then check more. If you do not have many participants, check the data for them all just to make sure.

Once you are satisfied that the data no longer contain mistakes, it is a good idea to use graphs and other techniques to check whether the data meet the assumptions of the tests that you hope to use. Look in your statistics textbook for ways of displaying data using histograms, bar graphs, scatter plots, stem and leaf plots, and box plots. Most statistical software packages will provide ways of producing such displays and may even contain useful programs to help you with this (e.g., EXPLORE in SPSS for Windows). You will learn more on your statistics course about what to do and what to look out for. The latter include extreme values that are unduly influencing the means and standard deviations (known in the trade as *outliers*) and any *missing data*. If **screening** your data in this way ever leads you to change or transform the data, make sure that you report what you did and why in the opening paragraphs of your RESULTS.

Only once you have done these things should you begin the analyses. You must get into the habit of inspecting your data *before* you compute *any* statistics. Otherwise you risk basing your RESULTS on nonsense.

Summary of Section 13.9

1 Where possible, it is a good idea to have more than one trial per condition – that is, to measure your participant's performance more than once in any given condition of the experiment.

2 A good habit to get into is to pilot test your experiment by trying it out on a few participants *before* you start to record any data. This enables you to spot any flaws in your design and gives you the opportunity to fine-tune the procedure. Pilot testing can save you a lot of wasted time and effort.

3 You must, however, run the pilot test on a sample of participants from the same population as the one that you will use in the experiment proper.

4 In some experiments a post-experimental interview with participants can give you useful insights into the variables controlling their behaviour in the experiment. This may help you to interpret your findings and can give you ideas for follow-up studies.

5 Make sure that you check that the data have been entered accurately before analysis. As you become more experienced, learn also how to screen your data thoroughly before analysing it.

13.10   Above all, randomize properly

Finally, here's a note to all you budding experimenters out there: *Randomize properly!* The random assignment of participants to conditions or of orders of conditions to participants is the key to the whole experimental enterprise. At all times and in all experiments use *truly* random procedures for assignment or else the exercise is in danger of being pointless. So, how you go about randomization is a central issue (see Appendix 2). You must take this problem seriously and not do it casually. Think carefully in advance about how you will do the randomization. Use random number generators or tables. Do *not* make the numbers up yourself or use a procedure that can be influenced consciously or even unconsciously. Learn to differentiate randomization *with* replacement from randomization *without* replacement and use the procedure that you require. Subsequently, describe in sufficient detail in your reports the way in which you randomized so that your readers can judge for themselves whether the randomization was effective.

That's it! Good luck. I hope that you enjoy finding things out with and about experiments in psychology.

Commentary

Chapter 1

1 The WWW puts an enormous amount of material at your disposal. Be warned, however: some of the stuff that you access will be rubbish. The whole point of the WWW is that people can put what they want on their pages. This is why I recommend accessing Web sites linked to your department's home pages or those of the professional bodies. Although no guarantee, it offers some hope that the Web sites that you access will contain useful material and not garbage.

2 When you have only just begun to write reports in psychology, however, at first you need to concentrate on the basics. At this stage, make sure that you have grasped the essentials of those papers centrally relevant to what you have done, and don't concern yourself about when they were published. It is no good throwing in an up-to-date reference or two just to impress your marker when you have failed to write about something older but more relevant.

Chapter 3

1 If you have used a lengthy questionnaire in your study or for some other reason have a large number of dependent variables, this may be difficult. Advice on writing your DESIGN under these circumstances can be found on the Web site that accompanies this book. Likewise you can find there advice on how to write a DESIGN when your study is not experimental.

2 A **pretest** is a useful thing. It is designed to enable us to assess whether overall performance in the conditions of our experiment is about the same *before* the introduction of the IV. It provides, therefore, a useful check on our randomization. For example, in this experiment our pretest will tell us whether the memory performance of participants in the mnemonic and no mnemonic conditions was equivalent before introducing the mnemonic. In situations in which we suspect that performance among the participants

might be highly variable at the outset, we can sometimes give participants *practice* on the experimental task to get them to a common baseline level of performance before starting the experiment. These are called **practice trials**. A **manipulation check** is a measure that tells us something about whether the manipulation had the qualities that we presume. For example, by including a manipulation check here we will be able to check whether the participants agreed that the easily imaged words were indeed easier to image than were the hard-to-image words. You can find more about *pretests, practice trials* and *manipulation checks* on the Web site that accompanies this book.

3 In some studies, especially those using lengthy questionnaires, it can be hard to work out what the IVs and DVs are or there may seem to be a large number. Sometimes this is because you are not in fact running an experiment but instead have non-experimental data. You can find more about how to report studies that used questionnaires on the Web site that accompanies this book.

4 Of course, I go over the gist orally in a standardized way!

Chapter 4

1 You need to do these things when you are testing for statistical significance. If you are *not* testing for statistical significance, then you need to report instead the probability of the obtained value of your statistic arising by sampling error (this is the probability associated with the statistic), and report and comment on the effect size(s) and relevant confidence interval(s). Once you know how, it is of course a good idea to report the effect size(s) and confidence interval(s) even if you *are* also testing for statistical significance (see Chapter 12).

2 Among other things, reporting the *exact* probability allows other people to see for themselves how close your results were to being (or to not being) statistically significant. This enables them to make a more informed assessment of your results.

3 Follow this advice until you understand about statistical power. Then you will learn that the outcome of the analysis depends in part on the power of the test. However, until you are quite confident that you understand about power and its implications, it is safer to follow this advice.

4 The paradox is resolved if you think of your reader as someone who in fact knows about psychology in general, but not about the specific area that you investigated in your study. Thus they understand the procedures involved in significance testing, as these are by and large the same regardless of the area of psychology under investigation. However, you still need to explain to them the psychology relevant to your study.

5 However, note also that the more tests of significance that you run on a set of data the more you run the risk of making a type I error. You will find this issue discussed in most textbooks of statistics. (If in doubt about what to do, see your tutor.)

6 Of course, you should not attempt to use and report any of these statistics without first reading your statistics textbook.

7 Remember that the terms *unrelated samples* and *related samples* are only two of a range of terms that you can use to describe these types of IV. You might have been taught to use different terms (see Section 10.2). The terms *pretest* and *manipulation* check are explained in the commentary to Chapter 3. You can also find them described on the Web site that accompanies this book.

8 I have assumed that you have yet to be taught how to conduct these further tests (known as tests of simple effects). Obviously, if you do know how to conduct them, they should be reported here. The Web site that accompanies this book has an example RESULTS section for this experiment containing such tests to see how to report them.

Chapter 5

1 Of course, if the designers of the experiment had obtained reports of the number of nightmares experienced by each participant in the weeks leading up to the experiment, they could have been even more confident here. One possibility would have been to allocate participants to conditions based on the number of nightmares that they reported experiencing (Section 10.7). Alternatively, after randomization had taken place, they could have tested statistically to see if there was a difference between the conditions in the number of nightmares reported by the participants before the experiment.

Chapter 8

1 What I have to say here is about graphs that you put in the report, primarily in the RESULTS, and when you are reporting *experiments*. If you are reporting non-experimental data then you will probably need to include different types of graph in your reports than those I describe here. Also, the graphs that you put in the report should not be confused with those that you use to help you to make sense of your data (Section 13.9.5). Graphs that you use to help you to make sense of the data do not necessarily need to appear in the report.

2 This use of the term "error" may strike you as odd. Let me try to explain. In an ideal world we would expect *all* of the participants in a particular condition of our experiment to get *exactly* the same scores on the DV. The fact that, in reality, they do not we assume reflects "noise" or *error* in our data. The fact that there is any variation in scores within a condition thus indicates the presence of error. Error bars tell us visually something about this spread and thus something about how much error there is. See your statistics textbook for more about this.

Chapter 9

1 Although there are alternatives, this "no effect" null hypothesis is the one used most commonly in psychology and the one that you will most probably be testing.

Chapter 11

1 Be careful here not to make an easy and common mistake. These statistics do *not* tell us the probability that the null hypothesis *is* true. I wish! Unfortunately, this we can *never* know. Instead, they tell us the probability of getting results like ours (at least as extreme as ours) *assuming* that the null hypothesis is true. Our assumption may be right. Our assumption may be wrong. As you will soon see, in the end we have to make an informed guess about whether our assumption is right or wrong. I will explain more about this later in this chapter. So, for now, just remember that inferential statistics do *not* tell us the probability that the null hypothesis is true. Boy, would life be simpler if they did!

2 Once you are comfortable with the issues discussed in the next chapter, you can add to this list:

8 Estimate the *effect size* of the IV.

9 With results that are not statistically significant, think about the likely *power* of the experiment.

Chapter 12

1 The opposite is also the case. If our studies look like they will be too powerful for our needs, we can take steps to reduce their power. For example, studies involving hundreds or thousands of participants can be so powerful that even relatively tiny and unimportant effects can become highly statistically significant. This can be a waste of resources. It can also lead to confusion over whether statistically significant effects are important or trivial. However, given that effect sizes in psychology are often smaller than we imagine, having underpowered studies is usually more of a problem. As a student, therefore, it is much more likely that you will be in danger of running a study that lacks sufficient power – especially with unrelated samples.

2 Have you spotted an apparent paradox here? If we know the effect size, then why are we running the experiment? Surely, the whole point of the experiment is to detect whether there is an effect of the IV on the DV? If we know this already, then why bother to find it out again by running another experiment?

This is a *very* good question. The answer is that you *inevitably* make assumptions about the effect size of the IV whenever you design an experiment in psychology. For example, if you decide to run an experiment with a two-level unrelated samples IV using only 10 participants overall, you are automatically assuming that the effect size is very large. This is because your experiment has little or no chance of rejecting the null hypothesis if the effect size is small or medium. If you decide to run the same experiment with 100 participants overall, however, you are assuming that the effect size may be much smaller than in the 10-participant version. Otherwise, why are you using so many participants? It therefore makes sense to formalize this process and to make calculated estimates of the number of participants that are needed, rather than to do this implicitly.

Making calculated guesses about the likely or possible effect size in our experiment does not beg the question of the *true* effect size: we may be wrong. The effect size may turn out to be bigger than we estimated, smaller, or zero. However, if we estimate sensibly in advance the likely effect size we can at least ensure that our experiment has the power (e.g., has enough participants) to enable us to stand a reasonable chance of rejecting the null hypothesis *if* the effect size is at least as big as estimated.

3 It is easy to work out the percentage variance. Simply multiply r^2 by 100. So, for example, I got the value of 4 percent from calculating $.04 \times 100 = 4$. Thus, with $r = .5$, $r^2 = .25$ and the percentage variance that is shared is 25 percent ($.25 \times 100 = 25.0$). *Do* think about r^2 when you use Pearson's r. Even some researchers fail to do this, so don't be fooled by what you may find in published papers. I have sat through talks at conferences and even read papers in which the authors reported correlation coefficients that were statistically significant but trivial. Had they looked at r^2 as well, they would not have made this mistake.

4 The reason why the percentages do not add up to 100 is that partial eta squared involves an adjustment to improve the accuracy of the effect size estimate. One effect of making this adjustment is that the percentages no longer add up to 100.

Chapter 13

1 However, as I said earlier, avoid here just trotting out the vacuous statement in your DISCUSSION to the effect that "our findings would have been significant if we'd had more participants". Remember that *any* difference between your conditions will become statistically significant if you use enough participants, no matter how small it is numerically and how trivial it is psychologically. Instead, look at your design and try to assess, if you can, whether your experiment was likely to have been powerful enough to detect any noteworthy effect of the IV on the DV. Section 12.3 has advice on how to do this.

Recommended reading

Further coverage of most of the statistical issues raised in this book can be found in almost any statistics textbook. The texts below are the ones that I know of that I happily recommend. (See the Web site for updates.)

To those of you who would benefit from a very straightforward and basic introduction to statistical tests with simple "cookbook" guidance for their hand calculation, I would recommend *Learning to Use Statistical Tests in Psychology* by Judith Greene and Manuela D'Oliveira (1999) or *Statistics Explained* by Perry Hinton (1995).

Clear and user-friendly coverage is also provided in each of the following: *Research Methods and Statistics in Psychology* by Hugh Coolican (1999), *Statistics for Psychology* by Art and Elaine Aron (1999), and *Statistics without Maths for Psychology* by Christine Dancey and John Reidy (2001). These texts include good coverage of issues to do with power and effect size. *Doing Psychological Research* by Nicky Hayes (2000) provides a broad but clear coverage of a wide range of methods in psychology, including qualitative methods.

An excellent guide to using the statistical software package *SPSS* for Windows to analyse your data is provided by Julie Pallant in her *SPSS Survival Manual* (2001). The survival manual covers a wide range of analyses and includes material on calculating effect sizes. A good, simple and straightforward guide to using *SPSS* for Windows is also provided in *A Simple Guide to SPSS for Windows* by Lee Kirkpatrick and Brooke Feeney (2001). (Dancey and Reidy (1999) also cover how to use SPSS.)

The following manage to be both authoritative and yet accessible: *Doing Quantitative Psychological Research: From Design to Report* by David Clark-Carter (1997) and *Fundamental Statistics for the Behavioral Sciences* by David Howell (1999). David Howell (2001) also produces *Statistical Methods for Psychology*, which is where I often turn when I'm stuck. For those using multivariate statistics, a good introductory source is *Reading and Understanding Multivariate Statistics*, edited by Laurence Grimm and Paul Yarnold (1995).

For more on how to write in psychology, *The Psychologist's Companion* by Robert Sternberg (1988) is both informative and entertaining. If you want clear and authoritative information on how to lay out your tables, see *Presenting your Findings* by Adelheid Nicol and Penny Pexman (1999). Of course, the ultimate reference for matters to do with paper writing and layout is *The Publication Manual of the American Psychological Association* (5th ed., APA, 2001).

Appendix 1:
Confusing predictions from the null hypothesis with those from the experimental hypothesis

Suppose that you are interested in biological theories of personality. On reading around the area you come across two theories concerning the biological basis of extraversion. Theory 1 predicts that, after exposure to ultrasound, the blood pressure of extraverts will be higher than the blood pressure of introverts. Theory 2, however, predicts that the increase in blood pressure that comes from being an extravert is offset by the increase in blood pressure among introverts that occurs when introverts are exposed to ultrasound. Thus this latter theory leads to the prediction that there will be no difference in the blood pressure of extraverts and introverts after exposure to ultrasound.

Now, for personal reasons, you favour the theory that predicts that there will be no difference in the blood pressure of the extraverts and introverts. So, you design an experiment to test this. You expose extraverts and introverts to ultrasound and measure their blood pressure. On analysing the data, you find that there is no reliable evidence for any difference in blood pressure between extraverts and introverts following exposure to ultrasound. That is, you fail to reject the null hypothesis in your experiment.

Now you are happy with the outcome. It is evidence against the theory that you dispute. Don't be *too* happy, however – it is not evidence *for* the theory that you favour. Although the evidence is *consistent* with what you'd expect under your favoured theory, it does not count as a test of it. This is because findings of no difference are exactly what we'd expect if extraversion and introversion had nothing to do with blood pressure whatsoever. That is, in your experiment, the predictions from theory 2 coincide with those under the null hypothesis and are thus not tested by your experiment.

Let's take another example. Suppose that someone argues that babies are brought by storks who drop them down chimneys to their mothers. Suppose, however, that you don't like this explanation. Instead you favour one that proposes that the doctor or midwife brings the babies with them in their bag. Now, you and I can devise a simple test of this. If babies *are* dropped down chimneys by storks, then we would expect to find women having babies only in houses with chimneys – not, for example, in high-rise flats, or houses with chimneys that have been blocked up. However, if the midwife or doctor brings them, then there should be no such difference.

So, imagine that we conduct this study and find that there is no difference in the relative frequency with which babies are born in houses with chimneys and houses without chimneys. This is evidence *against* the stork theory. However, is it evidence *for* the midwife/doctor theory? Really??

The point is that such studies – such experiments – are actually only tests of the ideas that lead us to predict differences. They are not tests of ideas that lead us to predict *no* differences. If you want to test these, then you must create a situation (i.e., design an experiment) in which the ideas that you want to test predict a difference at least somewhere between the conditions.

? SAQ 48   There's only one way in which an experiment designed to test an idea that predicts differences between conditions can tell you something about an idea that predicts no differences. Can you imagine when this is?

If you are confused, don't worry unduly. Just remember that *failing to reject* the null hypothesis at the end of your experiment tells you something about the ideas that led to the prediction of a difference and nothing about any ideas that you had that led to the prediction of no difference. If the predictions derived from a theory coincide with those derived from the null hypothesis, then you are not actually testing the theory.

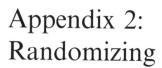

Appendix 2:
Randomizing

This is an *essential* skill of the empirical psychologist. Do *not* treat this casually. The capacity of the experiment to allow us make causal inferences depends critically on assigning participants to conditions or conditions to participants randomly. Make sure that you use a *truly* random procedure, therefore, not one that is even remotely open to conscious or unconscious influence. If you fail to randomize properly you will undo all of the time and effort that you have otherwise spent on the experiment.

There are a number of occasions on which you will need to randomize. One is when you need to allocate different participants to conditions. Another is when you need to randomize the order in which you present the conditions to participants. You may also need to use randomization when preparing your materials. Finally, if you go on to do research, you may eventually find yourself selecting participants randomly from a hypothetical statistical population.

You will find advice on how to do some of these things below. It is important for you to realize, however, that the basic principle of randomization is the same in all of these cases (although the method by which you realize this principle may differ). Thus, whatever you are randomizing – be it orders or participants or words in a stimulus list – any given item should have an equal chance of selection *at all times* (i.e., the prior selection of one particular item should not affect in any way the chances of any of the other items being subsequently selected). So, for example, if you are selecting orders for your participants, the chances of any given order being selected must not be affected by any selections that you have made previously. Similarly, when assigning participants to conditions, the chances of a given participant appearing in one particular condition should not be affected by previous allocations to that or any other condition.

What this means in practice is that we don't simply sit down and juggle our orders around or assign our participants to conditions in what seems to us to be a suitably random order. Neither do we generate numbers from our heads. Such methods do *not* give us truly random results. Instead, we employ *tools*, devices that enable us to generate truly random sequences and whose results *we obey*, however non-random they appear.

Now, all that is required of these tools is that they make the choice for us in an unbiased way: that is, that they do not favour some outcomes more than others. Consequently, if used properly, things like coins, playing cards, dice, and so on, can be adequate for the purpose. However, it is sometimes possible to influence consciously or even unconsciously the outcome of a coin toss or dice roll or card selection. Therefore you are best advised to avoid using these things for most purposes. (You can use, say, a fair coin for some small aspects of the procedure, such as choosing where to start in a table of random numbers.) For most of your randomizing, however, use either *random number tables* or (if you know for sure that it is well designed) a *random number generator* on a computer. The examples below use random number tables.

Tables of **random numbers** can be found at the rear of most statistics textbooks. These tables have been produced by a program that enabled the digits 0–9 to have an equal opportunity of appearing at any given position in the table. So, at any given position, you have no idea which of these digits is likely to appear. Even if the previous twelve digits have all been "7" (which is extremely unlikely, but still possible) the chances of "7" appearing as the thirteenth digit are *exactly the same* as if there had been no "7" among the previous twelve. You can see, therefore, that such tables are ideally suited for the purposes of randomizing.

You can use these digits singly, in pairs, groups of three and so on. The important thing is to make sure that you don't keep entering the tables at the same place. If you do, then you will simply be using the same sequence of numbers and your lists will not differ.

Finally, you should learn to recognize the difference between randomization *without* replacement and randomization *with* replacement. You are already familiar with both. In lotteries or draws for cup competitions, when a number has been selected, it is not put back into the pot to be selected again. This is **randomization without replacement**. With this technique numbers, once selected, are no longer available for reselection. (Consequently, the chances of each of the remaining numbers in the pot being selected will have increased. Nevertheless, the process still meets our requirements for a truly random procedure, for the chances of each of the remaining numbers being selected should still be equal.) In **randomization with replacement**, in contrast, the numbers *are* available for reselection. The previous number selected therefore has the same chance of coming up again. Roulette wheels and fair die are devices that use randomization with replacement. These devices have no memories. The number that came up previously has *exactly* the same chance of coming up again on the next spin or roll and *exactly* the same chance as have all the other numbers.

Using the tables

Enter the tables at a random position. Toss a coin to decide whether you will proceed diagonally (heads) or along lines (tails). If tails, toss a coin to decide whether you will move horizontally (heads) or vertically (tails). Then toss a coin to decide whether you will move up or down (if moving vertically) or left or right (if moving horizontally). Proceed similarly if the original toss had returned a head. This procedure is standard for the use of tables.

Allocating participants to conditions

Suppose that we wish to allocate 10 participants to Condition A and 10 to Condition B. One way of doing this is as follows. Number your participants 1–20, with numbers 1–10 in Condition A and 11–20 in Condition B. Enter the tables and proceed as directed above. Step through the tables reading *pairs* of digits. The order in which you come across these numbers will dictate the order in which you run your participants. For instance, with the sequence

  23 53 04 01 63 08 45 93 15 22

the first three participants will be allocated to Condition A (04, 01, and 08), the fourth to Condition B (15), and so on. Once a number has been encountered, however, you should disregard it on future occurrences (randomization *without* replacement). This technique can obviously be extended to more than two conditions.

Allocating orders to participants

Even with a counterbalanced design you must allocate the orders to participants randomly. For example, with our study in SAQ 44(a), we have six different orders. Suppose that we wish to allocate these orders to 12 participants. One way of doing this is as follows. Enter the tables and proceed as directed above. Number the participants 1–12. Step through the tables looking for pairs of digits, allocating the participants to the orders in sequence. For example, with the digits

  23 53 04 01 63 08 45 93 15 22

Participant 04 would do order 1, Participant 01 would do order 2, Participant 08 would do order 3, and so on until all 12 participants had received an order. Again, you should disregard repeats of particular numbers (randomization *without* replacement).

Constructing materials

Suppose that you need to randomize the order in which a set of 30 questions appears in a questionnaire. Number the questions, and then step through the random number tables as directed above to obtain the order in which the questions should appear. For instance, with the sequence

23 53 04 01 63 08 45 93 15 22

question 23 would come first, question 04 would come second, question 01 would come third, and so on.

To control for order effects you would probably need to produce more than one version of the questionnaire, so you would need to repeat the above process.

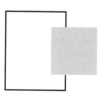

Appendix 3:
How to use tables of critical values
of inferential statistics

Before the development of statistical software packages, people would use **tables of critical values** of statistics to find the probability associated with their obtained or calculated value of the statistic. These tables contain different values of the statistic – the tabled or critical values – and the probability for each of these values under the null hypothesis. You can still find yourself on occasion needing to use these tables – such as when you have calculated a statistic by hand. This appendix summarizes the procedure involved for those of you who are unfamiliar with the use of these tables.

The tables can be found at the rear of most statistics textbooks. Sets of tables are also published in their own right. In order to use them, you need to know which statistic you are using and additional information such as the number of observations or participants or the degrees of freedom. Section 4.6 describes the additional information required for some of the statistics that you are likely to use as a student, and more information can be found on the Web site that accompanies this book. This information is also contained in your statistics textbook. For significance testing, you will also need to know whether your obtained value needs to be greater than or less than the tabled value. This information is also available on the Web site and in your statistics textbook.

Using tables to test for statistical significance

The tables are designed primarily for significance testing and therefore will always contain at least the critical values for the conventional significance levels – 5 percent and 1 percent. To use them to test for statistical significance:

1 Look for the tables containing the distribution of the statistic that you are using. These will be described as tables of the distribution of F or t or χ^2 or whatever. Note whether you are using a one-tailed or two-tailed test and the significance level that you have adopted. Most of you, most of the time, will be testing two-tailed hypotheses at the 5 percent level.

2 Find the additional information necessary to locate the critical value for the test. (For example, look in Section 4.6.) Most of the time this will be either the *degrees of freedom* or the *numbers of observations*. Whether the obtained value has to be greater than or less than the critical value for significance will also depend on the test.

3 Locate the **critical value**. These values are called critical values because they are the values that your statistic has to equal or exceed in the relevant direction in order to be statistically significant.

4 The **obtained value** is the value of the statistic that you have calculated. If your obtained value differs from the critical value in the direction required for statistical significance, or if it is *equal* to the critical value, then your data are statistically significant. Under these circumstances, *reject* the null hypothesis.

5 If your obtained value differs from the critical value in the direction opposite to that required for significance, then your data are not statistically significant. Under these circumstances, *do not reject* the null hypothesis.

You must be clear about what you are doing at each stage. *First*, you compare your obtained value with the critical value. For some statistics (e.g., the Mann–Whitney U test, the Wilcoxon signed-rank test) the obtained value has to be *less* than (or equal to) the critical value for statistical significance. For other statistics (e.g., χ^2, t, F) the obtained value has to be *greater* than (or equal to) the critical value for statistical significance. However, the *probability* associated with the obtained value will *always* be *less* than (or equal to) the *probability* associated with critical value if the obtained value is statistically significant.

? SAQ 49

Below are a number of results of statistical analyses. Look these up in the appropriate tables. For each of these state whether the result is significant at the 5 percent level, two-tailed.

(a) A researcher analysed a set of data using the Wilcoxon signed-rank test and found that $T(22) = 45$. Is this result statistically significant?

(b) A researcher analysed a set of data using the Mann–Whitney U test and found that $U(10, 12) = 8$. Is this result statistically significant?

(c) A researcher analysed a set of data using chi-square and found that $\chi^2(1, N = 82) = 3.80$. Is this result statistically significant?

(d) A researcher analysed a set of data using the independent t test and found that $t(16) = 2.20$. Is this result statistically significant?

(e) A researcher analysed a set of data using two-way analysis of variance for unrelated samples and found that, for one of the IVs, $F(2, 25) = 5.20$. Is this result statistically significant?

Using tables to establish the probability associated with the obtained value

Statistical software packages have programmed into them the equations for calculating distributions of statistics. They are therefore able to print out the *exact* probability associated with any particular value of the statistic. Unfortunately, when using tables it is very unlikely that you will be able to establish the exact probability for your obtained value. Instead, you will most probably find that your obtained value falls between two of the tabled values. The probability associated with your value will therefore also fall between the probabilities for these two values.

For example, in Chapter 11, the obtained value of $\chi^2 = 4.89$ does not appear in the table of values of chi-square (Table 11.2). However, using Table 11.2 (which is in fact a table of critical values of chi-square with one degree of freedom) we were still able to establish an upper and a lower level for the probability associated with $\chi^2 = 4.89$. The value immediately greater than $\chi^2 = 4.89$ in the table is $\chi^2 = 5.02$. This has a probability of $p = .025$. The value immediately less than $\chi^2 = 4.89$ in the table is $\chi^2 = 3.84$. This has a probability of $p = .05$. So, the probability associated with our obtained value lies between $p = .05$ and $p = .025$. (As you can see, this agrees with the $p = .03$ that we obtained from the statistics package, but is less exact.)

You do this the same way with any tables of critical values. However, if your obtained value equals the tabled value (which happens occasionally) then, of course, the probability is *exact*. For it is the probability associated with the tabled value.

Reporting probabilities that are not exact

Although the tables cannot tell us the exact probability associated with our statistic, for statistically significant results we can find out the next *highest* probability and report that our obtained value is lower than that probability. In the case of the above $\chi^2 = 4.89$ with one degree of freedom, we know that the probability associated with this value of chi-square lies between $p = .05$ and $p = .025$. We can, therefore, say that it is *below $p = .05$* and indicate this using the following shorthand: "$p < .05$". The $<$ sign means "less than", so the statement "$p < .05$" is shorthand for "probability less than .05". It is "less than" because the smaller end of the symbol points towards the p. You can, of course, do this for probabilities smaller than this, for example, $p < .01$, or $p < .001$. Probabilities as low as $p < .001$ are striking enough, so there's rarely any need to go below this (e.g., there is no need to report "$p < .0001$").

Alternatively, you might report *both* the upper and lower probabilities. For instance, in the above example you could write $.025 < p < .05$. This tells us *which* probabilities the probability associated with our obtained statistic lies between. Some authors recommend doing this (e.g., Clark-Carter, 1997). See what your tutor thinks.

If the findings are not statistically significant, just change the direction of the sign for your chosen significance level. For example, if you used the 5 percent significance level and your obtained value has a probability higher than this, you can write "$p > .05$". This reads "probability greater than .05", because now the broader end of the symbol points to the p.

Output where $p = .000$

It can be the case that you have probabilities so extremely small that the output from your statistics package doesn't print out enough decimal places. However, when it prints $p = .000$, this does not mean that there is no probability associated with the outcome! (For example, it may be $p = .00032$.) Under these circumstances you can use the first method described above. For example, you know that $p = .000$ is below $p = .001$, so you can write "$p < .001$".

Answers to SAQs

SAQ 1

(a) Results. (b) Discussion.

SAQ 2

False. Even if this is true of those who mark your reports, it is certainly not true of the person for whom the report should be written: the hypothetical reader who is intelligent, but unknowledgeable about your study and the area of psychology in which it took place.

SAQ 3

You could write the INTRODUCTION and the METHOD *before* conducting the experiment. This is because you will report in these sections material that you should have decided upon *before* starting the experiment.

SAQ 4

The DISCUSSION, because it is there that you assess the implications of your findings. It is precisely for their implications that we run experiments in the first place.

SAQ 5

You should attempt to *substantiate* it. The preferred method of doing this is by *referencing* previous work in the area.

SAQ 6

These conventions are designed to facilitate the conveying of information about a study clearly, precisely, quickly, and concisely.

SAQ 7

In the INTRODUCTION you introduce your *study* to your *reader*. But remember that you must assume that your reader *is psychologically naive* (Chapter 1). Which means that, as well as telling the reader all about the study that you conducted, you must also put it into its context – that is, you must show how your study relates to previous work on the topic.

SAQ 8

Because you must assume that your reader knows nothing about the area of psychology relevant to your study. In order to understand and evaluate your study, therefore, he or she has first to be told about previous relevant work in the area.

SAQ 9

Because the researcher will return in the DISCUSSION to the material summarized in the INTRODUCTION and will reassess this material in the light of the study's *findings*. To the extent that these findings improve, otherwise illuminate, or qualify the picture presented in the INTRODUCTION, we have made progress.

SAQ 10

Because, as pointed out in Chapter 1, your report reflects the sequence in which you (theoretically) designed the experiment. The INTRODUCTION, there-fore, should provide your reader with an outline of the reasoning that led to the design of your experiment in the first place. Consequently, it should describe the position that you were in *before* running the experiment and, of course, could have been written at this stage – before the data were in.

SAQ 11

The INTRODUCTION serves to introduce your study to the reader. There are two aspects to this: first, an introduction to the area of psychology relevant to the study that you conducted; and second, a brief description of your own study.

SAQ 12

An exact replication of a study occurs when the experiment is repeated in *exactly* the same way in order to examine the *reliability* of the findings ob-tained (i.e., to see if the same results are obtained). The whole point of the METHOD section is to provide readers with sufficient information to enable them to undertake such a replication.

SAQ 13

The DESIGN serves to give the reader a brief, formal account of the precise design employed in your experiment. This information is essential for anyone who wishes to replicate your study.

SAQ 14

Because this would be a *confounding* variable. See Chapters 9 and 10 for information on how to eliminate confounding variables.

SAQ 15

They need to know (a) what kind of participants you sampled and (b) how they were distributed across your experimental conditions. They need to know (a) in order to assess the generalizability of your findings. They need to know (b) in order to establish whether there are any confounding variables arising from the way in which the participants were distributed across the various conditions.

SAQ 16

It is in the form of a list, when it should be coherent sentences. It has been labelled "Apparatus", when it contains both apparatus and materials. The precise makes and models of the equipment used are not given. Although a number of pieces of equipment have been used, we are given no idea of how they were linked together – a diagram would have been useful here.

SAQ 17

If they weren't – if there *were* differences between your conditions other than those involving your manipulation of the IV – there would be a confounding variable in your experiment.

SAQ 18

Because if the instructions vary *between* conditions in aspects other than those involved in manipulating the IV, this would constitute a confounding variable. Similarly, if the instructions vary *within* conditions, this might not only increase the variability within that condition, but again, if uncontrolled, might constitute a confounding variable. Indeed, there is evidence to suggest that participants' behaviour can be strongly influenced by even quite subtle changes in instructions. So if you want to be able to make any sense of the results that you obtain, you need to keep the instructions as constant as you can within any given study.

SAQ 19

Readers need to be able to satisfy themselves that the data that you gathered were appropriate to the question that you claim to be examining, that the inferential statistics that you used are appropriate given your data, and that the outcomes of these analyses appear to be consistent with the data as described by the descriptive statistics. They need this information in order to evaluate your findings.

SAQ 20

What is wrong: First, we are not told which data are being analysed. Second, the description of the analysis is imprecise. Third, we are not told the value of F, either of the degrees of freedom, the associated probability, or the significance level. Finally, we have no idea what these results mean in real terms. A more appropriate statement would run as follows:

> The data in Table 1 were analysed using one-way ANOVA for unrelated samples with presentation rate (fast, moderate, or slow) as the independent variable. Recall was significantly influenced by presentation rate, $F(2, 15) = 7.45$, $p = .006$.

Indeed, this statement could be improved yet further if it were possible to specify the way in which presentation rate affected recall (e.g., did it improve it, make it worse?).

SAQ 21

The purpose of the DISCUSSION is to enable you to assess the implications of your findings for the area of psychology relevant to the study that you undertook. It is, therefore, the key section of the report, for it is at this stage that we are able to discover how much progress the findings have enabled us to make.

SAQ 22

They serve to alert potential readers to the existence of an article that may be of interest to them.

SAQ 23

What is wrong: For the first reference "&" is used instead of "and", even though it is a direct reference. No parentheses are used for "1994", even though it is a direct reference. The list of references within parentheses should come immediately before the full stop, not after it. The list of references within parentheses should be in alphabetical order. There are two references to Bennett and Bennett (1981), neither of which is suffixed. The word "and" is used for an indirect reference. Colons, rather than semicolons, are used to separate the references. "Blake, Perry & Griffith" is repeated in full when "et al." should have been used. No page numbers are given for the quotation. Corrected, the text should read:

> Blake, Perry and Griffith (1994) found that performance on the experimental task improved considerably when participants were in the presence of a group of peers. This contradicted previous findings in the area (Bennett & Bennett, 1981a, 1981b; Buchanan & Livermore, 1976; Pike, 1992; Scoular, 1964, 1973). As Blake et al. put it, "it is not clear why this happened" (p. 27).

SAQ 24

The variable that we manipulate is called the independent variable. The variable that we measure is called the dependent variable.

(a) The IV is the frequency of the words (high, medium, or low). The DV is the participants' reaction time in milliseconds.
(b) The IV is whether the rat had been injected with oestrogen or saline. The DV is change in the body weights of the rats in grams.
(c) The IV is the level of anxiety induced by the programme (high, moderate, or low). The DV is the number of those in each group who take up the opportunity to make a dental appointment.
(d) The IV is the nature of the violence depicted in the programme (realistic, unrealistic, or none). The DV is the mean level of shock that the viewers subsequently give to their victims in volts.
(e) The IV is whether the participants were working alone, or with one, two, four, or eight co-workers. The DV is the number of cereal packets put into boxes during the 20-minute period.

SAQ 25

The IV is whether or not the participant consumed the standard quantity of cheese 3 hours before going to bed. The DV is the number of nightmares reported by the two groups. What we have done here, in essence, is play around with the amount of cheese eaten by the members of the two groups, and looked to see if this has any effect on the incidence of nightmares. Thus eating cheese is the suspected cause and nightmares the measured effect.

SAQ 26

The control condition in our cheese and nightmare experiment is the one in which *no* cheese is given to the participants.

SAQ 27

There are five conditions in this experiment, four of which are *experimental* conditions (Cheddar, Caerphilly, Red Leicester, and Cheshire). The *control* condition has no cheese.

SAQ 28

(a) Three (high, medium, low word frequency). No control condition.
(b) Two (oestrogen, saline injections). Control condition: saline.
(c) Three (high, moderate, low anxiety arousal). No control condition.
(d) Three (realistic, unrealistic, no violence). Control condition: no violence.
(e) Five (alone, one, two, four, eight co-workers). Control condition: alone.

SAQ 29

No. There are in fact two other possible outcomes. This particular piece of folk wisdom might be the wrong way around. That is, instead of giving you nightmares, eating cheese might actually enhance sleep and suppress nightmares. In which case we should find that those in the cheese condition report *fewer* nightmares than those in the no cheese condition. On the other hand, it may be that cheese has no effect upon the incidence of nightmares. In which case we should find little or no difference in the number of nightmares reported by the two groups.

SAQ 30

(a) The reaction time of the participants will not be the same for the high, medium or low frequency words.
(b) The changes in body weight among those rats injected with oestrogen will be different from the changes in body weight among those rats injected with saline.
(c) The number of viewers making dental appointments will not be the same among those who watched the high, moderate or low anxiety-arousing programmes.
(d) The mean level of shock administered by the participants to the victim will not be the same after viewing programmes which depict realistic, unrealistic or no violence.
(e) The number of packets of breakfast cereal packed by the workers will not be the same when they work alone, or with one, two, four or eight co-workers.

SAQ 31

Because this would be a confounding variable. If we found a difference between the cheese and no cheese conditions in the number of nightmares, we would not know whether this was caused by the cheese or by the alcohol or both.

SAQ 32

Because the nightmares may not be due to cheese itself but to the act of eating something before going to bed. This may not be as far-fetched as it sounds. In a culture in which there is a belief that eating cheese before sleep can induce nightmares, this belief itself might be sufficient to increase the numbers of nightmares in the experimental conditions. That is, the belief would be **self-fulfilling**. Our current experiment does not rule out this explanation. A control condition involving a cheese-like but inactive substitute would. Beliefs about the effectiveness of the things that we take and consume can be very potent. This is one of the reasons why trials of drugs or treatments include *placebo* conditions. A **placebo** looks like the pill or tablet or resembles the treatment but does not contain the active or key ingredient thought to make the difference.

On the other hand, it may be that eating *anything* too close to going to bed might induce nightmares – that the simple act of eating something is what makes the difference. Our simple design does not rule out this possibility either. Our "placebo cheese" condition would control for both possibilities.

SAQ 33

No. This relationship probably occurs because of a third variable – temperature. That is, as the temperature rises, so more ice cream is consumed and, quite independently, so more people go swimming. As more people swim, so more people die in drowning accidents. So any apparently causal link between these variables is spurious.

SAQ 34

Our original cheese and nightmare experiment had different participants in the two conditions. Hence it had an *unrelated* samples design. We could also have run it by comparing the number of nightmares reported by the same participants on nights in which they had eaten cheese with the number reported on nights in which they hadn't eaten cheese. This would have been a *related* samples design. The advantage of having the same person in both conditions is that it controls for individual differences in the tendency to experience nightmares. This would be a considerable advantage. However, getting people to sleep sometimes with and sometimes without having eaten cheese would give them strong clues about the nature of the experiment and this might affect the way that they responded – a potentially confounding variable.

SAQ 35

(a) Related samples.
(b) Unrelated samples.
(c) Unrelated samples.
(d) Unrelated samples.
(e) Related samples.

SAQ 36

Otherwise there is the possibility of a *confounding* variable arising from the non-random assignment of participants to conditions, just as with non-matched participants.

SAQ 37

No. It may be that at other temperatures – for instance, chilled – they *can* taste the difference. Indeed, temperature appears to markedly affect the flavour of a drink, as any beer or wine drinker can tell you. In order to test this possibility, of course, we would need to *manipulate* the temperature variable, rather than hold it constant. So our findings may only hold for the conditions employed in the experiment. Moreover, whether people *in general* are unable to taste the difference, of course, depends on how representative the group of students at this summer school is of the population at large.

SAQ 38

A value of $p = .03$ is nearer to zero than to one. It is, therefore, nearer the impossible end of the continuum. Thus it is an event that is *unlikely* to occur under the null hypothesis. However, note that it does not have a probability of zero. Thus it is *still possible* for it to occur under the null hypothesis – and (sigh!) that's the rub.

SAQ 39

Yes. The probability associated with our obtained version of chi-square is less than $p = .05$. It is therefore statistically significant at the 5 percent significance level.

SAQ 40

The probability for a two-tailed t test is twice that for the one-tailed version. The probability associated with $t = 1.73$ with 20 degrees of freedom, two-tailed, is therefore $p = .10$, or 10 percent.

SAQ 41

A type II error – failing to reject a false null hypothesis. Remember, power is the probability of *not* making a type II error.

SAQ 42

(a) 6, 12 and 18 are all possible. Why? Because you need a minimum of six participants to ensure that the design is fully counterbalanced (because there are six possible unique combinations of three conditions). When thinking of the number of participants to run in this experiment, therefore, you need to think in multiples of six or else the design will not be fully counterbalanced.

(b) Six participants are unlikely to be enough to give you sufficient power to detect an effect of the IV on the DV (see Section 12.2.2). Twelve may also be too few. Eighteen *may* be sufficient, depending on how big an effect the IV has on the DV. If you need more than this, then what is the next highest number that you could use? (24.)

SAQ 43

(a) 24. Because there are 24 unique combinations of four conditions – see Table 13.1.

(b) 48. (2×24). This may well be too many with a related samples IV. Of course, whether this number of participants *is* too many depends, among other things, on the effect size (see Section 11.8).

SAQ 44

(a) As we have three conditions, there are only six different ways in which we can order these conditions. Thus, it is quite feasible to *counterbalance* them. The orders are:

Hi	Med	Lo
Hi	Lo	Med
Med	Hi	Lo
Med	Lo	Hi
Lo	Med	Hi
Lo	Hi	Med

As you can see, therefore, each condition appears an equal number of times in each position, and an equal number of times before and after each other condition – that is, the experiment is fully counterbalanced.

As we have six different orders, then we need a minimum of six participants for our experiment. Of course we would use more than this. However, our total number of participants would have to be divisible by six. That is, we would have to work in multiples of six participants. So, 24 participants might be acceptable – 25 or 26 would not.

(e) There are five conditions. There are, therefore, 120 different ways of ordering these conditions (5! = 5 × 4 × 3 × 2 × 1 = 120). We would therefore require a minimum of 120 participants to fully counterbalance this experiment. Consequently, we would probably have either to use a method of partial control or otherwise randomize the assignment of orders of conditions to participants. We could randomize by allocating one of the 120 possible orders randomly to each of our participants using randomization without replacement. This method of controlling for order effects does not limit the number of participants that we can employ, so there is no minimum. However, the more we employ, the more effective will be our randomization, and – other things being equal – the more reliable the data.

SAQ 45

(a) The variables are: alcohol, sex, and time since passing driving test. Hence there are three. The first of these, alcohol, is a related samples IV; the other two use unrelated samples. Thus it is a mixed design. One way of describing it is as a three-way, mixed design.

There are four levels on the alcohol IV (0, 2, 4 or 8 units), two on the sex variable (female or male), and three on the driving experience variable (passed in the previous 6 months, passed in the previous 7–18 months, or passed more than 18 months previously). The other answer, therefore, is a 4 × 3 × 2 (Alcohol × Experience × Sex) mixed design.

(b) The IVs are: type of stress and nature of task. Hence there are two IVs. Stress is an unrelated samples IV, the nature of the task a related samples IV. Thus it is a mixed design. One answer, therefore, is a two-way, mixed design.

There are three levels on the stress IV (heat, noise, or light), two on the type of task IV (demanding or undemanding). The other answer, therefore, is a 3 × 2 (Stress × Type of Task) mixed design.

(c) The variables are: sex and extraversion. Hence there are two. These are both necessarily unrelated samples variables. Thus it is an unrelated samples design. One answer, therefore, is a two-way, unrelated samples design.

There are two levels on the sex variable (female or male), two on the extraversion variable (extravert or introvert). The other answer, therefore, is a 2 × 2 (Sex × Extraversion) unrelated samples design.

(d) The IVs are: driving conditions, nature of listening material, and volume. Hence there are three IVs. All of these use related samples. Thus it is a related samples design. One answer, therefore, is a three-way, related samples design.

There are three levels on the driving conditions IV (easy, moderate or difficult), two levels on the listening material IV (talk or music), and three levels on the volume IV (low, moderate or loud). The other answer, therefore, is a 3 × 3 × 2 (Driving Conditions × Listening Material × Volume) related samples design.

SAQ 46

Because a mixed design has *at least* one IV that uses related samples and *at least* one IV that uses unrelated samples. You cannot, therefore, have a one-way, mixed design.

SAQ 47

(a) Up to three: alcohol, sex, driving experience.
(b) Up to two: type of stress, nature of task.
(c) Up to two: sex, extraversion.
(d) Up to three: driving conditions, nature of listening material, volume.

SAQ 48

If you *reject* the null hypothesis. This means that you have found evidence enough to persuade you that there is a reliable difference between your conditions on the DV. So this is *potentially* evidence *against* the proposition that predicted that there would be no difference. Thus, in this sort of experiment you can only ever find evidence that goes against propositions that predict no difference, not evidence in favour of them.

SAQ 49

(a) The critical value of T for $N = 22$ at the 5 percent significance level (two-tailed) is $T = 65$. As the obtained T of 45 is *less* than this, the result is statistically significant at the 5 percent significance level.
(b) The critical value of U for $n_1 = 10$ and $n_2 = 12$ at the 5 percent significance level (two-tailed) is $U = 29$. As the obtained value of U of 8 is *less* than this, the result is statistically significant at the 5 percent significance level.
(c) The critical value of χ^2 with 1 degree of freedom at the 5 percent significance level is $\chi^2 = 3.84$. As the obtained value of χ^2 of 3.80 is *less* than this, the result is *not* statistically significant at the 5 percent significance level.
(d) The critical value of t with 16 degrees of freedom at the 5 percent significance level (two-tailed) is $t = 2.12$. As the obtained value of t of 2.20 is *greater* than this, the result is statistically significant at the 5 percent significance level.
(e) The critical value of F with $df_1 = 2$ and $df_2 = 25$ at the 5 percent significance level is $F = 3.39$. As the obtained value of F of 5.20 is *greater* than this, the result is statistically significant at the 5 percent significance level. (Note that df_1 refers to the degrees of freedom for the *numerator* of the F ratio, df_2 refers to the degrees of freedom for the *denominator* of this ratio. With tables of the distribution of F you have to make sure that you read the columns and rows correctly and do not confuse df_1 and df_2.)

References

American Psychological Association. (2001). *Publication manual of the American Psychological Association* (5th ed.). Washington, DC: American Psychological Association.

Aron, A., & Aron, E. (1999). *Statistics for psychology* (2nd ed.). Upper Saddle River, NJ: Prentice Hall.

British Psychological Society. (2000, November). *Code of conduct, ethical principles & guidelines*. Leicester: The British Psychological Society.

Clark-Carter, D. (1997). *Doing quantitative psychological research: From design to report*. Hove: Psychology Press.

Cohen, J. (1988). *Statistical power analysis for the behavioral sciences* (2nd ed.). New York: Academic Press.

Coolican, H. (1999). *Research methods and statistics in psychology* (3rd ed.). London: Hodder & Stoughton.

Dancey, C. P., & Reidy, J. (2001). *Statistics without maths for psychology* (2nd ed.). London: Prentice Hall.

Glassman, W. E. (1995). *Approaches to psychology* (2nd ed.). Buckingham: Open University Press.

Greene, J., & D'Oliveira, M. (1999). *Learning to use statistical tests in psychology* (2nd ed.). Buckingham: Open University Press.

Grimm, L. G. & Yarnold, P. R. (Eds.). (1995). *Reading and understanding multivariate statistics*. Washington, DC: American Psychological Association.

Hayes, N. (2000). *Doing psychological research*. Buckingham: Open University Press.

Hinton, R. P. (1995). *Statistics explained*. London: Routledge.

Howell, D. C. (2001). *Statistical methods for psychology* (5th ed.). Belmont, CA: Duxbury Press.

Howell, D. C. (1999). *Fundamental statistics for the behavioral sciences* (4th ed.). Belmont, CA: Duxbury Press.

Kirkpatrick, L. A., & Feeney, B. C. (2001). *A simple guide to SPSS for Windows*. Belmont, CA: Wadsworth.

Murphy, K. R., & Myors, B. (1998). *Statistical power analysis*. Mahwah, NJ: Lawrence Erlbaum Associates.

Nicol, A. A. M., & Pexman, P. M. (1999). *Presenting your findings: A practical guide for creating tables.* Washington, DC: American Psychological Association.

Pallant, J. (2001). *SPSS survival manual: a step by step guide to data analysis using SPSS.* Buckingham: Open University Press.

Sternberg, R. J. (1988). *The psychologist's companion* (3rd ed.). Cambridge: Cambridge University Press.

Index of concepts

LEARNING TO USE STATISTICAL TESTS IN PSYCHOLOGY
SECOND EDITION

Judith Greene and Manuela d'Oliveira

Praise for the first edition:

> An excellent textbook which is well planned, well written, and pitched at the correct level for psychology students. I would not hesitate to recommend Greene and d'Oliveira to all psychology students looking for an introductory text on statistical methodology.
> *Bulletin of the British Psychological Society*

The second edition of this widely acclaimed text is an accessible and comprehensible introduction to the use of statistical tests in psychology experiments: statistics without panic. Presented in a new textbook format, its key objective is to enable students to select appropriate statistical tests to evaluate the significance of data obtained from psychological experiments. Improvements in the organization of chapters emphasize even more clearly the principle of introducing complex experimental designs on a 'need to know' basis, leaving more space for an extended interpretation of analysis of variance. In an important development for the second edition, students are introduced to modern statistical packages as a useful tool for calculations, the emphasis being on understanding and interpretation.

This book shows psychology students:

- how psychologists plan experiments and statistical tests;
- why they must plan them within certain constraints;
- how they can analyse and make sense of their results.

The approach is that:

- theory is always presented together with practical examples;
- theoretical points are summarized and understanding of them tested;
- statistical principles are introduced as part and parcel of the principles of experimental design.

Contents

240pp   0 335 20377 9 (paperback)   0 335 20378 7 (hardback)

DOING PSYCHOLOGICAL RESEARCH
GATHERING AND ANALYSING DATA

Nicky Hayes

> . . . covers a wider spectrum than many introductory texts on methods in psychology and has a stronger emphasis on qualitative methods than others . . . it will be particularly attractive to students seeking a lifeline into methods at first year undergraduate level. Nicky Hayes' reputation will strengthen the demand for it, particularly among undergraduates who have already used her texts at 'A' level.
>
> Professor Nigel Lemon, University of Huddersfield

> . . . there are other research methods textbooks for 'A' level students currently on the market . . . Nicky Hayes has written a book which renders most of these obsolete. The new 'A' level specifications allow students to venture into areas of research that require different forms of qualitative analysis. These are hardly addressed in competing texts and are given thorough treatment by Nicky Hayes. I admire her ability to offer depth of treatment to complex issues without losing her audience. This is an interactive textbook, and I am pleased to see that every chapter contains worked examples, definitions and activities . . . I can highly recommend this book.
>
> Mike Stanley, Gordano School, North Somerset, UK

Research methodology is one of the most important and also one of the most difficult aspects of psychology for many students to grasp. This new textbook, written by one of the most experienced and respected writers of psychology textbooks in the UK, provides a comprehensive account of both qualitative and quantitative methods. It does so in the friendly, lucid style which has made Nicky Hayes' other textbooks so popular with students and teachers.

Doing Psychological Research has been carefully written and designed to help students grasp complex concepts and to provide them with a sound methodological 'toolkit' for carrying out their own projects. The book is divided into data-gathering and analytical sections, and covers the main methods used in psychology for each of these purposes. Exercises and activities, worked examples of statistical tests, and self-assessment questions all help to deepen understanding and illustrate the relevance of the material. A full bibliography and index and a useful glossary of terms complete the package.

This is the accessible but comprehensive introductory text which many students and teachers of research methods in psychology have been looking for. It is likely to become essential reading for introductory courses.

Contents
Introduction – Approaches to psychological research – Part 1: Gathering data – Gathering data for psychological research – Experiments – Observational studies – Questionnaire studies – Psychometrics – Interviews – Case studies and ethnography – Analysing documents – Part 2: Making sense of data – Introducing qualitative analysis – Grounded approaches to qualitative research – Conversations, discourse and images – Protocol analysis and other techniques – Introducing quantitative analysis – Numbers as descriptive statistics – Descriptive statistics in visual images – Two-sample tests – Correlation and regression – Analysis of variance – Glossary – Statistical tables – References – Index.

420pp   0 335 19512 1 (Paperback)   0 335 19513 X (Hardback)